THE

HISTORY OF HYDER SHAH,

ALIAS

HYDER ALI KHAN BAHADUR

THE

HISTORY OF HYDER SHAH,

ALIAS

HYDER ALI KHAN BAHADUR:

AND OF HIS SON,

TIPPOO SULTAUN.

BY M. M. D. L. T.,

REVISED AND CORRECTED

BY

HIS HIGHNESS PRINCE GHOLAM MOHAMMED

GYAN

Published by

Gyan Publishing House
5, Ansari Road
Daryaganj, New Delhi-110002
Phone: 011-47034999, 9811692060
E-mail: books@gyanbooks.com

Distribution Network
gyanbooks.com
India, USA, Canada, UK, Australia

ISBN: 978-81-212-2401-7 (PB)
First Published, 1784

2nd Impression 2024

Printed at: Gyan Press, Delhi.

THE HISTORY OF HYDER SHAH, ALIAS
HYDER ALI KHAN BAHADUR

Author: M. M. D. L. T., PRINCE GHOLAM MOHAMMED

THE HISTORY OF HYDER SHAH,

ALIAS

HYDER ALI KHAN BAHADUR:

AND OF HIS SON,

TIPPOO SULTAUN.

By M. M. D. L. T.,

GENERAL IN THE ARMY OF THE MOGUL EMPIRE,

REVISED AND CORRECTED

BY

HIS HIGHNESS PRINCE GHOLAM MOHAMMED,

THE ONLY SURVIVING SON OF TIPPOO SULTAUN.

LONDON:

W. THACKER & Co., 87, NEWGATE STREET,

CALCUTTA: THACKER, SPINK AND CO.; BOMBAY: THACKER AND CO.

1855.

THE

AUTHOR'S PREFACE.

THOUGH it is not usual to write the history of a living prince, the great distance which, in the present instance, permits the historian to speak with freedom, will serve as an excuse for the infringement of so just a rule, in the eyes of those who may read the following sheets without prejudice. The writer has adhered to the strictest impartiality, in relating the exploits of the most famous conqueror India has beheld since the time of Thamas Kouli Khan; a prince very much superior to that usurper, as well for the extent of his genius as for the propriety of his conduct, which far exceeds that of the other Indian sovereigns.

It will be easily perceived that the Author has neither endeavoured to flatter nor to calumniate. If the English should find that they are not spared, it will not be in their power to reproach him with having invented any untruth: and there are very many individuals of that nation, who know that he could speak much more effectually to the disadvantage of the English administration in India, if he thought it necessary to reveal such particulars as he himself has seen.

Whether the tyranny which these men have exercised in India be a crime of their nation, or purely their own, is of no importance to the Author in his capacity as an Historian, since he has not made any reflections on the subject in the ensuing pages.

The Generals Coote, Smith, and Goddard, are spoken of with the justice they deserve; which circumstance ought to be of weight to vindicate his impartiality from the reproaches that interested and prejudiced readers will doubtless be ready to make.

If any of his recitals should be contrary to the ideas of certain persons acquainted with the same events, he begs they will please to make a distinction between the facts he himself has been witness to, and those he could only learn from the information of others.

The persons cited in the course of the history, and who may be now in Europe, are appealed to with confidence to assert the truth of what is here attributed to them. With regard to other facts, it is requested that they will believe this narration in preference to what may have been written to them by men who have not been in the same confidential situation as the Author, and have likewise reasons for disguising the truth, that can have no influence upon him.

The true dignity and importance of history is placed in truth. It has not therefore been in his power to spare such of his countrymen as have behaved unworthily: but, out of consideration for their respectable families, he has been careful to omit mentioning their names; which is the only tenderness he has indulged himself in. The following work is not strictly confined to the actions of Hyder Ali Khan; but is likewise intended to give an accurate idea of the revolutions that have taken place in India, previous to the aggrandizement of that great prince: for the purpose of satisfying the reader on this head, it is thought proper to prefix an Historical Introduction, that will render him acquainted with the genius and character of the personages spoken of.

The account of particular circumstances relating to the Life of Hyder Ali Khan, that follows the Introduction, gives an idea of his person, considered as a man, a general, and a soldier. The Author hopes that it will serve to make the private character of the Prince better known than those of most European sovereigns A perfect acquaintance with the men that surround a king, will often give the most accurate knowledge of his own manners and inclinations. With this intention, the portraits of some of the relations as well as of the intimate friends of Hyder are given.

There has not yet appeared any work that explains the principles of government of the princes now reigning in Hindostan: it is therefore hoped that the Public will receive with pleasure the detail here given of the establishment's laws, customs, and forms of government that prevail in Hyder's dominions. The English have lately published the laws and customs of the Hindoos: but Hindostan has been so long governed by Mahomedan princes, that this code of the ancient Hindoo laws instructs us in the present government of India, nearly as much as the laws of the ancient

Druids are capable of explaining the administration and government of the present French nation.

The author can with justice indulge the hope that these Memoirs will not be confounded with those rhapsodies that have appeared within the last three or four years, under the title of *Essais sur la Vie*, and *Abregès de l'Histoire d'Hyder Ali*, which were evidently fabricated by people who have not only been totally unacquainted with Hyder, but even entirely without any memoirs, except those tales that have occasionally appeared in the public papers. From these materials, copied with servility, they have formed compositions which they have had the assurance to offer as original to the Public, under a variety of pompous titles. It was from a view of these inaccurate and fictitious compilations, that the Author was induced to write the History he now presents to the world. As an eye-witness of his conquests, and of the glory that surrounds him, he thought it a kind of duty incumbent on him to make this sovereign known, at an instant in which he has become so interesting to Europe, and to France in particular.

Engd on Steel by C. Morrish

HYDER SHAH

ALIAS

HYDER ALI KHAN BAHADUR.

THE

HISTORY OF HYDER SHAH,

ALIAS

HYDER ALI KHAN BAHADUR.

INTRODUCTION.

BEFORE we enter upon the History of Hyder Shah, alias Hyder Ali Khan, it is necessary to give an account of part of those revolutions, which the invasion of India by Nadir Shah, king of Persia, commonly called Thamas Kouli Khan, occasioned in that extensive empire; and more especially in those provinces that were the theatre of the various scenes we are about to relate.

Nadir Shah, previous to his quitting Delhi for the purpose of returning to his own states, concluded a treaty with Mohumed Shah, emperor of the Mogols, in which it was ordained that the charge of Grand Vizier, and all the Subaships or viceroyalties,* then

* The title, power, and prerogatives of a Suba cannot be better defined than by translating the word into the terms Vicar-general of

nine in number, should be hereditary in the families at that time in possession of them. This article was doubtless a stroke of politics in the Persian conqueror, to divide the force of an empire, whose strength was sufficiently exhibited in the army of 1,200,000 men assembled to oppose him; and which, under an emperor of another disposition, might revenge the insult sustained by Mohumed Shah. But it is likewise to be presumed, that he had previously settled this point; and in putting it in execution, he only forwarded the ambitious views of Nizam El Moulouc, Grand Vizier and Suba of Decan, who, in revenge for an affront put upon him by Mohumed Shah, had invited the king of Persia into the empire, and had been the means of preserving him from the probable effects of so rash an undertaking.

The Subaship of Decan, then in possession of Nizam El Moulouc, constituted at least a third part of the Mogol empire. All the country that extends from the gulf of Cambaya to Bengal, formed part of this Subaship, whose chief cities were Aurungabad and Hyderabad; and it extended to all the coasts of the hither peninsula, from Cambaya to the gulf of Bengal.

This vast government was divided into many others. Among these were many kingdoms governed by their own kings and particular laws, being no more than tributaries to the empire; except that they were obliged to furnish a certain number of troops to the army of the Suba, which the kings themselves very often esteemed it an honour to lead in person. The principal of these kingdoms were those of the Marattas, of Canara, and of Mysore.

---

the Empire. For this charge bestows a supremacy over the kings and vassals of the empire, which the Suba exercises in the same manner as the emperor himself. Similar to this would be the power of a vicar-general of the empire in Italy, if this dignity were at present possessed of activity and energy.

Many of these kingdoms and states were scarcely in subjection; and among them Canara, a country difficult of access from its numerous forests and mountains. The Marattas were no otherwise subjected, than by means of the treaty with the Suba, respecting the payment of the Chauth, or fourth part of the revenue of Decan, which the emperor Aurengzebe had granted them; and the great population of their country furnished them with numerous and powerful armies, especially of cavalry, whose incursions were not easily checked: and lastly there were states, which, though comprised in the Subaship of Decan, were not yet subjected. Such were the small kingdom of Calicut, or of the Samorins, and the other states of the black princes on the coast of Malabar; into which the armies of the Mogols were unable to penetrate, by reason of the narrow and difficult entrances through forests and mountains.

Besides the kingdoms and other tributary countries, the Subaship of Decan comprehended several governments, of greater or less magnitude, which were not hereditary, but in the gift of the Suba; whose nomination, however, required to be confirmed by the emperor.

When the Subaships became hereditary, the Subas pretended to the right of irrevocably nominating those governors, which the Europeans call Nabobs, without the necessity of any confirmation from the court of Dehli.

The Nabobship of Arcot* held the first rank among all those

* This History of the Nabobship of Arcot is very different from that given by the Editor of the Memoirs ascribed to General Lawrence. It is necessary, in that work, to distinguish the reports of the Author himself from the account of the expeditions of General Lawrence. The latter is generally true, excepting that the French forces are magnified in number, and the English diminished; so as frequently to produce contradictions. As to the Editor of those Memoirs, it will be sufficient to form a judgment of him, if we recollect that he affirms,

governments comprised in the Subaship of Decan, as well for its extent as for its riches and population. For it contains all the country, known by the name of Coromandel, that lies between the mountains and the sea coast, from Cape Comorin to Kisna, a river which, after running over a course of more than five hundred leagues, all within the Subaship of Decan, falls into the sea near Mazulipatam.

This government, though held only at the pleasure of the Suba, had been very long in possession of the same family, a branch of the Syuds, or descendants of Mohumed, by Ali his cousin and Fatima his daughter. The princes of this illustrious family were adored by their subjects, for having rendered the country rich and populous by the mildness and moderation of their government.

Several lords of the same family, as the Nabobs* of Valore, Vandevachi, &c., possessed small tracts of country, which they had received *en appanage*;† but they acknowledged the Nabob of Arcot as their superior, and the chief of their family. This Nabobship of

---

that, previous to the time in which M. Bussi followed Mouzaferjung, the Europeans were ignorant of what passed at the court of the Indian princes, their nearest neighbours. He affirms, likewise, in his introduction, that his work is designed to exhibit or make known the rights of Mohumed Ali Khan. With this intention, he is careful to avoid every thing that can serve to render him odious, as well as his father Unvurudeen Khan. To shew, from an incontestable fact, that this Editor was not in possession of accurate information, we need only observe, that he gives Nizam El Moulouc no more than four sons, though he left six. The two that are omitted by him are still living. The one is named Bazaletjung, and the other Mirs Mogol.

* The signification of the word Nabob will be hereafter explained.

† Lands are given *en appanage*, when they are in lieu of the future right of succession to the whole, of which they are a part.

Arcot comprehended also several less states, as that of the Rajah of Tanjore, of the Naies of Madura, and of Mazara, &c., who were tributaries, and obliged to furnish a quota of troops to the Nabob's army.

In the year 1740, the Marattas made an incursion into the Subaship of Decan, in the absence of Nizam El Moulouc, Grand Vizier and Suba; and, spreading like a torrent, they arrived at the country of Arcot, under the conduct of Ragogi their general.

The Nabob of Arcot* having collected his forces, which were by no means equal to those of the Marattas, marched against them, and lost both the victory and his life.

This unfortunate Nabob left an only son,† who succeeded him in his government. The rest of his family sought an asylum at Pondicherry, where the Sieur Dumas, then governor, received and promised to protect them, in return for the repeated advantages the French had received from the Nabobs of Arcot, since their first establishment in India.

Ragogi laid siege to Pondicherry, whose fortifications were in a very indifferent state. He demanded the governor to deliver up to him the family of the Nabob, and to pay him tribute. The spirited answer of the governor is well known. He replied, that *the dominions of the King of France had always been the asylum of unfortunate Princes; and that the French had no other tribute to give than bullets and balls.* A piece of gallantry made to the mistress of the Maratta general, contributed, together with the activity of the besieged, to induce Ragogi to raise the siege.

The same general, in the following year, besieged Trichnapoli, a strong place on the river Caveri. It surrendered for want of provision; and Chanda Saeb, the Nabob of the country, became prisoner, and was carried to Sattara. Nizam El Moulouc, being

---

* Dost Ali Khan.

† Sufder Ali Khan.

informed of the irruption of the Marattas and the death of the Nabob of Arcot, who was assassinated, nominated Unvurudeen Khan, one of his best generals, a man of address and of consummate knowledge in politics and the science of government, regent and administrator of the government of Arcot, during the minority of the young prince, Syud Mohumed Khan, grandson of Dost Ali Khan. Unvurudeen Khan, who then (in 1742) commanded the forces of the Suba of Decan to the northward of Masulipatam, very soon arrived at Arcot. On the other side, Nizam El Moulouc advancing by forced marches to the relief of his dominions, Ragogi abandoned the country of Arcot, and retired into the country of the Marattas.

Unvurudeen Khan restored tranquillity and good order to the country entrusted to his charge, and made his government beloved both by the people and the army. He seemed at first to be exceedingly attached to the young prince, and was very attentive to the care of his education. But this insidious politician, whose desires tended solely to the acquisition of his pupil's territories, was careful to inspire the young prince with a degree of haughtiness and avidity capable of rendering him odious, at the same time that he was himself courting every day more and more the affection of the people and the army.

When the young prince became of an age proper to marry, he advised him to espouse the daughter of the Nabob of Valore, one of his near relations. This Nabob having accepted the alliance with joy, proposed to give superb entertainments on the occasion of the marriage, according to the ordinary custom of the Indians, who are much attached to pomp and ceremony in circumstances of this nature.

During the time of the preparation for the nuptials, at the beginning of the year 1744, Unvurudeen Khan inspired the young prince, who had the highest confidence in his tutor, with the absurd idea of profiting by the tumult of the occasion, to get possession of Valore, and rob his future father-in-law of the fortress, which was the strongest in all the country, and contained, as it was said, a great mass of treasure. The young Nabob, whose heart was already corrupted, approved highly of this advice, and resolved to put it in execution. He repaired to Valore, where it was concerted that Unvurudeen Khan should cause soldiers to come as simple spectators, who, joining at once with the prince's retinue and those who accompanied Unvurudeen Khan, should put the garrison of Valore to the sword, and take possession of the place, according to the orders of the young prince. But the perfidious tutor, who had devised this conspiracy with no other intention than that of betraying his pupil into destruction, sent but a small number of soldiers; and caused the Nabob of Valore to be advised secretly of the design of his nephew, the evening before he had appointed to come himself to the place. His hope was, that the Nabob, enraged at the perfidy of his future son-in-law, would put him to death. In this, however, he was disappointed; for the Nabob contented himself with reproaching the young man publicly with his crime; and caused him to leave the place immediately, with all his followers.

The event of this contrivance having turned out contrary to the expectations of Unvurudeen Khan, he soon after formed another plot, which succeeded in accomplishing the destruction of the young Nabob.

Nizam El Mouloue being desirous of possessing an army, which, though composed of different Indian nations becomes effeminate by a long peace, should nevertheless be fit for the purposes of war, had with that intention invited into his dominions a great number of Patans, or inhabitants of Candahar, the remains of those Affgans who had conquered Persia, and whom Nadir Shah, after having chaced them out of that fertile kingdom, had pursued even to their own mountains. He had even bestowed among the chiefs of them Nabobships, or fiefs of the empire; whence arose the Patan Nabobs of Carpa, Canour, and Sanour,—a numerous corps of these Patans, who composed part of the Nabob of Arcot's army, and to whom, at that time, considerable sums were due for pay. These people are courageous; but ferocious, cruel, and perfidious, when they believe themselves ill-treated. Unvurudeen Khan assembled these Patans at Arcot, under the pretence of causing them to pass in review before their prince; and, by his secret agents, excited them to demand the arrears of pay due to them. He did not fail to advise the young Nabob, that the method to enforce respect from his troops, was to threaten them with the chastisement due to their insolence. The prince, who was but too much inclined to speak with haughtiness and contempt, treated them in the severest manner. A revolt was the consequence; and, in their fury, they did not spare even the Nabob himself, but put him to the sword. This event happened early in the year 1745.

Unvurudeen Khan, arrived at the height of his desires, affected to be oppressed with the utmost despair and sorrow. He continued for some time to deplore the loss of his pupil; but at length becoming gradually more moderate, and the Patans appearing to be concerned for the effects of their ferocity, he persuaded them that he would refer the affair to the decision of Nizam. But in the mean time he secretly assembled the chiefs of all the other corps of the army, and represented to them, that, since the Grand Vizier would confound them all with the criminals, there was but one way of justifying themselves, namely, to extirpate the Patans. The insolent ferocity of those soldiers had rendered them odious to all the other Indians; and the advice of Unvurudeen Khan was, therefore, universally approved of. The effect of their deliberation was kept a profound secret; and they seized an opportunity so favourable to their purpose, that all the Patans, to the number of 3000, were massacred, the women and children only being spared.*

* As these anecdotes are differently related elsewhere, it may happen that many, who think themselves intimately acquainted with

Unvurudeen Khan, having at length finished this horrible carnage, wrote to Nizam El Moulouc the history of the catastrophe of the young Nabob of Arcot, and the punishment he had caused to be inflicted on the Patans; arranging the whole account to his own advantage. The Grand Vizier, Suba of Decan, concluded that he could not do better than to bestow the Nabobship on Unvurudeen Khan; as the family of the ancient Nabobs was extinct, and Chanda Saeb, who by right of his wife might pretend to it, was prisoner among the Marattas.

At the end of the year 1745, Unvurudeen Khan was established Nabob of Arcot, but did not succeed in procuring the same respect for his government as had attended his regency. He had several children. Maffous Khan, his eldest son, was designed for his successor; but his predilection was in favour of a son whom the law

---

the history of India, may demand, how the Writer of these Memoirs could acquire his knowledge of them? To anticipate this question, it is answered, that they cannot but know that the court and army of Hyder are filled with the relations and servants of the ancient family of the Nabobs of Arcot. Such are Razasaeb, the Nabob of Vandevachi, the son-in-law and nephew of the Nabob of Valore; Assinsaeb, an old man of great merit, formerly grand-treasurer of the Nabobs of Arcot, and exercising the same office under Hyder Ali Khan. In the same army are likewise Baoud Khan and Savay Khan, brothers, and chiefs of the Patans, strongly attached to the French; and, by reason of their youth, spared in the massacre caused by Unvurudeen Khan. The Author of this work being desirous of informing himself in the history of India, cultivated the friendship of all these persons; who took a pleasure in relating the history of the misfortunes of their family, their nation, and their ancient masters. It is from them that he has learned the facts he relates in this place.

excluded from the succession, as being born out of the house, and by a Bayadere, or woman reputed common. He gave Trichnopoli, a strong place on the Caveri, with a considerable territory, to this son, who was named Mohumed Ali Khan.

Unvurudeen Khan was in quiet possession of the fruit of his crimes, when Providence raised up an avenger of the family of the Nabobs of Arcot. This man was the famous Dupleix, whom the French King and East India Company, in 1746, called from the employment of director and commandant of Chandernagore, and appointed governor of Pondicherry.

This great man, after having acquired much glory by his brave defence of Pondicherry against Admiral Boscawen, whom he forced to raise the siege, received the news of the peace between France and England in the year 1747. In this juncture he thought it necessary, for the honour and advantage of his nation, to punish Unvurudeen Khan for the assistance he had afforded the English during the siege, by furnishing them with troops on that occasion: being likewise well assured, that this new family would always oppose the interests of the French, who had shown so strong an attachment to the family of Syud. His first step was to procure an antagonist to Unvurudeen Khan, by his negociations with the Marattas; who were by that means induced to set at liberty Chanda Saeb, Nabob of Trichnopoli, who had espoused the sister of the last Nabob of Arcot, and whose wife and son had taken refuge at Pondicherry.

Chanda Saeb being thus restored to his liberty, repaired immediately to the court of Naserjung, who succeeded his father Nizam El Moulouc in the Subaship of Decan in 1748. It was in vain that he solicited this young prince to re-establish him in the Nabobship of Arcot, as the inheritance of his wife, or at least in his town and fortress of Trichnopoli: the intrigues and the money of Unvurudeen Khan prevented his success with the Suba. But he was more fortunate in his application to Hedaet Mohyoddeen Khan, king of the little state of Adonis, and nephew of Naserjung. This young prince, the son of an elder brother of the Suba, had been designed by Nizam El Moulouc as his successor; but that Vizier perceiving himself at the point of death, and his grandson very young, nominated and caused his son Naserjung to be acknowledged his successor.

Chanda Saeb persuaded the young prince of Adonis, that it was proper for him to request the Nabobship of Arcot of his uncle; the extent and value of this last being much more considerable than the territory of Adonis. The nephew consequently made his request, which met with a refusal from his uncle, whose jealousy made him averse to a step that tended to increase the power of his nephew. Hedaet Mohyoddeen Khan, urged on by Chanda Saeb and M. Dupleix, raised an army of 60,000 men, with which, accompanied by Chanda Saeb, he arrived in the country of Arcot in July 1749, where he was joined by the French, to the number of 600 men and 2,000 Sepoys, commanded by the Comte D'Auteuil. This army marched against Unvurudeen Khan, who had assembled all his force, and encamped near Ambour. After having repulsed his antagonist for two successive days, his entrenchments were forced by the French on the third; and he lost the victory and his life at the age of eighty-two years. His two sons, Maffous Khan and Mohumed Ali Khan, were present at this battle. The first was made prisoner, and the other fled to the fortress of Trichnaopoli. Every other part of the country acknowledged the grandson of Nizam El Moulouc, as Nabob of Arcot.

Naserjung, jealous of the accession of power that Hedaet Mohyoddeen Khan had acquired, contrary to his orders assembled his army, and marched into the country of Arcot against him, Chanda Saeb, and the French who had assisted him in his undertaking. And in the month of February 1750, he arrived within six leagues of Pondicherry, with an innumerable army.

The ancient ministers and courtiers of Nizam El Moulouc, shocked to behold this dissension, attempted to reconcile the uncle and the nephew. They concerted among themselves, that the nephew should repair to his uncle's camp, and make his submission; and that the uncle should invest him with the authority of Nabob of Arcot. Hedaet Mohyoddeen Khan, on the assurances of the lords who had offered themselves as mediators, repaired to the camp of Naserjung; who, instead of giving him the appointment of Nabob, caused him to be arrested.

This treachery of the Suba of Decan occasioned a general disgust in his whole army. The lords conspired his destruction, and corresponded with the governor Dupleix, who caused the French army, consisting of 800 French and 4,000 Sepoys, under M. de la Touche, to march against the army of Naserjung, consisting of more than 300,000 fighting men. But this handful of French, aided by the conspirators, were sufficient to decide the fate of so powerful a prince, who was slain on his elephant by the Patan Nabob of Curpa, one of the conspirators. His nephew Hedaet Mohyoddeen Khan succeeded to his government, as Suba, in the month of December, in the same year.

It is at this æra that the history of Hyder Ali Khan commences in these Memoirs. He was then at the head of a quota of troops in Naserjung's army. It would be difficult to trace his actions from a more remote period; because, no person has taken the pains to collect the facts that relate to his infancy. They were far from beholding the avenger of India, in the soldier of Naserjung; or the scourge of the English, in the army that then fought against the French.

Hedaet Mohyoddeen Khan, who assumed the name of Mouzaferjung, expressed his gratitude to M. Dupleix and all the French, and gave the Nabobship of Arcot to Chanda Saeb. In his return to Hyderabad, his capital, he was accompanied by M. de Bussi, at the head of a body of French troops; but he was not fortunate enough to arrive at the end of his voyage, the Patans having slain him in a sedition. At the beginning of 1751, his uncle Salabutjung, brother of Naserjung, succeeded him, and had the same affection for the French as his nephew. Mr. Lally having recalled M. Bussi, in 1758, from the court and army of Salabutjung, this prince, whose disposition was good, though his abilities were not great, was assassinated by his brother Nizam Ali Khan, who is at present Suba of Decan, and will frequently be mentioned in the course of the following History.

The English having always supported the family of Unvurudeen Khan, preferred Mohumed Ali Khan to his eldest brother; and caused him to be acknowledged Nabob of Arcot in the treaty of Fontainbleau, after having assisted him to impoverish all the princes of the ancient family of the Nabobs of Arcot. Chanda Saeb had the misfortune to fall into the hands of the English, who were cruel enough to deliver him to Menagi, general of the troops at Tanjore, who caused him to be beheaded in the month of June 1752. This crime, though yet unrevenged, will not pass unpunished; for Hyder Ali has promised the dominions of the Raja of Tanjore to Raza Saeb, son of Chanda Saeb.

This succinct account of the revolutions in India, is sufficient to serve as an introduction to the History of Hyder Ali Khan.

Note.—The coss is an Indian measure of distance, which answers nearly to 2,500 toises, or a few yards more than an English league.

PARTICULAR CIRCUMSTANCES

RELATING TO THE

PERSON, HABITS, AND MANNERS

OF

HYDER SHAH,

ALIAS

HYDER ALI KHAN BAHADUR.

HYDER SHAH, alias Hyder Ali Khan, whose precise age is not known, ought to be about fifty-four or fifty-six years of age, if we may depend on those who have known him from his infancy. He is about five feet six inches high, and very lusty, though active, and capable of bearing fatigue as well on foot as on horseback. His complexion is brown, as is that of all Indians who expose themselves to the air and the sun. His features are coarse, his nose small and turned up, his lower lip rather thick; and he wears neither beard nor whiskers, contrary to the custom of the Orientals, especially the Mohumedans. His habits, like those of all the natives of India, are of white muslin, with a turban of the same. His robe is fashioned nearly the same as those of the European ladies, which are called *à l'Angloise.* The body and sleeves fit neatly, and are drawn close by strings; the rest of the robe being ample, and in folds: so that when the Indian great men walk, a page supports their train, from their first stepping off the carpet to their entering into their carriages.

In the army, Hyder Ali wears a military habit invented by himself for his generals. It is an uniform composed of a vest of white satin, with gold flowers, faced with yellow, and attached by cords or strings of the same colour: the drawers are of the same materials; and the boots of yellow velvet. He wears a scarf of white silk about his waist; and, with the military habit, his turban is of a red or aurora colour. When he is on foot, he commonly uses a gold-headed cane; and sometimes on horseback he wears a sabre, hanging by a belt of velvet embroidered with gold, and fastened over his shoulder by a clasp of gold, enriched with some precious stones.

He never wears much jewellery either on his turban or his clothes, and never uses either necklace or bracelets. His turban is very long, and flat at top. In this particular he follows the ancient mode; as well as in his slippers, which are very large, and have a long point turned back, resembling the roofs of the buildings in some countries up the Levant; or those slippers anciently worn in France, and called *Souliers à la poulaine.* The *petits maîtres* of his and other Indian courts affect to wear little bonnets which scarcely cover the tops of their heads, and slippers so small as scarce to admit the points of their feet: but though in these and other respects their taste is so different from that of Hyder and his son, yet to imitate him as much as possible in the article of beard and whiskers, without infringing the precepts of the Alcoran, they reduce their beard and moustaches to a moustache scarcely discernible.

The countenance of Hyder, though not handsome, is open, and calculated to inspire confidence. He has not acquired the habit of disguising his aspect, which is either gay or overspread with chagrin, according to the occasions that present themselves. He possesses a facility of conversing on any subject; and has none of that stateliness and taciturnity which almost all the other princes of the East affect to preserve. When he receives a stranger, he is reserved, and appears to speak with gravity, but soon recovers his usual ease, and converses with all the world, repeating himself the news and common conversation of the day with the greatest affability. It is most astonishing, that this sovereign asks questions, gives answers, hears a letter read, and dictates an answer to another, beholds a theatrical exhibition, and even seems to attend to the performance—at the same instant that he decides concerning things of the utmost importance.

There is no sovereign more easy of access to every one that has business with him, whether strangers or subjects; and the former, whatever may be their quality, are always sure to be introduced into his presence, by demanding an audience, by a Soutahdar, or mace-bearer, of which there is always a sufficient number at the gate of his palace. The Fakirs, a species of begging monks, are alone excluded from this indulgence; but when one of these appears, he is conducted to the Peerzada or grand almoner, who supplies his wants. The court of Hyder is, in this point, absolutely different from those of all the other princes in India; who hold these Fakirs in such high veneration, that they suffer them to enter their palaces at any hour, and even admit them to their table. They have the assurance to take the first place at table, nearest the prince; though they are most commonly disgusting, filthy, and covered with vermin.

When business or parties of pleasure do not prevent Hyder Ali from going to rest at his usual time, which is after midnight, he rises with the sun, that is to say, about six o'clock. As soon as he is risen, the majors of the army,* who have been on duty the preceding day

* These majors of the army are like adjutants-general. They are not persons of distinction, but men of approved diligence and fidelity, chosen out of the subaltern officers of cavalry and infantry.

and night, and likewise those who relieve them, enter, make their reports, and receive orders to be transmitted to the ministers and generals, who themselves have the privilege of entering his dressing-room, if they have anything extraordinary or pressing to communicate. The couriers that have arrived during the night, or in the morning, also come and lay their despatches at his feet. It may be esteemed a weakness in a prince so occupied, that his toilet takes up a considerable part of his time. It lasts commonly two or three hours; and is chiefly taken up by his barbers, who pluck the hairs from his beard.

But justice requires us likewise to observe, that when any military operation requires his attention, the toilet is no more thought of.

Between eight and nine in the morning he quits his apartment, and repairs to a saloon, where a number of secretaries wait for his appearance. Into their hands, according to their respective departments, he puts the letters received; giving them at the same time instructions for the answers. His sons, his relations, and those lords who are honoured with his intimacy, enter; and if it be nine o'clock, they take the usual refreshment. If he has leisure, he appears at a balcony, and receives the salute of his elephants,* that are led before him, as well as his horses. His tigers of chace likewise pay him a visit. They are led by hand, and are covered with a mantle of green and gold hanging to the ground, and a bonnet on their head, of cloth embroidered with gold, with which their eyes can be immediately covered, if they should chance to prove mischievous. Hyder himself gives each of them a ball of sweetmeats, which they take very adroitly

---

* When the prince appears at the balcony, his officers cry out, "Your elephants salute your Majesty;" and at the same time those animals, who are ranged in a semicircle round the palace, make three genuflections.

with their paws, being exceedingly tame. These are the spotted tigers, and their keepers lead them every day into those places where the greatest crowds are: but the grand tiger, or tiger royal, has never been tamed by any attempts yet made.

After the repast, which ends about half after ten, Hyder enters into the hall of audience; or the grand tent, if at the army. He is seated on a sopha, beneath a canopy, and very often in some balcony that fronts an open place or court of the palace; and some of his relations sit on each side of him. All persons who have permission or access, of which the number is very great, may come to this audience; and those who have affairs to transact, may either request admittance by means of the Souquedars, or put their request into the hands of those officers by whom it is carried to their chief, who is always present, and who places it at the feet of the prince, where it is immediately read and answered. It is not customary here to stop the prince by the offer of petitions, when he goes out, unless the affair be very urgent and extraordinary, or the petitioner has been prevented from forwarding his request at the usual hours of audience; a circumstance that very rarely happens.*

---

* In the year 1767, Hyder being at Coimbatoor, and going out with his retinue about five in the evening, to take the air, an old woman prostrated herself, and cried out, Justice!—Hyder immediately caused his carriage to stop; made a sign to her to come forward, and demanded her request. She answered, "My Lord, I had but one daughter, and Agha Mohumud has ravished her from me." Hyder replied, "Agha Mohumud has been gone hence more than a month; how does it happen that you have waited till this time without complaining?"—"My Lord, I have given many requests into the hands of Hyder Sha, and have received no answer."—This Hyder Sha, who was the chief usher, preceded the Nabob, bearing a large collar

At this audience thirty or forty secretaries are seated along the wall to his left, who write continually. Couriers arrive almost every instant, and are conducted with great noise and bustle to the feet of the prince, where they lay their despatches. A secretary kneeling takes the packet, and sitting on his hams before the prince, opens it and reads the letter. Hyder immediately dictates the particulars of the answer, and the letter is carried to the office of a minister, contrary to the customs of the princes of the East, who affix their names by means of a seal. Hyder signs the despatches in order as they are completed, as well as a number of private orders. Many writers report the contrary to this, which only proves that they have never seen Hyder half an hour at a time. The orders that issue from the offices of the ministers have no other signature than that of the great seal, of which they are the depositories; and the despatch is closed with the private seal of the minister. The letters signed by

---

of gold as a mark of his dignity. He advanced, and said, "This woman, as well as her daughter, are of infamous repute, and live in a disgraceful manner." The Nabob gave orders to return instantly to the palace, and commanded the woman to follow him. All the court were in great apprehension for the officer, who was much beloved; and no person daring to intercede for him, the son of Hyder begged the commandant of Europeans to endeavour to procure his pardon. He accordingly requested it of Hyder, who refused it with much severity. "I cannot grant your request," said he: "there is no greater crime than that of interrupting the communication between a sovereign and his subjects. It is the duty of the powerful to see that the weak have justice. The sovereign is the only protector God has given them; and the prince who suffers oppression to pass unpunished among his subjects, is deservedly deprived of their affection and confidence, and at last compels them to revolt against him." He

Hyder are closed by the seal of the sovereign, of which the principal secretary is guardian. When this Nabob writes any interesting letter, or gives an order of importance, he affixes a particular or private seal, which he always wears on his finger; and in that case he himself carries the packet to one of his couriers, who conveys it as far as the first station. To the packet is joined a paper, denoting the hour it was sent off; and at every station the time of its arrival is marked. We shall afterwards have occasion to speak of these posts, which have been since imitated by the English.

If Hyder purchases horses or elephants, or if new pieces of cannon have been founded or brought from any port or arsenal, he inspects them during this audience; the animals or pieces of cannon being brought into the court or square of the palace.

Ministers, generals, ambassadors, and other great men, rarely appear at this audience, unless commanded, or unless urged by extra-

---

then gave orders to punish Hyder Sha with two hundred stripes on the parade; and at the same time commanded an officer of his Abyssinian horse-guard to repair immediately with the woman to the country seat at which Agha Mohumud then was. If he found the girl, his orders were to deliver her to her mother, and return with the head of Agha Mohumud; but if she was not found, he was charged to conduct Agha Mohumud to Coimbatoor. The girl was found, and the head of the criminal was brought to Hyder. Agha Mohumud was then sixty years old, had been chief usher to Hyder Ali twenty-five years, and was succeeded in his office by Hyder Sha, at which time the Nabob had given him a jaghir, or considerable district of land, as a reward for his services. This man was enamoured of the girl, and had carried her off, upon her mother's refusing to sell her to him, because she subsisted by prostituting her. —The Alcoran condemns the ravisher of a girl or woman to death.

ordinary affairs. It is peculiar to their dignity to see the prince only in the evening, when none but men of consequence are admitted, and nothing else is thought of but to make their court to the sovereign, or to share his pleasures. The great have agents, who are usually Bramins, who solicit their affairs either with the prince or his ministers; and these agents, who have the title of Vakeels or envoys, have their leave of admission to the presence when they have been presented by their masters, and are honourably received. The ministers send one of the principal secretaries of their department to the prince, who, sitting before him in the same posture as the other secretaries, communicate their business, and converse with him.

A great ambassador, or other person of consequence, is announced in a loud voice by the chief of the ushers, in these terms, "Your Majesty, the Lord of —— salutes you." Ministers, secretaries, vakeels, or other men of business are not announced, but go in and out without particular observation, except that they are careful to salute the Nabob. When a great man is announced, the prince returns the salute, and begs him to be seated: the friends and other great men who surround the sovereign, salute him also; and, in proportion to the esteem or favour he is in with the Nabob, they give place, that he may approach him. A person of ordinary rank, who has requested an audience, makes three reverences in entering, by moving his hand from his forehead almost to the ground; and afterwards places himself on one side of the chief usher, continuing silent, with his hands joined before him. The Nabob returns the salute by simply touching his turban with his hand, and affects to continue the discourse with those about him; after which he makes a sign for the person to advance, and demands, in an engaging and affectionate manner, the subject of his visit: and upon the exposition of the affair by the suppliant, he receives a decisive answer. If he be a stranger of a genteel rank or employment, as a trader or merchant of consequence, he receives orders to sit; and his place is usually on the right, fronting the secretaries. The Nabob asks him some questions respecting his state of life, his country, or his voyage, and appoints a time when he will see his merchandize. Betel is then presented to the stranger, and is understood as equivalent to a permission to retire; which is done with the same ceremony as at the entrance.

This audience continues till after three o'clock, which is the hour he returns to his apartment to sleep, or make the siesta, as it is called in Italy.

About half-past five, the prince returns into the hall of audience, or some other large apartment, where he places himself in a balcony to see his troops exercise, and his cavalry defile before him. He is, as in the morning, surrounded by some of his friends or relations; and the secretaries are busied in reading letters, or writing.

About half-past six, when the day closes in, a great number of Mussalchys or bearers of flambeaux, appear in the court of the palace, and salute the prince as they pass on the side of the apartments where he is. They illuminate all the apartments in a moment, especially that in which the Nabob is, with tapers in chandeliers of exquisite workmanship, ornamented with festoons of flowers of the utmost lightness and delicacy. These chandeliers, on account of the wind, are covered with large shades of English glass. There are, likewise, in some parts of the palace, large glass lanthorns, painted with flowers of all colours. The great men, ministers, and ambassadors, visit the Nabob only at night. They are usually perfumed with the most costly perfumes. Besides the men in power and employment, the apartments are filled with the young nobility; and everybody assumes the most polite and engaging manners. After having saluted the prince, the salute is paid to his sons and relations, in an easy unaffected manner. Among the young nobility, there are a certain number who have the title of Arabsbequi; which answers nearly to that of chamberlain, in Germany. There are ordinarily four in waiting each day: they are distinguished by their sabre, which they carry in their hand in the sheath, using it nearly as a walking-stick. All the other company leave their arms in the hands of their pages and other attendants, who are very numerous, and fill the avenues of the palace. The pages alone are permitted to enter: they follow their master, bearing his train into the apartments, till they quit their slippers at their stepping on the carpet; the pages then let fall the train, and put the slippers in a bag. His apartments are commonly covered with white muslin, spread upon the most superb Persia carpets. He has such a predilection for white, that he causes wainscotting, that is painted, gilt, and varnished, to be covered with white muslin; and even chairs and sophas of embroidered velvet or gold stuff.

There is, for the most part, a comedy every night, that commences about eight in the evening, and lasts till eleven: it is intermixed with dances and songs. During this comedy, the Arabsbequi continue near the strangers, and politely inform them of everything they may desire to know; as the subject of the comedy, the news of the day, etc. They are careful to ask, if he chooses to drink or eat; in which case, they cause sherbet, fruits, or confectionary to be presented to him; but they seldom eat. If the stranger chooses to play chess, they play with him, or propose a party. Hyder, to whom the entertainments of the stage are very indifferent, discourses with his ministers or ambassadors, sometimes passing into a cabinet to speak with more secrecy; and continues, as in the morning, to dispatch business, without seeming to be busy. Almost always, before the end of the performance, flowers are brought to him in a basket of filigram, out of which he himself gives a few to the lords who are about him; and afterwards the basket is carried into the apartments of the theatre, every one taking a small flower from them, and returning a profound reverence to the prince. This takes place even to the lowest secretary. When Hyder wishes to give a particular mark of his esteem, he himself makes a collar of jasmine flowers, knotting them with silk as he converses, which he himself adjusts round the neck of the happy mortal to whom he gives this glorious mark of his esteem and favour. He has several times conferred this honour on the chiefs of his Europeans, knowing well that the French, above all nations, esteem themselves well paid by this sort of money. He who has received this honour is visited the following day by the first people of the court to compliment him.

If a battle has been gained, or any other glorious event has happened in favour of the prince, the poet of the court arrives, announcing himself, at his first entering the apartments, by the pompous and extravagant titles he bestows on the prince: as, "Health "to the greatest king on earth, whose name alone causes his enemies "to tremble," etc. All the world, at the voice of the poet, becomes silent and attentive. The comedy or dance is interrupted; the poet enters, seats himself in the place immediately opposite the prince, and recites a poem, which every body affects to hear with the utmost attention, except the prince, who seems at that time to be more particularly busied in conversing with his ministers. The poet usually, after speaking of the prince, proceeds to his relations, and the generals or principal officers; not forgetting the ministers and favourites. The young courtiers, or *baras ā demi*, who are usually included altogether in the praises bestowed by the poet, often turn it into ridicule; and their derision extends even to those who are the highest spoken of. They and the secretaries, or other inferior courtiers, often parody the words of the poem very pleasantly, sparing nobody but the prince and his son: but as they have no printing, both the poem and the criticism are of short duration. We cannot speak of their public entertainments, without mentioning the Bayaderes, of whom the Abbé Raynal has drawn so advantageous a portrait in his Histoire Philosophique.

At the present time, the court of Hyder is the most brilliant in India; and his company of performers is without contradiction the first, as well on account of its riches, as because the Bayaderes are the women to whom he gives the preference. Being sovereign of part of Begapore, he has every facility of procuring, among this class of women, those who are most remarkable for their beauty and talents.

The comedians of the court are all women. A directress, who is likewise manager, purchases young girls at the age of four or five years, who are chosen on account of their beauty. She causes them to be inoculated, and then provides them with masters both for dancing and music. They are taught every accomplishment that can inspire the prince and his court with the love of pleasure; and their success is such, that they delight and seduce the most insensible men. They begin to appear in public at the age of about ten or eleven years. They have generally the most delicate features, large dark eyes, beautiful eye-brows, small mouth, and the finest teeth; their cheeks are dimpled, and their black hair hangs in flowing tresses to the ground; their complexion is a clear brown, not such as that of the Mulatto women, who are incapable of blushing; but like that of a country girl in the flow of health, who has preserved the roses, after suffering the lilies to fade. These are the yellow women, that the Orientals prefer to all others: they give themselves that tinge by painting their cheeks of a jonquil colour, in the same manner as the French women use rouge; and it is remarkable that in a very short time one becomes habituated to this colour, and finds it agreeable. Their habit is always a fine gauze, very richly embroidered with gold; and they are covered with jewels; their head, their neck, their ears, their breasts, their arms, fingers, legs, and toes, have their jewels; and even their nose is ornamented with a small diamond, that gives them an arch look, which is far from being unpleasing.

The comedies are all pieces of intrigue. They personate either women who league together to deceive a jealous husband, or young girls that conspire to deceive their mother. It is impossible to play with more art or with more natural ease. Their songs are gay and agreeable. The words that are sung by a single voice are almost always the complaint of a lover. Those which are sung in chorus are much gayer; but they have no second parts, and are always repeated.

The dancers are superior in their performance to the comedians and singers; it may even be affirmed that they would afford pleasure on the theatre of the opera at Paris. Every part is employed when these girls dance; their heads, their eyes, their arms, their feet, and all their body seem to move only to enchant and surprise. They are very light, and very strong in the legs; turning round on one foot, and springing up immediately after with a surprising force. They have so much accuracy in their movements, that they accompany the instruments with bells that are on their feet; and as they are of the most elegant figures, all their motions are graceful. No Bayadere of the prince's company is more than seventeen years old. At this age they are dismissed; and either travel over the province, or attach themselves to the Pagodas.*

The directress of this company is paid by the prince; but her emoluments are not known. She has always a number of pieces ready in rehearsal to be played at a moment's notice. Though there is every reason to think she is well paid by Hyder for the pleasures she procures him, the emoluments she receives from private individuals of fortune, are still more advantageous to her. When a great man gives a set supper, he has usually a comedy ornamented with songs and dances. The directress of the prince's company is paid one hundred rupees for every actress that plays, sings, or dances. The number of these actresses is often more than twenty, the instrumental music not being charged.

If a supper is given to a few private friends, the singers and dancers are likewise employed at the same price of one hundred rupees. Besides which, they must be furnished with supper, and abundance of fruits, sweetmeats, and warm milk. If the friends are

* Every Pagoda maintains a number of Bayaderes, whose charms produce one of the most certain revenues of the Bramins.

retained to sleep (as is often done, where their suppers are more friendly than ceremonious), they choose each a companion for the night among the performers, for which the directress is likewise paid one hundred rupees each; and the master of the house must present his friend with some trinket, or piece of stuff, to be given to the damsel when she is sent away in the morning.

Besides the prince's company, there are several others in the town where the court is kept, and in the armies. There are even some that are composed of men only; but the people of the court never have recourse to any but the prince's company.

At eleven o'clock, or about midnight, every one retires but those that sup with the Nabob; who, except on grand festivals, are always his friends and relations.

This mode of life pursued by Hyder, is, as may be easily imagined, interrupted in the army. It is likewise occasionally interrupted by hunting parties, by excursions on foot or horseback, or by his attending to assist at the exercises and evolutions made by considerable bodies of his troops.

When he is obliged to remain a month in camp, or in any town, he usually goes to the chace twice a week. He hunts the stag, the roebuck, the antelope, and the tiger. When notice arrives that this last animal has been observed to quit the forests, and appear in the plain, he mounts his horse, followed by all his Abyssinians, his spear-men on foot, and almost all the nobility armed with spears and bucklers. The traces of the beast being found, the hunters surround his hiding place, and contract the circle by degrees. As soon as the creature, who is usually hid in some rice ground, perceives his enemies, he roars, and looks every where to find a place of escape; and when he prepares to spring on some one to force a passage, he is attacked by Hyder himself, to whom the honour of giving the first stroke is yielded, and in which he seldom fails. Thus the pleasures of the sovereign are varied to infinity.

THE

TITLES ASSUMED BY

HYDER SHAH,

ALIAS

HYDER ALI KHAN BAHADUR;

WITH

THEIR EXPLICATION.

HYDER ALI KHAN, Nabob Bahadur,* Nahondas,† Suba of Scirra,

---

* Nabob Bahadur signifies incomparable Knight; the Bahadurs in India being what the knights were in Europe. A great sovereign or general among the Mogols, after a battle, gives the dignity of Bahadur to a man of distinction, one of the principal officers who has behaved with honour. If there has formerly existed any ceremony for the creation of a Bahadur, it is now out of use: all that is done at present is, that the general publicly praises his actions, and in his discourse always calls him Bahadur; which title is afterwards given him by all the world indiscriminately. A Bahadur has great privileges; he may go everywhere completely armed, causing a gilt mace to be carried before him, and may appear thus even in the

† Nahondas implies one who is worthy of all the titles of honour.

King of the Canarins and Corgues, Dayva* of Mysore, Sovereign of the Empires of Cherquile and Calicut,† which contain the kingdoms of Cananore, Cochin, Trevancour; Nabob of Bangalore, Ballapour,

---

presence of any sovereign. When a Bahadur arrives at court, he demands an audience, which is always granted; he presents himself with a helmet on, and armed in every other respect: the sovereign seeing him enter, rises and salutes him, and in conversation uses the term *My brother;* because all the sovereigns dignify themselves with the title of Bahadur. Hyder was surnamed the Incomparable Bahadur; the true signification of the word *Nabob* being *incomparable;* for it is a title of honour, not of dignity; however, by common custom Nabob of Bangalore is used instead of Lord or Prince of Bangalore; but literally it only signifies incomparable, or without equal, in Bangalore. This title being exclusive, it must in no case be given to an inferior in presence of his superior. Hyder, to shew that the title of Bahadur, which we have rendered Knight, but which literally implies Great Warrior, is above all other titles, signs, instead of his name, the two letters B. B. for Bahadur Bahadur, or Knight of Knights. He was also styled Hyder Shah or Bahadur Shah.

* Dayva, or regent. It will be hereafter seen how Hyder became regent of this kingdom.

† Sovereign of the empires of Cherquile and Calicut. The Portuguese were the first Europeans, who, arriving with their ships on the coast of Malabar, gave the title of Emperors to the sovereigns of these two countries. The name answers very ill to the power and extent of the states of Cherquile and Samorin. The only resemblance they have to emperors is, that they are the chiefs or heads of two confederations of petty princes, or Rajas, to whom the Portuguese gave the title of Kings, because they have a diadem and purple mantle, having the head wrapped in red muslin, and a stripe of gold

Bassapatnam, or Bisnagar, &c. &c., Lord of the Mountains and Vallies, &c. &c.,* King of the Islands of the Sea, &c. &c.†

---

fastened to the back of their head; and wearing no other clothes than a kind of shirt of red gauze or muslin, reaching almost to their knees. Their pretended kings seldom possess a territory of more than two, or six leagues at the extreme. They go on foot, with their legs naked, followed by their courtiers barefoot, and armed with sabres and bucklers.

* Hyder is Lord of Malleaur or Carnate; which two words, in different languages, imply. The Country of Mountains and Vallies.

† We shall hereafter shew how this title of King of the Isles of the Sea was given, when his fleet made the conquest of the Maldives, which are said to be twelve thousand in number.

*** Mysore fell into the hands of Hyder Ali Khan about the year 1763, Bednore between 1763-5, Soonda in 1764, Malabar in 1765-6, Barah Mhal in 1764-5, the petty states of Hindoo Rajahs and of Purseram Bhow in 1774-7, Carnatic Balaghaut Bejapory in 1776, Carnatic Balaghaut Hydrabady in 1776-9. Tippoo Sultaun, on his accession to the throne, added Adoni, Sanore, Koorke, Anagoondy, Kurpah, Kurnool, and Imteazgur. This Prince inherited sovereign sway over a tract of country comprehending a space of not less than 80,000 square geographical miles, yielding a clear annual revenue of about three millions sterling, after deducting all cursory expenses; and peopled by upwards of six millions of inhabitants, including for the defence of the whole about one hundred and forty-four thousand (144,000) well-disciplined troops, together with a standing militia of one hundred and eighty thousand (180,000) men, under various denominations. The year 1786 appears to have been occupied by the Sultan in internal regulations; inspection of his forts, and examination of his treasures and stores. Soon after his return to Seringapatam, he ordered an inventory to be made of his property of every kind. The treasure, jewels, and other valuable articles, were estimated at eighty millions sterling. He had also 700 elephants, 6,000 camels, 11,000 horses, 400,000 bullocks and cows, 100,000 buffaloes, 600,000 sheep, 300,000 firelocks, 300,000 matchlocks, 200,000 swords, 22,000 pieces of cannon, of different calibres, and an immense quantity of gunpowder and other military stores. His regular army consisted of 19,000 cavalry, 10,000 artillery, and 70,000 infantry. He had besides 5,000 rocket men and 40,000 irregular infantry, and also a militia of 180,000 men. Tippoo Sultaun, at this period, formed a new code of regulations for his army. He reduced his cavalry, and augmented the infantry. He adopted Persian and Tartar terms for the words of command, which were formerly given in English or French, and gave new names to the different divisions of the army.

THE

HISTORY OF HYDER SHAH,

ALIAS

HYDER ALI KHAN BAHADUR:

OR,

NEW MEMOIRS CONCERNING THE EAST INDIES.

HYDER ALI KHAN, son of Nadim Saeb, general of ten thousand horse* in the army of the empire, was born in 1717 at Divanelli,

---

* General of ten thousand horse is nearly the same as lieutenant-general in France. In the army of the Mogols, all the degrees are conferred by patents, that give power and commission to raise ten thousand men for the service of the empire; with the prerogative to name all the inferior officers, to keep them in discipline, and to distribute justice among them. As the cavalry is the most esteemed service, the degree of general of ten thousand horse is the highest. This general has the right to cause any number of banners or streamers to be carried before him, and to cause a large square standard to be hoisted before his tent, which is, at the same time, a

a small fortress or castle between Colar and Oscota in the country of Benguelour. This land was given in fief to his father, who was particularly attached to Nizam El Moulouc, Grand Vizier and Suba of Decan. Hyder Ali claimed the honour of being by descent a Coreishy, and consequently of the same tribe as the Arabian Prophet Mohumed. When his ancestors emigrated from Mecca to India, is not known but to his family alone, and it is stated that they were much respected in the district of Kohir, which is situated about the middle of the Peninsula, between Hydrabad and Goolburgah; and that several of them held the honourable office of Judge.

After the death of Nizam El Moulouc, Nadim Saeb retired to Divanelli, with his two sons, Ismael Saeb and Hyder. Ismael Saeb was much older than his brother. He entered into the service of the king of Mysore; and in a short time became his first general. The king of Mysore, as a reward for a victory he had obtained over the Marattas, gave him the country and fortress of Benguelour; which put him into a situation of having a body of troops of his own, that composed part of the army of the king of Mysore, when Naserjung made a descent upon the coast of Coromandel in 1750. Hyder, then about thirty-four years old, had never quitted his father's house. His father gave him the command of the quota of troops he was bound to furnish to the army of the Suba, for his lordship of Divanelli. It consisted only of fifty horsemen, and two hundred soldiers armed with matchlocks. Ibrahim Saeb, the maternal uncle of Hyder, served him instead of a Mentor.

Hyder being at the battle where Naserjung was slain, the bravery

---

mark of his jurisdiction. A general, or commander-in-chief, causes two to be hoisted. When the grand army of a Subaship is assembled a large triangular standard is displayed at the head of the camp.

of the French, who, to the number of eight hundred, seconded by four thousand Sepoys, had the courage to attack the army of the Mogols, then more than three hundred thousand strong, made such an impression on his mind, that he was persuaded the French were capable of undertaking the most difficult enterprises. Having followed Mouzaferjung, successor to Naserjung, to Pondicherry, the observations he made in that city, upon the manners, discipline, fortifications, buildings, arts, and industry of the French, gave him the highest esteem for that celebrated and warlike nation, and more especially for M. Dupleix who was then governor.

In 1751, Mouzaferjung having withdrawn his army to Golconda, Hyder, whose father was dead, went to join his brother in Mysore. On the account the young man gave of the advantageous arms of the Europeans, and their address in managing great guns, Meer Ismael Saeb dispatched a Guebre to Bombay, to purchase cannon, and muskets with bayonets. This Persian, who died in 1767, purchased two thousand muskets, and six pieces of cannon, of the governor of Bombay. He likewise enrolled thirty European sailors, of different nations, that he collected on the coast of Malabar, to serve as cannoneers.

Meer Ismael Saeb, brother to Hyder, was thus the first Indian who formed a corps of Sepoys armed with firelocks and bayonets, and who had a train of artillery served by Europeans. This procured him new advantages over the enemies of the king of Mysore, and increased the esteem and friendship of that prince for him.

Nand Raja, brother to the king of Mysore, and Dayva,* having formed an army to make a descent upon the coast of Coromandel, and join that of the English, Hyder, at the recommendation of his

---

* Nand Raja was Dayva, which signifies regent, as Hyder is at present. It will hereafter be seen how this prince lost the regency.

brother, obtained the command of the cavalry of this army. The English, aided by the Mysorians, forced the French troops, combined with those of Chanda Saeb, to surrender themselves prisoners of war, and to give up the Pagod of Schirnigam, in which they had taken refuge. It was on this occasion that Chanda Saeb was made prisoner. Nand Raja afterwards quarrelling with the English, M. Dupleix formed an alliance with him; and it was agreed to lay siege to Trichnopoli, a strong place on the river Caveri, with an army composed of French forces, together with those of Mysore, and those of Chanda Saeb,* Nabob of Arcot. The English, who were the allies of Mohumed Ali Khan,† competitor of Chanda Saeb, had then a garrison in Trichnopoli.

When the French set out from Pondicherry, in 1752, to join Nanda Raja, they were harrassed in their march by a body of Mahratta cavalry, commanded by a chief allied with the English. On this occasion the commandant of the French troops wrote to the regent of Mysore to send him a reinforcement.

Hyder was sent to his assistance, at the head of eighteen hundred horse. It was then that Hyder began to be known to the French, and to acquire some reputation among the Europeans, whence he had his pretended name of Andernec. Before that time, the French, the English, and other European nations, had very little connection with, or knowledge of, the interior parts of the country; and there were not perhaps two Frenchmen at Pondicherry that could converse in the language of the Mogols, which is a kind of Persian, and is commonly called Moors. The officers and soldiers had no other interpreters than their Dabashis, or Malabar domestics, who knew

---

* Chanda Saeb, as has been shown in the Introduction, was the Nabob acknowledged by the French.

† See the Introduction.

only their own language and a sort of corrupt Portuguese. The Malabar language, though very regular, is perhaps the poorest language in being: so that the word *Dore* signifies Mr. or Sir; and to express the word governor, or general, or *the superior Sir*, they say *Peri-dore*, which is *the great Sir*, or *Master;* and in the same manner, to denote any chief whatsoever, the Malabar language has only the word *Naic;* and they use *Tanjaor Naic* to signify the king or Raja of Tanjaor; and *Narim Naic*, and *Chabri Naic*, to denote the serjeant Narim, or the corporal Chabri: and the name *Hyder Naic* implying the chief Hyder, the French have formed it into Andernec. It is this name of Naic that has caused it to be imagined that Hyder had been a corporal of Sepoys. He was then called Hyder Saeb, which is the same as Mr. Hyder. His name was enlarged in proportion as his power increased, as the custom is among the Mogols; and he is now called Hyder Ali Khan Bahadur or Bahadur Shah.

When the French army had joined that of Mysore, Hyder,* whose camp then formed the left wing of the Mysorian army, came and encamped himself to the right of the French, in spite of all the arguments of the French commandant, and the regent of Mysore; and, however disagreeable it was to the French to see themselves as it were cooped up, he would not remove from the station he had assumed. He informed the commandant that he wished to be near the French, that he might learn from them the art of war. In fact, he was very attentive and exact in observing everything that passed in the French camp; and caused several of their evolutions† to be

---

* M. de Maissin, who commanded the French at that time, is the author of this anecdote, which sufficiently confutes the several stories that have been circulated respecting Hyder's intentions.

† Hyder, though general of cavalry in the army of Mysore, had troops of his own.—The left is the post of honour in India.

repeated, as well as was in his power, in his own camp. This repetition caused some diversion to the French officers and soldiers, whom he was attentive to please by his politeness and good manners. But it was not with any satisfaction they observed that Hyder had drawn the most active and intelligent French soldiers into his service. He had still in his service, in 1770, the Sieur Stenet,* son of a *Cent-Suisse* of Versailles, who was a volunteer at the siege of Trichnopoli in 1753: he took him at that time into his service, and sent him to his brother in Mysore, as he did every other Frenchman that chose to engage in his service. These enrolments were made with some dexterity; and, as there was need of his services, the French commandant winked at the irregularity of the proceeding.

General Lawrence, who was then only major, attempting to throw some succours and a convoy into Trichnopoli, received a considerable check; of which, in his Memoirs, he gives all the honour to Hyder and his cavalry. English jealousy perhaps induced him to diminish the merit of the French; but it is certain that Hyder distinguished himself highly on this occasion.

In 1755, Nand Raja† having quitted the French to return to Mysore, Hyder made a particular treaty with M. Dupleix, by which he engaged to remain with his troops, forming a body of six thousand men, till the capture of Trichnopoli; and he did not return to Mysore till Mr. Godehen, successor to M. Dupleix, had made a truce with the English, and given orders to raise the siege of Trichnopoli. In 1756, Hyder being informed of the death of his brother, as he was on his

---

* He was then captain in the artillery.

† The cause of the retreat of Nand Raja with the army of Mysore, was, that M. de Bussi, with a body of French, had accompanied Salabutjung, Suba of Decan, when he came to Seringapatam, capital of Mysore, and exacted contributions.

way to rejoin him, hastened to receive the succession that had devolved to him by the law; his brother having no male children. This death put him in possession of a handsome fortress, a fertile territory, and a body of troops, which, joined to his own, amounted to above fifteen thousand men, including two hundred Europeans, and three thousand of excellent cavalry. The king of Mysore having the same confidence in him as his brother Ismael, appointed him generalissimo of his army.

The kings of Mysore being Bramins, had united the royal dignity and the priesthood; and, to be more venerable in the eyes of their people, they affected to appear in public only twice a year; namely, on those days when they presided at the solemn ceremonies of their religion. And in order to appear solely occupied with the sacred mysteries, which they celebrated with pomp and magnificence, they abandoned the government to a Dayva, or regent, who, till the time of Nand Raja, had always been one of the king's nearest relations. But a Bramin, named Canero, favourite of this prince, persuaded him to assume the government himself, and forsake his brother Nand Raja. This last, who had neither the capacity nor the application, nor even the firmness, necessary to support himself in this dignity, made no resistance; and preferred banishment to the frontier to the hazard of making the least remonstrance.

Canero having taken entire possession of the mind of the king, was declared his minister, and charged with the administration of affairs. Hyder kept his command of the army.

The power, the reputation, and the love of the soldiery that were possessed by Hyder, ought to have secured him from the envy and jealousy of this ambitious minister; but Canero, sacrificing every thing to those passions, ventured even to make a private treaty with the Marattas, enemies of the state. In consequence of this treaty, the Maratta army entered Mysore in the rainy season, at the moment when Hyder least expected them, and, deceived by Canero, had dispersed his troops.

The approach of the Marattas, and their superiority in number, obliged him to advance towards Seringapatam, capital of the kingdom, that offered him a sure asylum in the island on which the city is situated, and which cannot be entered, when the Caveri is swelled by the rains, but by the bridge of Seringapatam.

Canero, who in another situation, would have done his utmost to have prevented Hyder from entering the royal city, pressed him to pitch his camp on the island. Hyder fell into the snare of the perfidious Bramin. He passed the bridge and went through the town with his army, which he encamped at the opposite extremity of the island. The Maratta army soon appeared, and invested that part of the river, where it is fordable in the usual state of the waters.

Hyder, having no suspicion of the treachery of Canero, depended on the well-furnished magazines of the city for the subsistence of his troops. But he was in the highest astonishment, the day after the arrival of the Marattas, when he beheld the gates of the city shut; and was informed that Canero had determined that the whole army should perish, either by hunger or the cannon of the city, unless they delivered up Hyder to the king, who had strong reason for securing his person. This account convinced Hyder that Canero had sworn his destruction. He sent several officers to treat with him; but the day was consumed without effect. When the night was closed in, he sent for the chiefs of the different corps into his tent. He thanked them for their fidelity to him, and assured them that he would not be the cause of the loss of so many brave men. He advised them to arrange their affair, at the break of day, as well as they could, with Canero; and informed them that he should determine for himself in the course of that very night. At the same time he gave six month's pay and gratification to the whole army, which was distributed to the soldiers before any treaty was made with Canero. He then embraced the principal officers, telling them that he depended on their friendship when a favourable opportunity might arrive; and afterwards dismissed them. About midnight, assembling thirty of his men on whose fidelity and bravery he could rely, he committed a quantity of gold to the charge of each; and, putting himself at their head, attempted to pass the river by swimming. He succeeded; and happily eluding the Maratta army, kept a direct course, without stopping, till he arrived at Bangalore, which is thirty leagues distant from Seringapatam.

When he came near this fortress, he sent one of his friends to his uncle Ibrahim Ali Khan to whom he had entrusted the government, to inform him, that though he had formerly possessed lands, fortresses, treasures, and an army, he had now no more remaining than thirty friends, who were determined to share his fortune; that he therefore begged him to say, with sincerity, whether he could still rely on his friendship; and that his answer would determine whether he should come to Bangalore, or seek an asylum elsewhere. His uncle having received this message, mounted his horse, and returned with the messenger of Hyder. "Courage!" said he, on meeting his nephew, "nothing is lost that you have trusted in my hands; and God will assist you to recover the rest." Hyder embraced him, and they entered Bangalore.

Seeing himself thus in possession of a strong place, he began to hope for the re-establishment of his affairs; and his wishes were soon partly realized, by the unforeseen arrival of almost all his cavalry, which the brave Meer Mughdoom Ali Khan, his brother-in-law, brought after him.

At the time that Canero was in treaty with the chiefs of Hyder's army, Mughdoom seizing the instant of a sudden and unexpected decrease of the Caveri, crossed the river at the head of three thousand horse; and overthrowing every force the Marattas brought to oppose him, he opened a passage, and arrived at Bangalore by favour of the woods and mountains he was perfectly acquainted with, having lost a very inconsiderable number of men.

Hyder made use of every resource. He raised troops with the utmost celerity; and being necessarily on the defensive, he began a war of stratagem with the Marattas, seconded by his brother-in-law, and assisted by the nature of the country.

In the year 1760, at the time he was busied in defending his own proper home, Pondicherry being in great danger, he detached seven thousand men, at the request of M. Lally, to assist the French, under the command of his brother-in-law Mughdoom.

Mughdoom, in his way to Pondicherry, placed a garrison in the fortress of Thiagar, which the Sieur Mariol put into his hands, by order of M. Lally; and the garrison of that place, consisting of three hundred French and twelve hundred sepoys, having joined the army of Hyder, Mughdoom after repelling a party of the English, who pretended to dispute the passage of a river, encamped on the glacis of Pondicherry, where he remained two months; and threw several convoys into the place, without being able to prevail on M. Lally to encamp without the town. He returned to Hyder, bringing with him all the French cavalry under the Sieurs Alain and Hughel, and such workmen as were at Pondicherry: a precious acquisition, which has highly contributed to the success of Hyder, by furnishing him with skilful armourers, carpenters, and other workmen from the arsenal of Pondicherry, collected with much expense and trouble by the French. Mughdoom, on his return, passing by Thiagar, withdrew his garrison; and the French replaced some sepoys in the same; Mughdoom saying, with a generous spirit of integrity, that as the place was to have been the reward for delivering Pondicherry, justice required him to restore it, since he had failed in the attempt.

This action, however, may perhaps have been more political than generous. But the fact is, that Thiagar was not surrendered to the English till after the capture of Pondicherry.

During the absence of Mughdoom, Hyder made a truce with the Marattas, a nation very averse to long wars. This Nabob esteeming the French in the highest degree, saw with great satisfaction a fine corps of cavalry of that nation in his army; and he was still more rejoiced to behold them accompanied by a body of workmen, for want of whose assistance he was in no small distress. His brother-in-law, who had conciliated the affection of all who knew him, was doubtless entitled to the most honourable reception. Hyder, on the contrary, received him with coolness, and even with indignation; making it a crime that he had not accomplished the object of his mission, by raising the siege of Pondicherry; and, without waiting for his reply, he degraded him to the rank of simple cavalier, as being unworthy of any command. This treatment, which astonished all the world, was highly mortifying to the officers and soldiers who had borne a part in the expedition. Many of them, particularly the French, spoke to Hyder in favour of his brother-in-law; but he appearing always in anger, but at the same time willing to do justice, consented to assemble all the chiefs of his army, and allowed the friends of Mughdoom to give a detail of his conduct during the expedition to Pondicherry. The whole assembly unanimously extolling the merit of Mughdoom, Hyder ordered his grand sawari* to be immediately prepared; and being on his march to the house of his brother-in-law, followed by the whole assembly, he met him in the bazaar,† where he was walking on foot like a common soldier. As soon as Hyder saw him, he descended from his elephant, approached Mughdoom and embraced him cordially several times, and addressed him nearly in these words: "I find, by the account of your

---

* *Sawari* is a word that signifies the grand retinue of the sovereign on occasions of ceremony. It will be described in a future part of this work.

† The bazaar is that part of the city or camp where the shops of the merchants are situated. The streets of the bazaar being usually covered, it is common to walk there.

"friends, that I was wrong in blaming your conduct, and was going to "your house to make an apology for my error. I am happy that I "have met you, that the satisfaction I make may be the more public." Then causing him to mount the king's own elephant, he conducted him to his own house, riding before him on horseback, with all his attendants in procession, and followed by the people and soldiery; who, happy at the reconciliation of Hyder and Mughdoom, sang his praises, in which his brother-in-law was not forgotten.

The conduct of Hyder in this transaction was founded in justice; but, according to all appearance, it was not less the effect of policy. He was then looking forward at a great fortune, and was desirous of convincing his officers, that, as he had not spared his brother-in-law, who was his dearest friend, he should not fail in punishing any neglect of duty in them.

Hyder lost no time in turning the arrival of the French to his advantage. He spread the news by his emissaries, magnifying their number; and, avowing his intention to march to Seringapatam, he invited all the great men of Mysore to join him for the purpose of delivering the king from the power of the treacherous Canero, and to restore the government in conformity to the laws of the kingdom. Nand Raja, who had always held a secret correspondence with Hyder, quitted his exile and joined him; and it is said, that he furnished him with large sums of money to raise troops and increase his army.

Canero, knowing the activity of Hyder, was not remiss in his preparations. He collected an army vastly more numerous than that of Hyder; and, by virtue of caresses and rewards, gained to his party those Europeans who had managed the artillery of Hyder before his flight. His artillery was, besides, far superior in number and quality, so that he did not fear to go out of the town, and waited for Hyder at Cenapatam, an open village seven leagues distant from Seringapatam.

The two armies were encamped at the distance of three leagues asunder. The dependence of Hyder on his own troops, and hopes he had been encouraged to form from his French succours, did not prevent his employing stratagem against his enemy. Success attended his attempts.

There was a lady at Seringapatam, commonly called the old Dayva, because her husband, brother of the king and of Nand Raja, had been regent or Dayva of the kingdom.

This lady had possessed great power during the regency of her husband, who left her extremely rich. Nand Raja, her brother-in-law, on his accession to the regency, had not that respect and consideration she thought were due to her: from that moment she declared herself his enemy, and contributed much to his loss of the regency. This princess had always protected Hyder and his brother; and, as her conduct was not very exemplary, the scandalous chronicle affirmed, that Hyder and his brother shared her private favours. Though distant from Seringapatam, Hyder had always kept up an intimate correspondence with this lady, who was not a friend to Canero, though apparently, from policy, much attached to him. On the assurance that Hyder gave her, that Nand Raja should never be regent, she promised to serve him to the utmost of her power, and even supplied him with large sums of money.

Hyder, to make every advantage of the friendship of this lady, on whom he had an entire reliance, transmitted to her fictitious letters, addressed to the principal heads of the army of Canero, in which he appeared to prescribe, in consequence of an agreement long established, operations to be made by them upon certain signals appointed by Hyder. The intention of these manœuvres was apparently that of surrounding Canero at the commencement of the battle, and preventing his escape. The lady having received these letters, repaired to the camp of Canero the night preceding the battle: she gave him the letters; and, by an artful conversation on the business, increased the consternation of the minister: the consequence was, that he immediately retired to Seringapatam, leaving the command of the army to an old general named Peer Khan, whom he believed to be in his interests, but who was really the friend of Hyder.

Hyder, informed of every thing as it happened, marched with his army at the break of day to approach that of Canero, thrown into great agitation by his departure. The news of this precipitate march augmented the confusion, and the general was by no means desirous of removing it. A number of deserters from Canero's army arrived in the camp of Hyder, with the news of his flight. As soon as that Nabob heard their report, he caused his army to halt, and sent a messenger to the general of the other army to propose a conference, publicly assuring him, that his exertions were directed against the traitor Canero, and not the king and kingdom of Mysore. Peer Khan, after taking the advice of the principal chiefs of his army, consented to a conference with Hyder and Nand Raja, in the presence of the two armies; when it was resolved, to the great satisfaction of the soldiers, that they should unite, and form but one army; and that a deputation should be sent immediately to the king of Mysore, praying him to drive the traitor Canero out of the kingdom, as a declared enemy of the king and the state. When the two armies were united, Hyder, to the surprise of every one, commanded before him the Europeans who had formerly been attached to his service and that of his brother; he made them ground their arms, and, giving every one a stroke, after the manner of the Indians, when they dishonour or degrade any one, he drove them out of his camp. He was induced to this severity, as he said, because these soldiers, having been loaded with favours by his brother and himself, were the only men of all his troops who had presumed to carry arms against him. The French cavalry from Pondicherry were present at this execution, and pretended to approve it.

The deputation from the army being arrived at Seringapatam, the answer of the king, dictated, no doubt, by Canero, was, that they were traitors, and that the king would punish them. On this answer, it was resolved to lay siege to Seringapatam; which was immediately done, to prevent Canero from calling in the assistance of the Marattas.

The inhabitants of the city had no sooner heard the report of a few cannon, than they assembled, and remonstrated in strong terms against Canero, excited, most probably, by the dowager Dayva; who at length prevailed on the king to deliver Canero to the army, and to declare Hyder regent instead of Nand Raja, who expected the appointment, and supposed Hyder would be contented with the post of generalissimo.

Upon his accepting the regency, Hyder made every submission to appease Nand Raja. He gave him a considerable territory, and made a promise, both in writing and by oath, that he would never make any attempt on his liberty, property, or life, but would always regard him as his brother.

Hyder afterwards caused the Bramin doctors to be assembled to judge Canero. He was condemned to death for having invited a foreign enemy into the kingdom, and levying war against the king's most faithful subjects. By virtue of his power as regent, Hyder spared his life, and commuted his punishment into that of being shut up in an iron cage in the middle of the most public place of Bangalore; where it is still to be seen, with the bones of this unhappy favourite, who lived two years in the cage, exposed to the insults of a populace that adored Hyder.

As a beginning of his performance of the duty of a regent, Hyder caused an exact account to be made out of the royal revenues, together with the treasure and jewels. He found that the greatest part of the jewels, instead of being in the treasury, were in pawn with the court banker,* who had advanced money when Salabutjung,

* In every great city in Hindostan, especially those where courts are kept, there are rich bankers, named Sarcars. They are all

Suba of Decan, accompanied by M. Bussi, came as far as the gates of Seringapatam, and forced the king of Mysore to pay contributions.

Hyder being informed that this man had acquired the whole of his immense fortune in the service of the state, was displeased that he had demanded pledges on lending money to the government. He ordered the jewels to be taken out of his hands, and his due

---

Guzerats, or natives of that country. Their integrity or credit, as well as their skill in business, is much esteemed. Their business is properly that of bankers, borrowing or lending money, furnishing or taking letters of exchange on all places, not excepting even those at which they have no correspondence. In this last case, they make use of money porters, who carry money to any distance, charging their carriage at per league. These men may be depended on; and it is related, that one of them having carried off a considerable sum belonging to a banker at Madras, the rest of the people following the same occupation assembled, and reimbursed the banker, though under no obligation to do it; and two of them immediately repaired to Goa, where the thief had taken refuge, and, cutting off his head, brought it to Madras, where it was carried to all the bankers to be seen, in order that the punishment of the crime might ensure a continuation of their confidence. Letters of exchange are far more ancient in India than in Europe; but are not drawn to order, which creates a difficulty in case of the death or absence of the person in whose favour they are drawn. This difficulty is in some measure obviated by naming several persons in the same bill: so that the letter of exchange drawn by an Indian banker runs, "Pay to John, or in his absence to Peter, or in his absence to James, &c."

Besides dealing in money, these bankers traffic likewise in precious stones, coral, pearls, and gold and silver plate. Some of them are very rich; and there are insurance companies of great credit at Surat, at Madras, and at Calcutta, entirely composed of Guzerat bankers.

paid him; but at the same time nominated a commission to inspect his accounts. The commissioners having found him guilty of fraud and extortion in his dealings with the state, condemned him to perpetual imprisonment, and confiscation of all his property. The luxury of this banker was enormous. It is said that his children had cradles of gold suspended from the ceiling by chains of the same metal. Hyder caused the judgment to be put in execution, but gave him a pension to subsist on; and placed his sons in the service, where they have been preferred.

Order and regularity were soon established in the finances, and Hyder then proceeded to compel a number of petty tyrants, known by the name of Palleagars,* to evacuate their fortresses. He was under the necessity of using force with some of them, but the greater part treated with him in a friendly manner. He compelled likewise many Rajas, vassals and tributaries to the kingdom of Mysore, to acknowledge their dependence, and pay the tribute with punctuality and exactness. He likewise obliged many neighbouring kings, such as the kings of Canara, the Marattas, and the Patan Nabobs of Canour, Curpa, Sanour, and many others, to restore the lands they had usurped from the kingdom of Mysore. But he did not accomplish all this without declaring war, and obtaining many victories over them. The Patans were dreaded through all Hindostan, for their valour and their perfidy. Hyder acquired great reputation by the signal victory he gained over the three Nabobs, near Sanour; for which he was indebted to the bravery and spirited evolutions of the French cavalry under M. Hughel.

---

* The Palleagars are people who inhabit castles or small fortresses. There are many in India, but there does not exist one in all the dominions of Hyder. This name is given only to Hindoos, and is not properly applied to Mogols.

This victory of Sanour induced Busalutjung, Nabob of Adonis, and brother of Nizam Ali Khan, Suba of Decan, to send an embassy to him.

Those princes were at war with the Marattas, who had lately received a considerable check on the banks of the Kisna, in a battle they had lost against the united armies of the Grand Vizier* of the empire and of Abdali, king of the Patans,† in which sixty thousand Marattas were left on the spot.

---

* This Grand Vizier was Shahaboodeen Khan, or otherwise named Suja Dowla, who succeeded his grandfather Nizam El Moulouc, and his father Gawzoodeen Khan. He is, besides, sovereign of an extensive territory on the Ganges.

† This Abdali is king of Candahar. When he had joined his army to that of Suja Dowla, they drove the Marattas from Delhi as far as Kisna, where the fugitives crossed the river, and waited to defend the passage. The Patans and the Mogols several times attempted to cross the river, but could not succeed, many Patans being taken prisoners in the attempt. Ragogi, general of the Marattas, caused them to be brought before him, and proposed to them to join the Marattas. They replied, that Mahomudans were not made to serve, but to command other men. Ragogi demanded, if they were stronger or more courageous than other men? To which they replied, Give us arms, and you shall see. As they were very few in number, Ragogi caused arms to be given them; and they instantly fell upon the Marattas, who were obliged to put them all to the sword. Abdali and Suja Dowla, finding too much difficulty in forcing a passage over the Kisna, made use of stratagem. They pretended to quarrel, and Abdali departed, as if intending to return to his own dominions. Ragogi, being advised of this, passed the Kisna to attack Suja Dowla, who pretended to avoid him; but sending intelligence to Abdali, the

Busalutjung had laid siege to Scirra, a strong place situated between his dominions and the kingdom of Mysore and gives the title to a Subaship; of which the whole district has been either seized by the Marattas, or united to the Subaship of Decan. This prince imagined, that taking advantage of the defeat of the Marattas, he should easily get possession of Scirra, and, by that means, become of equal rank with his brother, by acquiring the title of Suba. But his army not being equal to the undertaking, he experienced a resistance that would have reduced him to the shameful necessity of raising the siege, if he had not been advised to form an alliance with Hyder; who was glad to assist him. He did not, however, consent to join his army till he had previously made an advantageous treaty. In this treaty it was agreed, that Hyder should appear before Scirra with his large army, and a numerous artillery; that Busalutjung and himself should carry on the siege conjointly, till the place was taken; that as soon as it should surrender, each army should take possession on its respective side of attack; that all the artillery, ammunition, and in general everything that could be carried away, should be the share of Busalutjung, who should either take it in kind, or receive the value from Hyder; and, that this last should take possession of the place.

---

two allies joined, and faced their enemy. The Marattas were attacked, and gave way; and, being vigorously followed, they lost sixty thousand men, for want of time to repass the Kisna. Ragogi was general only for the minority of Madharao, his nephew, whom he caused to be assassinated. The Mahrattas did not suffer him to retain the regency during the minority of the son of Madharao, but expelled him. He took refuge among the English at Bombay, who espoused his cause. This is precisely the event that occasioned the war between the Marattas and that European nation.

Hyder being arrived before the place with a well-disciplined army, and a grand train of artillery served by Europeans, made his attack in a manner very different from that made use of by Busalutjung. By successful undermining, he blew up two bastions and the curtain, which forced the besieged to surrender at discretion, and increased the terror his arms had spread over the extensive empire of India.

In the execution of the treaty between these two princes, Busalutjung, who was always afterwards called the Merchant by Hyder, preferred the receiving money for his share of the capture; and it was now that Hyder was declared Suba of Scirra, by the Emperor sending him an embassy with all the highest honours annexed to the title, and marks of the dignity of Suba, such as the rich round palankeen, and Mahee Muratib, the fish's head, set with precious stones, &c., &c., &c. It was thus that Hyder, born a private gentleman, found himself raised to the rank of the greatest princes of India! *

At the time of his receiving the title and honours of Suba of Scirra, he engaged to make war on the Marattas; who had then seen the end of their empire, if the sons of Nizan El Moulouc had possessed as much courage and intelligence as Hyder; and if, more especially, the king of the Patans had not abandoned his allies, and returned into his own country, satisfied with the immense plunder he had obtained.

Hyder, continuing the war with success against the Marattas, took Marksira and Maggheri, strong places in the district of Scirra, as well as the kingdom of Bisnagar or Bassapatam. But the Marattas having collected their forces against him, he, by the pusillanimity of his allies, had nearly lost his life, having received a stroke on the

* The Subas are at present the greatest princes in India, and regard themselves as the representatives of the Emperor. They are above the tributary kings of the empire.

head with a sabre, in a battle in which neither side gained the victory. A few days afterwards he concluded a truce for three years; and preserved his conquests by paying a sum of money to the general of that nation.

This war was scarcely finished, when a new opportunity presented itself for extending the power and reputation of Hyder. The son of the Queen of Canara had escaped from Rana Bidnoor, capital of that kingdom, and came to the Suba at Bisnagar, to implore his assistance, that his mother might be compelled to put him in possession of the kingdom of his ancestors—the regency of which she had held since the death of her husband, the late king, and father of the young prince, and still retained it, though her son had arrived at the age prescribed by law for him to take charge of the government himself.

As the kingdom of Canara was comprised in the subaship of Scirra, the prince could carry his complaint with propriety to no other tribunal than that of Hyder. The young prince was, therefore, favourably received, and his mother was cited, by an ambassador of Hyder, to appear before the Suba at a time fixed.

This woman, who possessed a degree of courage unusual in her sex, and who, from the anarchy that had long reigned in the Mogol's empire, was habituated to despise the orders of the emperor and his officers, replied to the ambassador of Hyder, that she was queen, and knew no superior. On this answer, which Hyder expected, war was determined on against the queen; but the nature of the country promised to throw many difficulties in the way of the expedition.

Rana Bidnoor, capital of the kingdom of Canara, is one of the largest and best-peopled cities of India. It contains at least sixty thousand souls; among whom are about thirty thousand Christians, who have great privileges. This considerable population is, however, by no means proportionate to the extent of the city, whose circuit exceeds three leagues. It will not be found that this is an exaggeration, when it is considered, that there are streets in it, nearly in a right line, of two leagues in length. Besides, the greatest part of the ground on which the town stands is inhabited by great men and nobility, whose houses are each in the midst of a large garden, inclosing vast basins or reservoirs of water, as well for the purposes of pleasure as utility. A prodigious number of trees, planted in these gardens, shade all the streets; which are watered on each side by a rivulet of clear and limpid water, and have no other pavement than a fine gravel.

This beautiful city is situated near a small mountain, at whose summit is a considerable fortress, since much more strongly fortified by Hyder. The mountain is in a plain about five or six leagues in diameter, environed by mountains and forests that extend for more than twenty leagues every way, and are not to be passed but by narrow passages, defended by forts at a small distance from each other. These circumstances render the access to the city extremely difficult for an army, that may be checked at every step by an inconsiderable force, and cannot encamp but in the length of a stony passage, where it is liable to be attacked by the people of the country, who know all the secret passages, and can continually lay in ambush to annoy their enemy. The woods cannot be cut down, much less burned,* without infinite labour; and they are filled with tigers, bears, elephants, and every species of venomous reptiles.

A mass of such almost insuperable obstacles as presented themselves to Hyder ought to have deterred him from his enterprise, if he had not been accompanied by the young prince, who was beloved by the people and the men in power, while the queen, his mother, was detested by them, as well for her haughtiness and pride, as for having contracted a second marriage with a Bramin, contrary to the law of

---

* In these forests are a prodigious number of bamboos, a tree that cannot be burned without first cutting it down and drying it.

the place, which prohibits the widows of their kings from marrying a second time.

Hyder, determined to make the attempt, left Bisnagar, carrying with him the Prince of Canara, at the head of 6,000 men of his best cavalry, and some Caleros, men habituated to traverse the mountains and forest. He was followed by a number of oxen,* loaded with rice; and, with no other baggage, he advanced by forced marches towards the capital of Canara. His movement was so rapid, that he passed on without finding any obstacle, and arrived on the plain of Bidnoor before the queen had received any news of his march. His cavalry, accustomed to every kind of ground, terrified the Canarins, who had never beheld a legion of that kind. The good discipline observed by his troops, and the sight of the legitimate prince, caused Hyder to be received everywhere as a tutelar divinity.

On his appearance in the plain, his cavalry easily dispersed a part of the queen's army that attempted to oppose his passage; and that princess, who had scarcely time to make her escape, was pursued, taken, and conducted into the presence of the conqueror.

Hyder used his victory with the greatest moderation. He received the queen in the most gracious manner, and reconciled her with her

---

* Oxen are of the greatest utility in India, both for draught and carriage. This species, which is but little varied in Europe, is very much so in India, much more than any other species of animals. There are some extremely tall, some middle sized, and some small. They work at the plough, draw all sorts of carriages, and go very fast. Some have their horns straight, others curved, and others have none at all. The greater number have a hunch on their back; and generally it is an animal of the greatest utility, which is still more enhanced by the consideration, that, after doing much service, its flesh is eatable, and its skin tanned for leather.

son; who granted her a considerable pension, allowing her to live with her husband. To satisfy the people, who ardently desired it, the young prince was proclaimed king; he made homage to the empire for his kingdom, and signed the treaty, as well as his mother, and the principal great men of the country.

While these transactions were performing in the kingdom of Canara, the army of Hyder advanced into the country, and his infantry took possession, without resistance, of all the posts that were necessary to secure his return, and the success of anything he might think proper to undertake.

Before he engaged in the war that was to place the Prince of Canara on the throne of his ancestors, Hyder made a treaty with him, by which the prince yielded to the Suba the port of Mangalore, with a tract of country to form a comunication from thence to the frontiers of the kingdom of Mysore. In execution of this treaty, Hyder, after causing the new king to be crowned, marched with a party of his troops to take possession of Mangalore, leaving a part of his army encamped at the gates of Rana Bidnoor.

The Queen of Canara, enraged to find herself deprived of the sovereignty, had pretended to be reconciled with her son, and to acknowledge him as king, with no other intention than to wait for an opportunity of destroying Hyder. With this hope, and completely to gratify her vengeance, she resolved on the death of this generous Suba. She therefore endeavoured to gain the confidence of her son, whose feeble and pusillanimous spirit she well knew. She reproached him, with a dissembled tenderness, that, to hasten the beginning of his reign, he had inconsiderately delivered up his kingdom to barbarians, the enemies of his religion, who would leave him only the empty name of king, after depriving him of the most valuable part of his dominions, and most probably would finish by entirely robbing him of the whole. At length, by force of insinuations, and under the appearance of a highly disinterested person, who had resigned a kingdom to him, she succeeded in her endeavours to make him regret the treaty with Hyder; and, continuing to act on his fears of the future intentions of the Suba, she acquired such an empire over his mind, that he was brought to consent to the assassination of Hyder, which she had projected in a manner that, in its own nature, was almost certain of success.

During his stay at Rana Bidnoor, Hyder had dwelt in the palace of the kings of Canara, and was, of course, to reside there on his return. From this palace to a famous pagoda there was a subterraneous communication, known to very few except the queen. The queen had resolved to undermine the palace, and to blow up Hyder the night of his return, when he should be at table with his principal officers,* hoping that, at the instant of the catastrophe, the people and soldiers of Canara, animated by her son, might easily put the troops of Hyder to the sword in their first confusion and disorder.

This project might have been easily put in practice by means of her husband, the superior of the Bramins, who belonged to the pagoda. The day of Hyder's return was come, and the moment approached in which this Suba and his retinue were to perish by treachery; when the plot first came to the knowledge of a Bramin, chief of a pagoda some leagues distant from the city. Whether he was actuated, as the Bramins affirm, by a detestation and horror for the crime—or whether his hatred for the queen and her husband, who were united contrary to their law, was his leading motive—he conveyed himself in secret to Rana Bidnoor, and, presenting himself before Hyder, as if to compliment him on his happy return, he advised him openly, in the presence of the king and queen, of the conspiracy, and the danger he was in. This astonishing recital made the whole

* Hyder, like all the other Indians, makes two meals a-day—the first at eight in the morning, the second at midnight.

assembly tremble, but made no impression upon Hyder, who, looking round, discovered the guilty persons without difficulty. He ordered them to be seized. The witnesses were heard, and the truth being established on the spot, the queen, her husband, and all their accomplices, were put to death, except the King of Canara, who was carried prisoner to Maggheri, near Scirra, and his kingdom was confiscated.

The discovery of this conspiracy was worth a fine kingdom to Hyder, rich in all sorts of productions, and having a valuable extent of sea-coast, with a good number of sea-ports. The immense quantities of rice, pepper, cinnamon, cardamoms, coral, sandal wood, and ivory, that abound in this kingdom, have caused it to be called the granary and warehouse of all India. In the mountains there are mines of gold, diamonds, rubies, and other precious stones; and even in the very fortress of Rana Bidnoor, there is a rich gold mine. When Hyder took possession of the place, he found an immense treasure in gold, coined and in ingots, in trinkets and precious stones, that was indeed stupendous, if credit may be given to the accounts of the French, who accompanied him in that expedition. They say that the prince caused pearls and precious stones to be measured in their sight with a corn measure; and that, having made two heaps of gold in ingots and trinkets, they surpassed the height of a man on horseback. On this happy occasion Hyder gratified all his troops with half a year's pay, not excepting those that were in garrison in different parts of his dominions. He changed the name of Rana Bidnoor into that of Hyder Naga, or Royal City of Hyder, and the name of Mangalore into that of Corial or Port Royal. He assumed at the same time the title of King of Canara and of the Corgues, a small kingdom situated at the southern extremity of Canara, and separated from that kingdom, as well as from the Malabar district, and the kingdom of Mysore, by mountains that entirely enclose it. It has long been in subjection to the kings of Canara.

Hyder, after taking possession of the capital, visited the several parts of his new dominions, and was everywhere acknowledged sovereign with scarce any opposition. But being desirous of re-uniting certain cantons of this kingdom, in possession of the Portuguese, he did not find the viceroy of Goa disposed to make this restitution; and, as he was far superior in force to the Portuguese, he did not hesitate to attack them. With little difficulty he got possession of the country of Carvar and its fortress of Opir,* situated in the country of Sunda, formerly dismembered from the kingdom of Canara. As he was preparing to lay siege to the fort of Rama, a fortress on the point of a cape of the same name, and the only barrier that could stop his progress to Goa, the French, who were under his command, refused to give him the least assistance, preferring rather to retire into the fort of Rama than to combat with the Portuguese: M. Hughel, siding with the French, abandoned him likewise.

Hyder, knowing it to be impossible to take this fort with his own troops, did not hesitate in making peace with the Portuguese, who yielded him the country of Carvar. This inconstancy of the French, and other similar events, gave Hyder to understand that he should not well support a war with any European power, and that he could not depend upon the Europeans in his service, excepting when they themselves were at war with his enemies.

When Hyder came a second time to Mangalore, at his return

---

* This fortress is much renowned for its strength. Hyder has augmented the fortifications. The Portuguese and the Marattas have besieged it without success. It defends the country of Carvar on the Portuguese side, and the entrance of the river Sangheri, that gives its name to a city at three leagues distance from its mouth, which is the capital of Carvar, and residence of a Catholic bishop.

from the war with the Portuguese, he received a solemn deputation from a nation originally from Arabia, but now dispersed over the whole coast of Malabar, and known by the name of Mapelets. At the head of this deputation was Ali, Raja or Prince of Cananore. This Ali, son of one of the most rich and powerful Mapelets, had the good fortune in his youth to be beloved by the daughter of the Raja of Cananore, a Nayre* prince. The father, in spite of the diversity of religion, and the prejudice of his nation, which forbids all alliance with a different cast, and much more with strangers of another religion, consented to the marriage of his daughter with Ali, and dying, left him his principality, or the small kingdom of Cananore.

---

* The Nayres are the nobility of the Malabar coast. We may affirm that they are the oldest nobility in the world; for the ancient writers mention them, and quote the law that permits the Nayre ladies to have many husbands; every one being allowed four. Their houses, which stand single, have as many doors as the lady has husbands. When one of them visits her, he walks round the house, striking with his sabre on his buckler: he then opens his door, and leaves a domestic with his arms in a kind of porch, and who serves to inform others that the lady is engaged. It is said, that one day in the week the four doors are all opened, and all her husbands visit her, and dine together with her. Each husband gives a sum of money, or portion, at the time of marriage, and the wife only has the charge of the children. The Nayres, even the Samorin, aud the other princes, have no other heirs than the children of their sisters. This law was established, that the Nayres, having no family, might be always ready to march against the enemy. When the nephews are of age to bear arms, they follow their uncles. The name of father is unknown to a Nayre child. He speaks of the husbands of his mother, and of his uncles, but never of his father.

The Mapelets seem to be Arabs of Marcate and Sahar, who have settled in India for the sake of commerce. This nation, forming no alliance with strangers, has preserved its peculiar manners, and a particular physiognomy, much resembling that of the Arabs of Marcate, who have generally the face long, the chin square and turned up, and the beard thin. They are lean, and of a short figure, not in the least resembling the other Arabs, who are large and handsome men, with black thick beards.

The inhabitants of the coast of Malabar having suffered the Mapelets to take possession of all the commerce of their country, as well by sea as by land, this nation has become rich and numerous, and that with still less difficulty, by reason that the princes and nobles of the country, having frequent occasion for money, have often had recourse to the Mapelets, who lent them large sums of money at exorbitant interest; sometimes upon pawns, and sometimes in advance upon the harvests of pepper, cardamoms, and rice. These repeated* usuries have increased the riches of the Mapelets, and impoverished the princes or Nabobs of the Malabar coast, known by the name of Nayres. The Mapelets grew proud in consequence of their wealth, and attracted the envy and jealousy of the Nayres. These last, especially the more powerful of them, were not very exact in fulfilling their engagements with the Mapelets; who, on their part, were still

* Though the religion of Mahumed forbids usury, the Mapelets make no scruple in that respect, notwithstanding they are great enthusiasts. The shocking effects of their fanaticism have been often seen at Mahé. In an excess of zeal for their religion, the Mapelets intoxicate themselves with opium, and devote themselves to death for the sake of killing Christians and other enemies of their religion. They furiously attack and kill all they meet, and do not cease till they are themselves put to death.

more arrogant, when they saw Ali, a prince of their nation, elevated to the rank of prince of the country.

In this state of things, Hyder became master of the kingdom of Canara; and, consequently, a neighbour of the Malabar coast, of which the principality of Cananore is the frontier on the Canara side. Ali Raja, and the Mapelets, concluded that they should insure the possession of their states by putting themselves under the protection of Hyder, who was of the same religion, and whose power and reputation were capable either to protect or subjugate them.

The deputation of the Mapelets was honourably received by Hyder. He loaded their deputies with magnificent presents, and assured them of his protection and good-will. The Mapelets are navigators. Ali Raja had many vessels then well-equipped and ready to set sail. Hyder, who had resolved to have a fleet, in order to defend his coast from the incursions of the Marattas and other pirates, created Ali Raja his high admiral, and made his brother, Sheik Ali, intendant of the marine, of the ports, and of the maritime commerce of his dominions.—He intrusted him likewise with considerable sums for the purposes of purchasing or of building vessels.

Hyder with justice regarded his kingdom of Canara as the most precious gift Providence had bestowed on him, and the best inheritance he could leave to his children. He designed Hyder Nagar to be the capital of all his dominions. He caused all his family to repair thither, except his first Begum, the sister of Mughdoom, and mother of Tippoo Sultaun, his eldest son, who desired to reside at Bangalore. The intentions of Hyder were, to establish in this kingdom a government calculated to make himself beloved by his people; and he succeeded beyond his hopes.—The government of his other states was shared among his relations.

He left the government of Bangalore and its dependencies to Ibrahim Ali Khan, his uncle, who had so long enjoyed it. To

Mughdoom Ali Khan* he gave the government of the kingdom of Mysore; to Mirza, that of Scirra, and all its district; and to a son of his uncle, named Amin Saeb, the government of the kingdom of Bisnagar.

Ali Raja having formed a fleet, at the commencement of the fair season made the conquest of the Maldive islands, under the pretence of some injustice done to his nation; and after taking their king prisoner, he had the cruelty to put his eyes out. This conquest was made in the name, and on the account of Hyder, whose colours were borne by the fleet. Ali Raja had embarked on board a number of Sepoys, or disciplined soldiers; so that Hyder's colours had no sooner appeared at sea, but they enforced respect.

Ali Raja having brought back his victorious fleet to Mangalore, came to Nagar to do homage to Hyder, and presented to him the unfortunate king of the Maldives. Hyder, whose character is far from cruel, was so irritated at the barbarity of Ali Raja, that he instantly deprived him of the command of the fleet; which he afterwards gave to an Englishman named Stanet. Shocked at the inhumanity of Ali Raja, he entreated the king of the Maldives to forgive the outrage his admiral had been guilty of; and after expressing how much he was afflicted at the event, and using every argument in his power to console him, he gave him one of his palaces for a retreat, with a revenue sufficient to procure all the pleasures his situation permitted him to enjoy.

The courtiers and poets of this conqueror's court, little acquainted with geography, having learned that their master was become king of

---

* In the patents given to his relations on this occasion, he prolonged their names. Thus, Nabob Meer Mughdoom Ali Khan Moctum, was called Moctum Ali Khan, or Nabob Moctum Ali Khan.

twelve thousand islands, added to his titles that of King of the Islands of the Sea.

The conquest of the kingdom of Canara, that had withstood the efforts of the Emperor Aurangzebe, and that of the Maldive islands, unknown to the greatest part of the Mogols, added so much to the reputation of Hyder, that almost all the princes of Hindoostan dispatched ambassadors to congratulate him on his numerous conquests. The poets,* likewise, did not fail, in their poems, to set him above Alexander and Timur.

It was now more than a year that Hyder had not quitted the neighbourhood of Nagar, and that, occupied with the cares of government, and his pleasures, he appeared to be delighted with a state of repose till then unknown to him. At this juncture it was that the protection he had granted to the Mapelets recalled him to the head of his troops, and gave him an opportunity of making new conquests.

The Mapelets, proud of the protection of Hyder, gave up that respect and complaisance they had till then preserved for the Rajas and the other Nayres; they even threatened to do themselves justice by force of arms, if the Nayres did not perform the engagements made with them. The Nayres, whose expenses had compelled them to multiply the sums borrowed of the Mapelets, were so beset by that nation of usurers, that they were unable even to pay the interest of the sums due, and saw nothing but ruin in the menaces of the latter.

---

* There are a great number of poets in Hindoostan, especially in the courts, though Hyder does not value himself for the protection of poets and men of letters. There is a poet at court by appointment, who enjoys about £125 per month, or a thousand rupees, and the rank of chief or general of a thousand men: he composes a poem on every event that adds to the reputation or glory of the prince.

Irritated as well by the arrogance as by the extortions of a race of people they were in the habit of despising, they resolved, at any rate, to dissolve the connection between them: for this purpose several assemblies were held at Calicut, where the Zamorin, or chief of the Nayres resides, at which it was unanimously resolved, that on an appointed day a general massacre of all the Mapelets should be everywhere made. This conspiracy was in part put in practice, and more than six thousand Mapelets were murdered; though the greater part escaped. Their vessels, spread over all the coast, favoured their escape; and in many places, being forewarned, they assembled in sufficient numbers to resist their enemies. The greater number took refuge at Cananore, where they found themselves in security, by reason of its vicinity to the dominions of Hyder, as well as from the two fortresses of Cananore, one of which belonged to the Hollanders,* and the other to Ali Raja. The Mapelets, in their distress, hastened to send deputies to Hyder, to inform him of the catastrophe, and implore his protection. This nation, being fanatic Mahometans, their deputies represented to Hyder in their harangue, that God, and the prophet whose relation he was, had made him powerful for no other reason,

---

* The Hollanders have since sold their fort and territory to Ali Raja, which gave Hyder an opportunity of doing an act of justice to many hundreds of Christians, inhabitants of Cananore, almost all of Portuguese extraction. When the Dutch took Cananore from the Portuguese they found a number of inhabitants round this fortress, whom they permitted to continue in the country. A great number of others have since come into Cananore, where they have built houses, cleared the ground, and cultivated the gardens and fields. The Portuguese and Dutch had granted the lands without any formality, and possession was the only title of these poor people: when the Dutch sold the fort and territory to Ali Raja, they made no stipulation in

than that he might protect the true believers; and that the crime of the infidels, which ought to be punished by their destruction, would give him an opportunity of forming new conquests.

Hyder, who was already instructed in the power and force of the empire of the Nayres, and was acquainted with the difficulties that might oppose him in the conquest of the country, did not hesitate to promise justice and protection to the Mapelets. He quickly assembled twelve thousand of his best troops, of which four thousand were cavalry, and the rest infantry, and began his march to the coast of Malabar, directing his route by Mangalore and Cananore. All the artillery he took with him consisted of four pieces of cannon; and he ordered his fleet to accompany him along the coast, to furnish him with assistance, as it might be required.

On his arrival at Cananore, he found more than twelve thousand Mapelets under arms; ill armed, it must be confessed, but superior in courage to the Nayres, and animated by the desire of vengeance and the hope of recovering their losses at the expense of their enemies.

Hyder encamped on the banks of the river at Cananore, and dispatched an embassy to Calicut, composed of the most distinguished

---

favour of the inhabitants. Ali Raja having demanded their titles, thought proper to force them to purchase the lands of which they supposed themselves to be proprietors. This avarice of Ali Raja gave occasion to the English to rail against the Dutch, of whom they had been desirous of purchasing the place. In their embarrassment the poor inhabitants had recourse to Hyder, who condemned Ali Raja upon the passage of the Alcoran, that says, "Thou shalt not take from "the infidel his house, his field, etc., because they were given him from "God; but thou shalt be content with causing him to pay tribute." Hyder fixed this tribute at a rupee, or nearly half a crown a head.

Bramins* of his court. They had orders to represent to the Samorin, and all the Nayre princes, the injustice of the cruelties they had been guilty of to the Mapelets; and to inform them, that he was come with his army to see justice done them: but that, before he employed force, he judged it expedient to offer his mediation; promising, that if they would punish the principal offenders, and give a just and reasonable satisfaction to the Mapelets, his army should not advance into their country; and that he would even undertake the troublesome office of rendering justice to every one. The Nayre princes had agreed to support each other; and upon the report that Hyder was coming against them to the assistance of the Mapelets, they assembled an army of more than one hundred thousand men. The deputies of Hyder having finished their harangue, the Nayre princes replied, that they were astonished at the conduct of Hyder, with whom they had never had any connection or dependence; and that if his troops did anything more than drink the water of the river of Cananore,—if they even presumed to set their feet in the river, they should be attacked and punished for their temerity. On this answer the ambassadors of Hyder returned to their master; and the Nayres, having collected all their forces, appeared with the firm resolution to prevent Hyder from passing the river.

The arrival of Hyder and his army on the Malabar coast induced

---

* The Bramins (who are the first caste of Indians, destined by their legislature to be the priests of their religion, as the Levites are by the law of Moses) being become a very numerous body, have been forced to apply themselves to other employs; and as they do not choose to undertake any servile employ, they are introduced into courts, where they do all kinds of business, from the post of minister to that of spy: they are generally writers. Every lord, general, and even the lowest officers, have them in their service; a great number being forced to acquiesce in the pay of a private soldier.

all the European nations who have establishments there to send deputies to him.

Upon the great reputation of Hyder, it was not doubted but he would make a conquest of the whole country. The deputies of every nation were in haste to treat with him for the security of their factories and their commerce. As they expected to find this great conqueror at the head of a numerous army, they were astonished to see so small a number of troops; many of them could not help expressing their surprise to the European officers of the army; magnifying at the same time, the forces of the Nayre princes, which they affirmed to exceed one hundred and twenty thousand men. The officers answered, that since the Nabob, who had it in his power to assemble a much greater army, had brought no more than twelve thousand men with him, it was to be presumed, that he was certain that the number he had brought was sufficient to defeat his enemies. This proper answer, which, to instructed and enlightened men, would have had its due force, made very little impression on the deputies, who had no notion of the military art, and still less of tactics; they made haste to return to their counting-houses, well convinced that the little army of Hyder would be destroyed by that of the Nayres, who had lined the opposite bank of the river with a numerous artillery, and were continually firing and making rhodomontades. Hyder, perfectly acquainted with the genius of all the people of India, held himself assured of the victory, and founded his expectation on his cavalry; which was a body of troops absolutely unknown to the Nayres, no foreign army having penetrated as far as the Malabar coast, where no horses had been ever seen, except a few belonging to the European chief of the factory, and purchased by them more for pleasure than utility: for this country, intersected by rivulets, and covered with woods, besides being subject to continual rains for seven months in the year, is absolutely improper for the breeding and keeping of horses.

To succeed in his attempt, in spite of this numerous army and the artillery, Hyder caused his fleet to enter the river. His vessels sailed up as far as possible; and, drawing up his infantry in order of battle in a single line in face of the enemy, with his twelve pieces of cannon, he waited for the ebb of the water. When the river was at the lowest he entered it full gallop, at the head of his cavalry, which he had till then kept out of sight of the Nayres: they were led on by fifty of the French hussars, lately arrived from Pondicherry. As the rapidity of the current was diminished by his vessels, he traversed the river without difficulty at a place where it was a league in breadth, sometimes swimming, and sometimes wading: he soon came to the other river, where the Nayres were busied in attempting to oppose the infantry, who pretended to be on the point of passing over. They were frightened at the sudden appearance of the cavalry, and fled with the utmost precipitation and disorder, without making any other defence but that of discharging a few cannon, which they were too much intimidated to point properly. Hyder, foreseeing this event, had given orders to pursue the fugitives full speed, cutting down all they could overtake, without losing time, either by taking prisoners, or securing plunder.

This order being executed with the utmost strictness, nothing was to be seen in the roads, for the distance of four leagues round, but scattered limbs and mutilated bodies. The country of the Nayres was thrown into a general consternation, which was much increased by the cruelty of the Mapelets, who followed the cavalry, massacred all who had escaped, without sparing women or children: so that the army advancing under the conduct of this enraged multitude, instead of meeting with resistance, found the villages, fortresses, temples, and in general every habitable place, forsaken and deserted. It was not till they were near the environs of Tellicherry and Mahé, French, and English establishments, that they began to find people, who had taken refuge near those places.

Notwithstanding this general defection, the army was in want of nothing: they everywhere found cows, oxen, poultry, rice, and all sorts of provisions that could be wished for in a fertile country; the fugitives having abandoned everything, without daring to load themselves with the least article that could impede their flight.

Hyder caused his army to halt near these settlements, and sent an offer of peace to the Samorin, and other princes, on reasonable terms. The Samorin, who was old, remained quiet in his palace, and sent word that he waited for the conqueror, and trusted to his discretion.

This halt of the army, the sending of several Bramins, and more especially the tranquillity of the Samorin, encouraged the inhabitants, who returned for the most part to their houses; they were still more encouraged at finding that the Mapelets committed no outrages, except on the persons or property of Nayres; but the Nayres continued to conceal themselves in the woods and mountains, from whence they carried on a kind of concealed war with the Mapelets.

Hyder marched for Calicut, and found no other resistance in his route but from a large pagoda, built on a mountain, and fortified. In this place the nephew and presumptive heir of the Samorin had taken refuge, and found means to make his escape from thence, though it was invested: after his departure, the Bramins opened the gates to Hyder. The conqueror continued his journey to Calicut, and took up his residence at the English factory, where his fleet arrived before him. He inquired for the Samorin on his arrival, and was informed that he was in his palace, without any guard, waiting the commands of the conqueror; from whom he hoped for mild treatment, as he had always formally opposed the resolution to massacre the Mapelets, and had foretold the consequences to his nephews.

On this intelligence, Hyder returned into his palanquin, and gave orders to advise the Samorin of his approaching visit. He met this prince, who came forth and threw himself at his feet; Hyder hastened to raise him, and the Samorin offered his presents, consisting of two small basins of gold, one filled with precious stones, and the other with pieces of gold, and two small cannons of gold, with carriages of the same metal. The two princes having entered the palace, Hyder testified his respect for the Samorin, and promised to restore his dominions (on condition of his paying a small annual tribute) as soon as his subjects had laid down their arms, and the affair of the Mapelets was amicably settled. These two princes parted, apparently much satisfied with each other; but the world was highly astonished, the next day, to behold the palace of the Samorin on fire; and though Hyder himself assisted in procuring help, it was impossible to save anything, the edifice being entirely wood; and the Samorin, with all his family, and, as it is presumed, much treasure, perished in the flames.

This prince had himself caused the palace to be set on fire, being resolved to terminate his life in that manner, on account of some letters he had received from his nephews and the kings of Travancore and of Cochin.* These letters contained the bitterest reproaches and execrations, treating him as the betrayer of his country, and apostate to his religion, which he had abandoned to the Mohumedans. The Bramin who had conveyed these letters to him, avowed to him at the same time, that he was degraded and excluded from his caste; and that all the Bramins and Nayres had sworn never to have any communication with him. The tragical end of the Samorin affected Hyder extremely; and he was so irritated against the nephews of that prince, that he publicly swore he would never restore their dominions.

---

* These two kings were not tributary to the Samorin; but being of the same caste as the Nayres, they made it a common cause.

The princes of Calicut, assisted by the kings of Travancore and Cochin, had collected a considerable army on the river of Paniani, twelve leagues from Calicut, where they appeared disposed to make better opposition than they did near the river of Cananore. They had even collected together some European cannoneers and Portuguese artisans; but upon the approach of Hyder, they had not the courage to face him, and saved themselves by precipitately withdrawing their whole army. Hyder passed the river, and attacked Pañiani, which made little resistance, though the best and almost the only fortress in the country. He continued to pursue his enemies till he arrived at the environs of Cochin, where, by the mediation of the Hollanders, he made peace with the king of that place, on his engaging to pay tribute.

The example of the King of Cochin was followed by the submission of all the Nayre princes; who sued for peace, and obtained it on condition of doing homage, paying tribute to Hyder, and rendering ample justice each to the Mapelets in his respective districts. On these terms they were all put into free possession of their dominions; the nephews of the Samorin only being excluded from theirs.

After putting garrisons in Calicut and Paniani, Hyder bestowed the government of this state on the Raja of Coimbatore, a Bramin, prince of a country dependant on Mysore, and separated from the Nayres only by the mountains. He hoped that this prince, entitled to respect from the Nayres, as being a Bramin, would be capable of maintaining peace and order, on account of his intimate knowledge of their manners and customs.

The rainy season, which is very long and tempestuous on the coast of Malabar, began to appear, and obliged Hyder to quit the country; but in order to be at hand to watch his new conquest, he retired only to Coimbatore, the residence of the raja, whose palace he occupied.

This country is beyond the mountains called *Gates*, and is not subject to the rains that overflow the coast of Malabar, from the middle of April to the end of September.

Passing by Madigheri, a large town and fortress on the frontier of the Malabar, at the distance of six leagues from Coimbatore, Hyder left Raza Saeb, son of Chanda Saeb, in quarters with three thousand infantry.

Hyder imagined that the Nayres, awed by his power and contented with his moderation, would peaceably support the yoke he had placed upon them; but he was not yet sufficiently acquainted with the characters of that haughty people, who, once offended, never pardon their enemies, however great their wrongs.

The month of May was not yet elapsed, when a general revolt of the Nayres manifested itself over all the coast of Malabar. It commenced by the massacre of a small garrison of about two hundred men, that were surprised by the inhabitants of a large town, called Pondicharry, situated at the foot of the fortress. They carried their cruelty so far as to cut off five French soldiers, deserters from Mahé, who, intending to enter in the army of Hyder, arrived in the town the day after the massacre: and, as a still greater instance of the inhuman rage by which they were actuated, they ripped up two women who accompanied these unfortunate soldiers.

According to every appearance, this revolt was the effect of the secret intrigues of the king of Travancore, and the nephews of the Samorin. It would doubtless have been less general, if the Raja of Coimbatore, Ali Raja, and his brother Sheik Raja, who were intrusted with the charge of seeing the Mapelets re-imbursed, had been more temperate in their rapines and exactions.

As the immense quantities of water that fall in the Malabar country convert the smallest rivulets into large rivers; and as this country offers an almost insurmountable obstacle, by the torrents caused by the overflowing of the waters, that are met with almost at every step, during the rainy season; the Nayres, habituated to their climate, and going absolutely naked in the stormy months, believed, with reason, that they should have time to take Calicut and Paniani, and destroy the Mapelets, before Hyder could enter their country; but they were yet to learn that their conqueror was not to be stopped by obstacles much greater than those they depended upon. They had taken their measures so effectually, that Raza Saeb, commandant at Madigheri, and Hyder, were still ignorant of their revolt.

Calicut and Paniani were already invested by the army of the Nayres, when the news came to Hyder, by means of a Portuguese sailor, who, on the promises of a handsome reward from the governor of Paniani, ventured to ascend the river of the same name alone, in a canoe made of bamboo,* and covered with skin. This sailor, travelling only in the night, notwithstanding the danger of wild beasts and noxious reptiles, and with no other guide than a pocket compass, arrived at Madigheri. He apprized Raza Saeb of the revolt, and the danger to which Hyder's troops at Calicut and Paniani were exposed.

This general, without loss of time, caused the Portuguese to be conducted to Hyder at Coimbatore; and himself immediately marched with his forces towards Paniani, in spite of the rains, and the

---

* These boats of bamboo, covered with skin, are in fact a kind of basket; and are of admirable use in armies, more especially in the Malabar country. Hyder had a great number in his army; two men carried the skeleton of one, and two more the skin: in a quarter of an hour they are ready for use; and one boat will carry twenty-five men, or a piece of cannon. The editor of the Memoirs of General Lawrence makes fifty horses enter one of these boats; but the fact is false; the horse swims, and the horseman, who is in the boat, holds the bridle.

inundation under which almost all the country was laid by the overflowing of the rivers. This precipitate march made some impression on the revolters, as soon as they were apprized of it; but hearing that he had brought no cavalry, they detached a party of their army, which harrassed Raza Saeb at the crossing of each river, and at length succeeded (perhaps by the fault of his guides) to draw him into a place between the meeting of two rivers that joined near Pondiaghari, where he found himself shut up, without being able to pass on either side, by reason of the depth and rapidity of the water; and cut off from returning by the defiles he had passed, which were every where rendered difficult to pass, by felling of trees, and the Nayres, who were in ambuscade in various parts.

Hyder no sooner heard of the revolt than he recalled a party of his cavalry that had been luckily cantoned near Coimbatoor. While he was thus collecting the strongest part of his army from Mysore and other parts of his dominions, he commanded a select party of his infantry to be in readiness to march on the shortest notice: however, in expectation that Raza Saeb might disperse the mutineers, he waited for news, before he exposed to so insalubrious a season troops designed for very different operations.

Raza Saeb having contrived to send advice of his situation, Hyder immediately marched with three thousand horse, and ten thousand Sepoys or Topasses. He ordered his cavalry, both officers and men, to ride without saddles; and commanded his infantry to quit their habits, and march naked, excepting a pair of light drawers and shoes. Each soldier was provided with a waxed cloth to wrap up his knapsack; and the three hundred Europeans lately arrived from Pondicherry and Colombo, were offered parasols, as they did not choose to quit their habits. Their refusal was the cause that they were almost the only persons in the army that were attacked by the dysentery.

All the artillery of this small army consisted in twelve light pieces of cannon, that were carried by elephants.

It is scarcely possible to form an idea of the species of war to which Hyder led his troops this campaign. Imagine an army of fifteen thousand men marching from the break of day through a mountainous country, in roads or passages scarcely admitting more than three men a-breast exposed from morning till night to a constant shower, equal to those that fall in the greatest storms, attended with frequent thunder and lightning, excepting for three hours after noon, in which the sun shone out with almost insupportable lustre and heat; frequently obliged to cross rivers up to the chin in water, and sometimes swimming; and passing the night in towns or villages deserted by their inhabitants, where, however, they found plenty of the necessaries of life. Their path was every where marked by ruin and destruction, for their orders were to burn and pillage, and they exerted themselves so much in this horrible work, that they left behind them nothing but heaps of ruins, where houses had formerly stood.

This unexpected march obliged the Nayres to collect all their troops, and gave some relief to the troops of Raza Saeb, though not sufficient to prevent his losing many of his men for want of necessaries, and in consequence of the hardship they were subjected to. The Nayre princes, though half defeated by the fear of the consequences of their revolt, nevertheless expected Hyder with confidence in a retrenched camp near Pondiaghari, which on its left wing had a village fortified with a ditch and parapet planted with pallisades, well furnished with artillery, and maintained by the most resolute, who had determined rather to perish than yield. Hyder,* for the

---

* Hyder, before he made the attack, was persuaded by his chief almoner, named Cakee Saeb, to suffer him to go near the Nayres,

attack of this retrenched camp, disposed of his army so that four thousand of his best Sepoys, forming the right wing, were charged to attack the village; this corps was commanded by a Portuguese lieutenant-colonel,* lately arrived from Goa, with different officers of his nation. The left wing, composed of Topasses, was commanded by an English officer; and Hyder himself commanded the main body, having behind him a reserve of Europeans almost all French, with whom were joined those who are called the *Bara Audmees*, or *Great Men*, a corps composed of all the young nobility and courtiers, without excepting even the generals, who have not appointed posts or command on the day of battle. They were all on foot, and armed with sabres and bucklers, having voluntarily put themselves under the command of the officer of Europeans, whom they promised to follow wherever he might lead them.

---

and persuade them to surrender. This Peerzadah (for so the doctors of their law are called) was sitting in a meadow with his brother, in conference with the deputies, when the enemy fired on him, and broke his brother's arm. Some horsemen, whom his brother (then captain of artillery) had brought with him rode up, and helped them to escape.

* Hyder being informed by Naza Saeb, who had resided at Colombo for two years after the capture of Pondicherry, that all the European powers had introduced the Prussian exercise among their troops, wrote to Goa, Bombay, Pondicherry, Madras, Colombo, &c., to send him officers to discipline his troops. The Portuguese lieutenant-colonel had arrived from Goa on this occasion. His improper manœuvre during the battle and an unfortunate affair that happened to him the following night, caused Hyder to speak harshly to him, at which, being affronted, he demanded his dismission, and immediately obtained it.

The cavalry, that could not be of service till after the entrenchment was forced, was formed behind the corps-de-reserve. According to the orders, the Portuguese officer attacked the retrenched village with his four thousand Sepoys, by conducting them bravely to the edge of the ditch; but, without advancing a step farther, he contented himself with causing his troop to fire as if at their exercise. These unfortunate Sepoys, totally exposed, were destroyed with impunity by their enemies, who fired from pent-holes, or from behind the hedges. This firing, which lasted upwards of two hours, highly enraged Hyder, who receiving every moment news of the state of the attack, learned with the utmost mortification the unavailing loss of his best troops. The French officer, commandant of the Europeans, who lately arrived, and had not yet had an opportunity of distinguishing himself, offered to advance with the corps-de-reserve, and put himself at the head of the Sepoys. Hyder answered, that he might do as he thought proper; and he immediately joined his troop, which was impatient for the combat, and burned with a desire to revenge the French who were inhumanly massacred at Pondiaghari. Headed by this active and courageous officer, and joined by the Bara Audmees, they ran with violent eagerness to the attack. The intervals between the battalions of Sepoys afforded them a passage: they jumped into the ditch, and hastily ascending the retrenchments tore up the pallisades, and were in the face of the enemy in an instant. They gave no quarter; and the enemy, astonished to the last degree at their impetuosity and rage, suffered themselves to be butchered even without resistance. The flames of the village on fire, and the direction of the cannon now pointed on the distracted Nayres, evinced to Hyder that the village was carried. The whole army, in consequence, moved to attack the retrenchment; but the enemy, perceiving that Hyder's troops had stormed their outpost, and catching the affright of the fugitives, fled from their camp with disorder and precipitation.

Hyder had supposed his enemies would have exhibited more firmness on this occasion. This brave and fortunate attack, which was much exalted by the young nobility that shared the glory, gave him infinite pleasure. He created the French commandant Bahadur upon the spot; and in the evening presented him with a patent, appointing him general of ten thousand horse, which is the highest military post among the Mogols; at the same time declaring him general in chief of his artillery. He likewise gave a gratification of thirty rupees to every soldier, and twice that sum to each of the wounded; of which there was a great number, though no more than one died. As the Nayres had no bayonets, the wounds were only cuts with the sabre, little dangerous where ready assistance is to be had. The Europeans inspired the Malabars with a new terror by this exploit; and Hyder, to increase it, spread a report that he expected many thousand men from Europe; he added, that they were a cruel people, and devourers of human flesh; and that his intention was, to deliver all the coast to their outrages. The rage and fury by which his small handful of French were urged on to revenge their murdered countrymen, gave much force to the belief the wretched inhabitants were disposed to afford to his reports. Wherever he turned, he found no opponent, nor even any human creature; every inhabited place was forsaken: and the poor inhabitants, who fled to the woods and mountains in the most inclement season, had the anguish to behold their houses in flames, their fruit-trees cut down, their cattle destroyed, and their temples burned. The perfidy of the Nayres had been too great for them to trust the offers of pardon made by Hyder, by means of Bramins he despatched into the woods and mountains to recall these unhappy people; who were hanged without mercy, and their wives and children reduced to slavery, whenever they were found in the woods by the troops of Hyder; severity and mildness being both equally ineffectual in making them return to their homes. Ali Raja and the Mapelets, who saw themselves thus involved in the ruin of the Nayres, persuaded Hyder to return to Coimbatoor, in hopes that his absence might remove the timidity of the people: and it is highly probable that the dysentery that raged in his army was a much more effectual reason that induced him to leave the country. The officers and Europeans, who had retained their clothing, and had more particularly abused the liberty of doing as they pleased, were the most exposed to this dangerous malady.

Before he quitted the country, Hyder, by a solemn edict, declared the Nayres deprived of all their privileges; and ordained that their caste, which was the first after the Bramins, should thereafter be the lowest of all the castes; subjecting them to salute the Parias and others of the lowest castes, by ranging themselves before them, as the other Malabars had been obliged to do before the Nayres; permitting all the other castes to bear arms, and forbidding them to the Nayres, who till then had enjoyed the sole right of carrying them; at the same time allowing and commanding all persons to kill such Nayres as were found bearing arms. By this rigorous edict Hyder expected to make all the other castes enemies of the Nayres; and that they would rejoice in the occasion of revenging themselves for the tyrannic oppression this nobility had till then exerted over them.

This ordinance being found to make the submission of the Nayres absolutely impossible, because they would have thought death preferable to such a degradation, he made a new edict, by which he re-established in all their rights and privileges such Nayres as should embrace the Mahumadan religion. Many of these nobles took the turban on this occasion; but the greater part remained dispersed and chose rather to take refuge in the kingdom of Travancore than submit to this last ordinance. Though the approach of the fine season, and the terror he had spread, might have left little apprehension of another revolt, yet he left several bodies of troops in the country, distributed in posts so situated as to assist each other in case of necessity, and quartered the rest of his infantry in the neighbourhood of Madigheri, taking only his cavalry with him to Coimbatoor, which he was obliged to spread over the country, on account of the scarcity of forage.

On his arrival at Coimbatoor, Hyder found there a body of four thousand Maratta cavalry lately arrived. More than a year had elapsed since he had ordered this corps to be raised, and since the chiefs had received the necessary sums of a Bramin, named Chamrao, formerly attached to Mons. Bussi, but since entered into the service of Hyder, whose confidence he had acquired. This Bramin had not been sufficiently sparing of the money; and when the Marattas had received it, they were in no haste to complete their engagements. Instead of three months, they were scarcely ready to march in eight. Their horses, instead of being of the height and quality agreed on, were mostly small. In short, instead of a regular body of cavalr it was nothing more than a collection of peasants and vagabonds, incapable of forming a line, or indeed of doing any thing, but rob and pillage. Secure in possession of the Bramin's money, they paid little regard to his complaints; and, in order to avoid losing the whole, he was obliged to take the troops, such as they were. When they were on their journey, they advanced very slowly, and made continual stops; so that instead of one month, they employed four in making their journey; and even that degree of expedition was not obtained, but in consequence of repeated sums advanced by the distressed Chamrao.

The Marattas would not have acted in this manner, if they had been acquainted with the character of Hyder; who, for the sake of economy, was in the habit of requiring an exact account of the sums expended for the maintenance of his troops, and was not easily deceived. In fact, having passed them in review the day after his arrival, he found them in so bad a state that he could not avoid expressing his surprise to the Bramin. Chamrao had long since written to Hyder, complaining of the mutiny and disobedience, not only of the private men, but of their officers. Hyder complained to the chiefs, that his orders were so ill executed: he signified to them, that, on account of their disorderly appearance and bad equipment, he would receive the troops, as his custom was with all his cavalry, and reform all those that were not agreeable to the agreements made with Chamrao, his agent; that he likewise expected they would account for all the money employed in raising the troop; and besides, to shew them his displeasure to find that, regardless of every thing that could be urged by the person intrusted with his orders, they had employed in their journey four times the space necessary to perform it in, he had given orders to his treasurer to deduct from their account the time they had voluntarily lost by passing through unusual roads.

These Marattas, who, according to their own account, had large sums to receive, murmured loudly at finding themselves obliged to renounce a considerable part of their claim. Not at all habituated, in their own country, to be commanded despotically, they resolved with one accord to return to their camp; with menaces to do themselves justice, if refused it by fair means.

They who knew Hyder, and how circumspect he is, could not conceive how he could so indiscreetly put himself in the power of these Marattas; having kept with him at Coimbatoor no more than five hundred Sepoys, and thirty Europeans, who were their commandant's guard.

Fortunately, the Marattas troops were not ignorant that Hyder was able, in a very short time, to collect military of every denomination; in the meantime they demanded payment within the hour, or in default they threatened to mount their horses, and return into their own country, destroying and pillaging all that might offer in their way.

Hyder reproached himself secretly for the vivacity that had led him to use menaces with those people, at an instant in which he was not prepared to give law to them. Though he had little to fear personally, it would have been more prudent in him to have retired at this juncture into the fortress of Coimbatoor; but that courage, which never abandoned him, led him to surmount the difficulty and danger that now presented itself.

In this embarrassment Mahfooz Khan, ancient Nabob of Arcot, and brother of Mohamed Ali, advised him to send for the French commandant, and give him the charge of reducing this mutinous cavalry to reason. Hyder approved of the thought, and sent for the officer; he explained the affair to him, and informed him that, by the advice of the Nabob of Arcot he requested he would undertake to bring those vagabonds to hear reason; whom he could easily reduce by force of arms, but that he wished to use milder methods. The French officer consented to shew himself worthy of the confidence Hyder honoured him with, though he saw all the difficulty attending the execution of the business: however, he undertook it with ardour, being desirous of continually rendering himself more useful and necessary.

To begin his negociation, he sent word to the Maratta chief, that he was desirous of paying him a visit, in order to cultivate an acquaintance with him and the other great men of his nation: at the same instant he sent an express for Madigheri, with orders for all the Europeans to march for Coimbatoor; and, together with his letter, he dispatched an order from Hyder to the commander-in-chief of the cantonment, to send off all the Topasses, which amounted to a body of above four thousand men.

The Maratta chief having accepted with joy the visit the French officer proposed, received him with the greatest politeness, as did the other chiefs who were assembled on the occasion. In order to obtain their confidence, the commandant, after making the usual compliments (that is to say, speaking highly of the valour and merit of the Maratta nation) proceeded to inform them, that he wished to visit them, because the French and himself were nearly in the same situation as the Maratta cavalry; and it might be found advantageous to unite their pretensions, and made a common cause. The fact in reality was, that the French troops arrived in Hyder's dominions at the very juncture in which the revolt of the Nayres demanded his attention, and had remained a considerable time at Seringapatam. It is true, that he had received considerable sums by order of Hyder; but, though he had already been engaged in actual service, no agreement had yet been made for the emoluments and pay of himself and his troops.

This overture having insured the confidence of the Marattas, they began to exclaim against Hyder, and accused him of breach of faith, by speaking almost all at once; their chief at last found an opportunity of speaking alone: he spoke highly of the conduct and behaviour of his troops, and placed their pretensions in the most favourable point of view; and the French officer, seeming to give credit to their words, was careful not to shew any intimation that he was charged with any commission from Hyder: he gave them reason to suppose the contrary; and even acquainted them (as in confidence) that he expected his troop the next day, who, impatient to know their fate, would come expressly to decide it: that therefore he judged it expedient fo them to wait till the Europeans were arrived; and in the meantime, he would go to Hyder, as if from himself, and offer his mediation: the Marattas unanimously approved this project, and accepted his offer with gladness. Things thus adjusted for the present, there was no question concerning the expediting of business: the Marattas promised the French officer, that they would return his visit the following day at the same hour, to learn the effect of his intended conference with Hyder; and they parted good friends. All the country resounded with the valour of the French; and the Marattas, who had the highest opinion of them, on account of the defeat of

Nazerjung, and the exploits of M. Bussi,* were highly flattered with this kind of alliance with them.

The following day the few Europeans that were at Madigheri, to the number of four hundred men, began to appear, but irregularly, in small numbers, consisting of three or four at most in a party. By this artifice, they appeared to be coming in all day, without its being possible for the Marattas to judge of their number; and those who arrived did not fail to acquaint the inquirers, that the main body would soon arrive: accordingly, at the close of the night, a column of infantry passed by the Maratta camp, with drums beating and colours flying, composed of Topasses,† who had

---

* This ought not to be taken for flattery. The Author has long ago assured the people in power, that M. Bussi enjoys the highest reputation in Hindostan; and it is certain, that a Frenchman among the Marattas, or in the army of the Suba of Decan, will be every moment asked *Moussa Bussiqu'an-e?* or, what is become of M. Bussi?

† The Topasses are black Christians, who call themselves Portuguese, and have the names of the first families in Portugal; but who, to all appearance, are descended from slaves, born and brought up in the houses of the Portuguese, who treat very favourably, and with great humanity, those slaves whom they call Creanza de Caza, or Children of the House. The Europeans have never been able to form good troops out of those people; which arises, no doubt, from the contemptuous manner they treat them with: instead of which, Hyder has always put them on an equality with the Sepoys, and even preferred them to his other troops; as will be seen in the course of this History. The officers of these Topasses, are Europeans; which circumstance, however, does not prevent those among them who distinguish themselves, from being promoted; in consequence of this treatment, they may be regarded as Hyder's best troops, and those he can most rely on.

been sent from Madigheri, and were headed by the Europeans who, by another route, had gone out of Coimbatoor to join them.

This artifice caused the Marattas to believe the Europeans were much more numerous than they really were; and their notion was strengthened by the hats of the Topasses, and their drums and fifes, which resemble the others; and as they played the same marches, and it was almost dark when they appeared, it was not easy to perceive the difference.

The principal Maratta chiefs waited on the French commandant; who receiving them with the most attentive politeness and regard, acquainted them, that he had found Hyder disposed to act in the most amicable manner with them, and had accepted his mediation; but that he had promised to keep strictly to the agreement made with his agent, Chamrao: that he consented, either that himself alone, or with such other person of consequence as the Marattas might choose, would pass in review, one by one, the horsemen and their horses, for the purpose of reforming those that were not according to the agreement: and likewise, that after having taken an account of the length of the journey they had had to perform, arbitrators should decide the time they ought to have employed. The French commandant added, that these propositions having appeared to him equitable, he had judged it proper to submit, and accept them; being well convinced of the candid and noble manner of thinking that distinguished the Maratta nation.

They, who did not find their account in this method of adjusting the affair, exclaimed much against the facility of the officer, and assured him that they would not consent to be thus passed in review; and more particularly because Chamrao, the envoy of Hyder, had seen and approved the horses, which had not since been changed; and that with respect to his demand concerning the time employed in the journey, it was at the very request of Chamrao, they affirmed, that they had so sojourned on the road, in order that they might not arrive at Coimbatoor during the absence of the Nabob, being informed that forages were very rare. These Maratta officers having persisted in their determination, maintained firmly that the propositions made to them were unreasonable; and that they could not accept them, nor abate their pretensions, without the consent of all the chiefs, of whom they would convene an assembly. The night approaching, they returned very dissatisfied with their visit, and the resolution of Hyder.

The French officer, not to render himself suspected by paying too great attention to the situation of their encampment, thought proper to commit that charge to one of his adjutants.* This officer reported that the camp was in a meadow situated between two banks, one serving to retain the water of a great tank, and the other as a passage at the time of rain; that the meadow was bounded at one end by a hill impracticable to cavalry, because covered with fruit-trees, and intersected by hedges and walls of earth, that divide the property of different persons; that at the extremity of the bank, that served for a road, there were some houses, and a small pagoda; and lastly, that he was of opinion, that two hundred men, and some pieces of cannon, placed in this hamlet, would be able to prevent the Marattas from going out of their camp. In consequence of this advice, cannon were conveyed in the night to this post, and 250 men, who entrenched themselves. A barbette battery of ten pieces of cannon was constructed, which was by no means an agreeable sight to the Marattas when day-light appeared. Their chiefs having sent to the officer who commanded the post, to demand with what intention those cannon were pointed at their camp, received answer, that they had been placed there by his

* This adjutant was M. de Lallie, who now commands a corps in Hyder's army of two hundred and fifty European horsemen; of which he is proprietor, as well as of a regiment of Sepoys.

commandant, with orders to fire on the first Maratta that should attempt to get on horseback; and that if they desired farther information, they must apply to the commandant. On this they dispatched two of their officers, who complained of this act of hostility, but with much politeness, and an air that sufficiently exhibited their fear. The commandant did not hesitate to answer, that having been so little satisfied the preceding evening with their reception of the propositions of Hyder, which to him appeared just and reasonable; and fearing that, by a precipitate resolution of returning into their own country, they might betray his faith and honour, pledged to the sovereign on their account, he thought it incumbent on him to take these precautions. But, nevertheless, he wished to continue his mediation, and would certainly join them, if Hyder refused to do them justice. This discourse having encouraged them, they protested they were ready to treat; and that, trusting entirely to his promises, all the chiefs would wait on him at an hour to be appointed, for a conference with Hyder's ministers.

On the assurance given them that no act of hostility should be committed, provided they remained quiet in their camp, they returned to their quarters. The commandant repaired to Hyder to inform him of their good dispositions; he found him alone with Mahfooz Khan, who likewise offered himself as mediator and interpreter, for which he was qualified by speaking very good Portuguese.

In consideration of the advanced age and high rank of this personage, the French officer begged he would consent that the meeting might be held at his house. Advice was given to the Marattas, who repaired thither at the close of the evening. Two Bramins, secretaries to Hyder, likewise attended, and everything was arranged in two days; Mahfooz Khan having removed all the difficulties with a degee of address and intelligence very uncommon, but acquired by fifty years' experience in this sort of negociations. It was agreed, that none should be dismissed but such horses as were absolutely incapable of any kind of service; that they should all pass in exact review; that such as should be judged in a state to serve as good cavalry, should be paid at the rate of forty rupees a month, man and horse, according to the agreement made with Chamrao; and that the others should be reduced to five-and-twenty, and should serve as irregular cavalry. The time allowed for the journey was set at three months.

After this review it was found that one hundred and fifty horse only were entitled to forty rupees, and the rest were reduced to five-and-twenty. The principal chief, whose troop was well mounted, and who alone possessed eight hundred horse, had none dismissed; perhaps there was indulgence shewn him, on account of the pains he had taken to accommodate the difference.

The affair being thus satisfactorily adjusted, Hyder made a present of twenty-two horses to the French officer, to mount twenty Europeans, to serve him as a guard, and accompany him everywhere: at the same time he gave orders to the Bacsi* and the secretary at war, to settle the pay and emoluments of all the Europeans; Hyder being in the custom never to settle pecuniary affairs himself, but committing the charge of them to ministers, who have no permission to conclude any business without the precise orders of their master. To make their court, the Bacsi and his colleague exclaimed against the exorbitant pretensions of the Europeans, and proposed abatements that were flatly rejected; but as the corps of Europeans was not numerous, the subject of these discussions was of small consequence to Hyder: to end them therefore, and to make a parade of generosity that he thought suitable to his rank, he ordered the commandant and principal officers before him, and addressing himself to the former, "I hear, with concern," said he, "that you do not agree with the Bacsi and Narimrao. Why did you not apply to me? have you

* The Bacsi is properly the minister at war, and the secretary is subjected to his orders, though generally he is the confidential minister of the Nabob.

forgot that I have, both by writing and conversation, informed you, that you may dispose of everything I possess; and that the French are highly esteemed by me?" Upon which he gave orders to Narimrao to prepare the Batis,* and he signed them before he dismissed the officers; at the same time inviting them to an entertainment to be given at the palace the next day.

As it could not be expected that the coast of Malabar would ever enjoy a state of tranquillity while the Nayre princes were on the frontiers, and in the country of Travancore, Hyder resolved to make the conquest of that kingdom; for which, however, he could urge no better reason than that the king of that country had assisted his enemies. Though this kingdom is of small extent, it is very populous; and its king, Ram Raja, has acquired a reputation for his valour and prudence, which gave reason to conclude that the undertaking would be attended with much difficulty.

Hyder knew that his enemy had long exerted himself in disciplining his army; that he had a numerous corps of Sepoys well armed, and a train of artillery, served by good cannoneers, procured from the Danes, the English, and the Dutch. He likewise knew that

---

* The Batis are small writings or warrants. Every person in the military service has one, from the general to the drummer. This writing contains the name of the person, and of his father and grandfather; a description of his person, and that of his horse (if he be a horseman); the day he entered the service; his station, and his pay; and as often as he is paid the sum is entered on the same: those of the officers contain simply the name, the station or degree, and the sums received. The Batis are triple, and in three different languages, Persian, Maratta, and Canarin; and as there are three chancellors, they are preserved in the greatest order. Hyder signs the state of accounts every month, as well as a particular state for every troop; for no payment is made without the signature of Hyder, or, in his absence, of the general commandant.

the country was not to be penetrated but by way of narrow passages through mountains, where Ram Rajah had caused fortresses to be constructed, which he was firmly resolved to defend to the utmost. Neither was he ignorant, that the English, jealous of his power, had assembled troops in Madura and Marava, countries dependant on Mohumed Ali Khan, and frontier to Travancore: but, habituated to overcome all obstacles, he was determined to pursue his intention. He trusted to the promises made by the English deputies, who had waited upon him on the coast of Malabar; to whom he had granted not only a confirmation of all their former privileges, but had, besides, given permission to establish a factory at Onoor; and he was likewise persuaded, that the English troops were assembled for no other purpose than to protect the dominions of Mohumed Ali from insult.

Mahfooz Khan had lately been induced to take the part of Nizam Ali Khan, who had sent him presents of great value. He knew that the Suba of Decan was engaged in wars with his vassals, in which he was assisted by a party of English, commanded by General Smith. He therefore concluded that he had nothing to fear on his part.

In order to secure himself from any interruption in the war he had projected, Hyder wrote to Mirza Ali Khan, governor of Scirra, and his brother-in-law, to renew the truce with the Marattas, which was on the point of expiring: a business not difficult to be performed, by means of a sum of money properly distributed among the chiefs.

The intended war, and the necessity of placing strong garrisons in the conquered country, obliged Hyder to make considerable levies for the augmentation of his army; and, being willing to derive every advantage from the time preceding that in which he intended to march against Ram Rajah, he caused all his troops and his artillery to be exercised by the European officers, he himself assisting every day with his sons and generals at the different exercises and evolutions.

After consulting the commandant of Europeans, whose knowledge and intelligence he greatly valued and depended on, he established, by his advice, a corps of five thousand grenadiers, divided into battalions of five hundred men, composed of four companies of one hundred and twenty-five men each. Two of these battalions were selected out of the Topasses, and the rest from the Sepoys; each being commanded by an European officer. There was, besides, in each company, an European adjutant or serjeant-major. The officers and private men of every company were chosen by Hyder himself, who regarded tallness less than a martial air, and the activity and robust temperament of the individual.

These grenadiers received ten rupees a month, instead of eight, which is the pay of the other Sepoys. They were exempt from all works of labour, and even mounted no guard, except that of their commandant; and, that nothing might prevent their being ready to march at the first signal, every escouade, composed of seven men, including an inferior officer, were allowed a cook servant, and an ox to carry their tent and baggage. Every company was augmented by an escouade of seven men, destined solely to guard the baggage. These were as it were apprentices, being youths of about seventeen years old, intended to replace the grenadiers who fell, and to render the corps capable of affording great advantages by the rapidity of their motions. From the time of their first establishment, they were exercised every morning in handling their arms, by their own officers; and every afternoon, from three till six, five battalions, by turns, were exercised in their evolutions by the French commandant; after which they were made to march from six to eight, marching out at the ordinary pace, and returning home with a quick step.

All the officers, without exception, were obliged to do this exercise as well as the common soldiers. This constraint at first occasioned much murmuring among them, but luckily it did not come to the hearing of Hyder. However, whether through a sense of duty, or from example, they became accustomed to it, and their assiduity afforded great encouragement to the soldiers. It was thus that this sovereign formed a body of troops, to whose rapid movements the English afterwards attributed all his successes.

The English had no sooner heard of Hyder's preparations, which fame had rendered still more considerable, than they conceived umbrage at them, as well as at the long stay he made at Coimbatoor, the capital adjoining to Madura, of which we have already made mention. In their uncertainty respecting his intentions, they resolved to dispatch his Ouaquil from Madras, a Bramin, named Menagi Pundit, to carry him a letter from the governor and council of that settlement. This letter announced a solemn embassy, composed of Colonel Call, chief engineer, and Counsellor Boschier, brother to the governor. Hyder being persuaded that they intended to make propositions to him, relative to Travancore and the coast of Malabar, contrary to his views and intentions, thought it necessary to elude the receiving the embassy. He immediately despatched an answer to the letter of the council, assuring them that he was very much flattered with their letter, and thanking them for the honour they intended him in sending so distinguished an embassy; but at the same time he added, that Coimbatoor, being only a camp or military station, by no means proper for the reception of ambassadors with those honours they were entitled to expect, he could not decently receive the embassy till he should arrive at Seringapatam, a royal city, to which he proposed to return in a short time; and that he would be careful to advise the governor of Madras of his arrival there.

Hyder was too well acquainted with English politics to suffer himself to be seduced by the pompous honour with which they hoped to dazzle his sight; and, far from being flattered by this embassy, he was determined no longer to defer his expedition against Travancore. The order was already given for the army to be in readiness to march, when an unforeseen event convinced him that he had more enemies than he suspected, who were anxiously intent upon his destruction.

There was an Irish officer in his army, named Turner, who had been admitted into his service by virtue of a letter of recommendation from Governor Boschier. He was a man of strong understanding; and who, possessing all the talents required in a good soldier, especially in the art of tactics, had in a very short time gained the affection of Hyder, who committed the most important operations to his care. This man, who was not in the slightest degree suspected, was commander of the first battalion of Topass grenadiers; and, in this quality, he was regarded as general of that military, which forms a body of about five thousand men.

It must be allowed that an officer recommended by an English governor ought to have been treated with less confidence and security; but this man had behaved so well in the war on the coast of Malabar, that, far from having any mistrust of him, he had acquired the confidence of his generals. Taking advantage of the good opinion they had of him, he waited till the time of payment, which is made the fifth day of every lunar month after the moon has appeared; and when he had received his appointments, and the pay of his men, he made his escape by the road that leads towards Cochin.

His quarters were a short league distant from Coimbatoor. The officers of his corps waited on him to receive their pay; but, under the captious pretence of his secretary being absent, he begged them to wait till the next day, which was without difficulty granted. To put his project in execution he mounted his horse, being accompanied by a young Swedish officer, to whom he had communicated his design, and disappeared, carrying every thing of value he possessed with him; taking the precaution first to acquaint his domestics that he was going to supper with the commandant-general at Coimbatoor.

The intensity of the heat in the day, and the beauty of the nights, in India, induce people of distinction to sit up very late, more especially as they have the custom of sleeping in the day from three till six. Some officers, who were in this habitude, called upon him, and were astonished to find he was gone to supper at Coimbatoor; but far from harbouring any suspicion, they concluded, on the contrary, that it was a gaming party, knowing him to be a great gamester; the night being fine, they resolved to take the advantage of it; and, thinking to surprise him agreeably, they mounted their horses, and repaired to the commandant's quarters at Coimbatoor, where they arrived about midnight. Their astonishment was highly increased, when they found everybody in the most profound sleep. They inquired to no purpose for Turner, as no one could give any account of him; and the suspicion that consequently arose in their minds induced them to apply to the commandant himself. On their account of the absence of their officer, the commandant sent to inquire of the posts that guarded the entrance of the passes, whether any one had passed them; and was informed that two European officers had departed three hours before. The first captain of Turner's corps, named Minerva, an Irishman, offered to pursue him instantly with a party of fifty Europeans: his offer was accepted, and he departed at two in the morning. At eight they had stretched over upwards of six leagues, and arrived at the frontier of the country of Cochin. They discovered the horses of the officers they were in quest of, and environed the house, in which they found them both asleep. They immediately secured their persons and conducted them bound to Coimbatoor.

Hyder being informed of the escape of Turner and the Swedish officer, and of their recapture, gave orders to judge them as in a similar case in Europe. In consequence, a court martial was assembled, at which the two criminals were tried, and convicted of carrying off the public money; sentence was accordingly pronounced, that they should be degraded and hung, and their bodies afterwards exposed on the high road. The council, in compassion to the youth of the Swedish officer (who, according to all appearance, had been seduced by the other, and still more, because he carried away no property of any other, and was only culpable in having departed without leave) thought proper to intercede with the Nabob in his favour, who commuted the punishment of death into that of imprisonment. As to Turner, he was conducted to the place of punishment, and there discovered to the council, that the English, conjointly with Nizam Ali Khan, intended to attack Hyder. He confessed that he was a Sepoy employed by the government of Madras, and begged pardon of the sovereign for having so long abused his confidence; that he should not have made his escape, if he had not lately been nominated major of a regiment on the Bombay establishment: he intreated his judges, in consideration of the importance of his discoveries, that they would spare him the indignity of being hanged, and, as he deserved to die, would give orders for him to be shot; this request was allowed him. Before he suffered, he distributed all his money to the soldiers appointed to put him to death; to the Sieur Minerva he gave his sword and watch. After his death he was suspended on a tree near the road-side conformably to the latter part of his sentence.

The discovery of the intentions of the English, caused the departure of the army for Travancore to be suspended. Hyder without delay caused Mahfouz Khan to repair to Hyderabad, where he was charged to attempt, by the intrigues of his friends and his creatures about the Nabob, who were in great number (Busalutjung, brother of the Suba, being the first) to avert the storm that threatened him from that court.

In the meantime he continued to exercise his troops, and train them to all kinds of evolutions. This spectacle, entirely new to the Indians, and the long stay of the sovereign of so many states in Coimbatoor, drew so great a concourse of people to that place, that their number amounted to more than 100,000, exclusive of the army, which exceeded 60,000: but it will scarcely be credited, that this country is so abundant with all the necessaries of life, that a sheep or a dozen of fowls never cost more than two shillings; and twelve measures of rice, one of which is sufficient to serve a man a day, were sold at the same price. The immense population of this country is proved by the two markets which are held weekly; where, at each, is commonly sold twenty thousand pieces of silk, each fourteen cubits long.* This country, through which lies the ordinary passage from Mysore and the coast of Coromandel to the coast of Malabar, produces a considerable revenue to Hyder, who enjoys the tolls, to the exclusion of the Rajas of the country.

It is estimated, that thirty thousand oxen, loaded with tobacco, annually pass through Coimbatoor: this assertion is rendered very probable, by the numerous magazines of that commodity at Pondiagheri. Besides tobacco, there are great quantities of silks of every kind, and pepper, cardamom, clove, ivory, &c., brought from the coast of Malabar.

During the long stay of Hyder at Coimbatoor, many events happened, which, though of no great importance, are yet sufficiently interesting to be related. They may serve not only to give the reader a more perfect idea of the genius and character of Hyder, but likewise to throw light on the manners of the people, of whom the Nabob is become the sovereign. The first of these events is a process or suit at law, carried on against the missionary Jesuits of the dominions of Hyder.

---

* The superior of the Jesuit missionaries, who resides at Zavier Paleam, one mile distant from Coimbatoor, has assured me, that he had ten thousand Christian weavers in his mission.

The news of the expulsion of the self-named Jesuits from Portugal and France having arrived in India, a missionary of that order, a Portuguese by nation, and residing in Mysore, quitted his cure in 1767, and retired to Goa; being determined, as he said, to shew himself a faithful subject of his king, by no longer continuing in a body of men declared to be enemies of his country. A year and a half after his departure, he wrote to a Portuguese lady, named Madam Mequinez, widow of a Portuguese officer, who had rendered signal services to Hyder, and was afterwards slain in a battle against the Marattas; Hyder, in return, had given his widow the regiment of Topasses her husband had possessed, with the appointment of colonel, till an adopted son of her husband's was of age to command the regiment himself.

This lady accompanied her regiment everywhere: the colours were carried to her house; and she had a private sentinel at the door. She received the pay, and caused the deductions to be made in her presence from each company. When the regiment was collected, she inspected them herself, as well as all the detachments that were ordered out; but she permitted the second in command to exercise the troops, and lead them against the enemy.

This dame Mequinez having received the letter of the ex-jesuit father, addressed herself to the Brahmin Narimrao, secretary at war, and much esteemed by Hyder. She complained that, during the life, and since the death of her husband, she had deposited in trust in the hands of the now ex-jesuit, all her jewels, and the money she and her husband could spare: that this father having departed to Goa, she, being in the army, wrote to him, and received for answer, that all the jewels and money she had deposited in his hand, were transferred, under the same title, into those of the provincial father resident at Xavier Paleam, to whom it was necessary for her to address herself for restitution: she added, that having carried this letter to the provincial father, he affirmed she had lost her senses: and that he had never heard either of her money or jewels: at the same time she placed in the hands of the secretary the letter received by her from Goa, together with a state of the jewels and money she reclaimed, amounting to a considerable sum. The Bramin acquainted Hyder with the particulars of this affair, and painted the Jesuits in the most odious colours, by reciting what had passed in France and Portugal concerning them.

On this complaint, Hyder immediately ordered a guard of four Sepoys and a corporal to every missionary found in his dominions, with orders not to lose sight of the reverend fathers; but at the same time to permit them to perform their functions, as well in their missions as in their churches, without impeding them in the least; but, on the contrary, they were commanded to treat them with every mark of respect.

Hyder commanded this restraint to be laid upon them, because the complaint was made at the very time when the revolt of the Nayres demanded his presence on the coast of Malabar. On his return to Coimbatoor, and the Bramin Narimrao having renewed the widow's complaint, he sent for the French commandant, of whose integrity and judgment he was well convinced: "You are, doubtless," said he, "acquainted with the suit urged by the widow Mequinez against the Jesuits; and, as I wish the affair to be terminated by an equitable decision, I have fixed upon you to take cognizance of the same, and shall give you every necessary power to be her judge." The officer answered, "That not being a man of the law, he could not pretend to undertake the distribution of justice, for fear of erring through ignorance." Hyder replied, "Certainly you, who are yourself a Christian, must be better acquainted with the law* of the

* Hyder, and all the Mahometans, believe that Jesus Christ, like Moses and Mahomet, has given laws to the Christians, which the judges are bound to follow in their decisions; and that Christian princes cannot evade them by contrary laws.

Christians than any judge in my dominions: and since my intention is, that every one shall be judged by his own law, you cannot avoid accepting this commission; but I permit you, if it be necessary, to select, as assistants jointly with yourself, such officers of your nation, and religion, as you think capable of seconding your own endeavours." There was nothing could be objected to this offer. The French officer, after thanking Hyder for the honour of his good opinion, consented to perform his orders to the utmost of his power: and the day following, Madam Mequinez and the reverend provincial father, being informed of the Hyder Bahadur's determination, did not fail to wait on the French officer as their judge.

The lady arrived apparently in the utmost distress. She lamented, with signs of great affliction, that poverty, to which, she affirmed, the perfidy of the Jesuits had reduced her, and against whom she vented numberless invectives: her oration was so specious that almost all the Europeans, especially the French, who were chiefly young men, were prejudiced in her favour, and were desirous that the Jesuits should be condemned to make restitution, and be burned, or at least hanged.

The provincial father was an Italian of about sixty years of age, of a commanding* and venerable aspect, though at the same time affable

---

* The Jesuit missionaries in India, who reside in the country not subjected to Europeans, call themselves Bramin Christians: they wear a habit resembling that of the Bramins, having the triple cord and the slippers made without the skin of animals: they wear their beard, and live in the manner of the Bramins, never eating publicly anything that has had life, and never going to the altar without first washing and purifying themselves. Virgins pour vessels of water on their heads, and afterwards, drying them, they put on the albe, the chasuble, and other sacerdotal habiliments. This provincial father, like the other missionaries of his order, resembled a Bramin.

and mild. He praised God for inspiring the sovereign with the choice of such a judge as his heart had long desired. After this short prayer he entreated the French commandant (making at the same time the most humble apology to the other gentlemen present) that he would be pleased to grant him a private audience, that he might be able to explain the affair in all its particulars; but which he could not do in public, because of certain persons who were involved in the business. The French officer made a sign for every one to retire; and the reverend provincial father, being alone with him, expressed himself in these terms; "You must be sensible, Sir, that, even in the "most regular and holy societies, it is impossible to prevent Judas "from sometimes appearing; and he who now has drawn this unex-"pected persecution on us, for the satisfactory termination of which we "depend on you, may justly be called by that name. Before that "man determined to retire to Goa, there were several scandalous "stories came to my knowledge concerning him, that obliged me to "reprimand him; for, in this country, when a man is once at the head "of a mission, the superior has no other right than that of reprimand"ing him, for fear of a greater disorder. Being informed that my "remonstrances produced no effect, I thought it my duty to watch "over all his actions. I was advised when he quitted his cure, and "that he had departed to Mangalore, in his way to Goa. I followed "him without delay, and coming up with him before he embarked, I "easily obtained an order from the commandant of Mangalore to "prevent his quitting the place before I had published, in all the "missions, that if any one had interests to discuss with that father,*

---

* All the Christian women in India that are married to Europeans have the madness to hoard up a private sum or fund, which they entrust to their priests, under the seal of confession. It is to the honour of the missionaries, that there is no instance of any complaint

"he should repair to Mangalore: many persons repaired thither, "and among them the dame Mequinez, who reclaimed two thousand "rupees, a pair of bracelets of rubies, and a collar of pearls, which "were returned to her; as was acknowledged by an authentic act "passed in the chancellory of the Portuguese factory at Mangalore, "and witnessed by the signature of the French and Portuguese "factors. Since the exhibition of the widow Mequinez's complaint "against us, I have applied to the chief and chancellor of the Portu-"guese factory* for a copy of the act, which they have constantly "refused.

---

of this trust having been abused. This custom is very ancient, and seems to have originated with the Portuguse. The monks, at all events, gain much money by the practice, because there are scarcely any women that die, who previously acquaint their husbands or relations where they have placed sums in this manner.

* The Portuguese had a factory at Mangalore, on an eminence that commanded the river. In this factory they kept a small garrison of thirty Portuguese soldiers, commanded by a lieutenant, who was at the same time factor, and a kind of consul; this settlement had two pieces of cannon, and displayed Portuguese colours. The king of Canara submitted to this, and the Portuguese levied a small duty, as toll on the entering or going out of the river of Mangalore, which they pretended to defend against invaders. When the English took Mangalore in 1768, the Portuguese had neither the inclination nor the power to defend the entrance of the river against the English army. Hyder being desirous of constructing a citadel at Mangalore, in 1774, M. Catini, his engineer, found that the site of the Portuguese factory was the most proper for building a citadel capable of defending the entrance of the river; and the Portuguese were obliged to resign their factory.

" To procure this deed, which is absolutely necessary for the " right decision of the cause, it will be proper, Sir, for you to make " use of the authority of the Nabob. The bearer of his order must " be a Frenchman who can be depended on, and who must compel " the Portuguese factor to exhibit the registers of his chancellorship, " in spite of all the resistance he may make, on account of the " honour of his flag and garrison. I must entreat you likewise, " sir, to conduct the business in such a manner as that the Bramin " Narimrao may not be apprised of the order given to force the " chief of the Portuguese settlement to communicate his registers: " for I have good reasons to suspect that this Bramin, whose avarice " you are no stranger to, is interested in the plot, as well as the " Portuguese chancellor and factor. The Bramin would not fail, " in that case, to advise them of the intended order, and they would " dispatch the registers to Goa. If you cannot clear up the affair " by means of these registers, you may write to Mahé, to know " who was the French gentleman who then resided at Mangalore.* " You may then apply to him, and perhaps his memory will furnish " you with means to do justice to the injured."

The French officer, after having heard the recital of the provincial father, said, "Be at your ease, my reverend father; I will do my utmost to search your affair to the bottom, without giving any suspicion of the communication you have made."

Madam Mequinez, impatient to know the result of the provincial father's conference with the French commandant, hastened the next morning to wait upon him. There were then several French officers with him: he no sooner saw her, than he said, "Madam, the

* There was not then, perhaps never was, a French factory at Mangalore. The French gentleman, of whom the reverend father spoke, was some merchant who was casually there.

provincial father made his confession to me yesterday; you must now absolutely make yours." The lady colonel, assured of the victory, consented with great readiness; and everybody having retired, he addressed her thus, "How could you thoughtlessly precipitate yourself into the abyss you are fallen in? You enjoy a great revenue by the bounty of the Nabob; and you have presumed to impose on that prince, whom you know to be severely just: you are a Christian, and you have not scrupled to invent the most odious imposture, in hopes of enriching yourself by the plunder of the churches and altars, and with the intention of sharing your unjust demands with a Bramin and a Monk, whose wickedness you are well acquainted with. But it is in vain that you hope any longer to conceal your conspiracy. I am informed of everything by the French gentleman who resided at Mangalore, and who will quickly arrive here, together with the chancellor of the Portuguese factory, who brings his registers, and is guarded by Sepoys. You have but a moment in your power to save yourself, by making a sincere declaration of the truth: for from this instant I will cause you to be arrested and guarded, without permission to speak to any one; and when your imposture shall be proved, you may expect that the Nabob will punish you as you deserve: but if, on the contrary, you make the confession I demand, I will find means of terminating the affair without noise." The woman, who now saw herself unmasked, was almost dead at hearing a discourse so unexpected; and finished by falling on her knees. She confessed the truth, and threw the blame on the Monk of Goa, and the Bramin, who had prompted her with this infamous contrivance. The officer raised her, with the assurance, that by her confession she had placed herself out of all danger: he then went out, and fastened the door behind him; but soon returned with two officers of known discretion, to whom he had communicated the particulars of what had passed: and the dame Mequinez, supposing them to be of the number of her judges, repeated before them everything she had before avowed to the commandant.

The provincial father being sent for, and informed of the confession of the widow, prostrated himself on the earth, and then raising himself, returned thanks to God, that the truth was cleared up, and his brethren justified from the accusation so maliciously urged against them. He nevertheless entreated the commandant to conceal the detail of the affair from the Nabob; fearing, as he said, the consequence that might ensue to the widow: but more probably wishing to avoid the enmity of the Secretary Narimrao.

The officer having informed Hyder that the affair was terminated, that prince was contented with saying, "I am persuaded that the whole is an iniquitous contrivance against the reverend fathers; for I am informed, that her conduct is such, as, if she does not take care, will finish by bringing no small mortification upon herself.* However," added he, "since you and the reverend fathers forgive her, I shall say no more of it." He immediately gave orders to

* Hyder proposed to the Swedish officer, accomplice of Turner, the Irishman, to espouse this lady colonel, as a condition upon which he would pardon and restore him to his former post. This young man, aged twenty-eight, but of a spirited disposition, absolutely rejected the offer; saying he would rather die than marry a woman who had prostituted herself to all the Topasses. His pardon, and permission to retire where he pleased, were the consequence of this answer. The lady colonel afterwards married a Mongrel Portuguese serjeant; but she was highly astonished, when the Bacsi sent for her to let her know that the Nabob had reduced her to serjeant's pay, because she had dishonoured the name of her former husband, whose services had demanded that the woman who bore his name should not be without the means of subsisting reputably.

remove the guard he had placed over the Jesuits. The good fathers were not, however, disposed to pardon the lady spiritually: she was excommunicated, and condemned to public penance; to which, though it may seem astonishing, she submitted, with much apparent resignation. The provincial father, in his letter, written to inform all the missions of the means by which his innocence was cleared up, spoke highly of the French officer; who, he said, was in the highest favour with the Nabob. This eulogium produced a letter from the archbishop of Cochin, who recommended to him a Malabar priest, of the number of the Christians of St. Thomas, whose diocesan the archbishop was. He was deputed, together with three other laymen of his country, to request of Hyder the permission to keep fire-arms, under the pretence that, by not being armed, they ran the risk of being robbed by the Nayres, and the soldiers of the Nabob. The officer, who imagined he might safely give credit to the archbishop's letter, was much surprised when Hyder said, he was no stranger to the antipathy that fomented their quarrel. "These people," said he, "have been disarmed, because they assassinated each other, being always at enmity on account of their priests, who are of different castes: I shall take care to place safe-guards in the country, to prevent my people from molesting them, and I shall send troops sufficient to disperse the Nayres."

These christians of Saint Thomas are of very ancient origin, being settled in India before the arrival of the Portuguese. It is demonstrated, that their St. Thomas was not the disciple of Jesus Christ. They are partly in subjection to the Pope, and partly under the patriarch of the Chaldeans, who resides at Merdin in Mesopotamia. This division causes them to detest each other; and, profiting by the troubles of their country, they were mutually engaged in a cruel war, when Hyder caused them to be disarmed. The deputies who came to Coimbatoor were stout men, with a ferocious air and manner: they had the figure of a small cross above their nose punctured in the skin, and a large scar on the right cheek, caused by the recoil of their muskets. The archbishop, in his letter, offered to the commandant two young slaves, who, he said, he had himself educated, and were qualified to render services both of utility and pleasure, being instructed in writing and in music. As he did not obtain his desire, he sent an inconsiderable present; with an excuse, that the young slaves, at the moment of their departure, had cried and wept so immoderately, that his feelings would not suffer him to part with them. To this present were added a vast number of benedictions, and a promise that he would write to the Pope, then Clement XIII.

The same officer was employed by Hyder in a law-suit between the French and English factors resident at Calicut. A merchant of that city had long been indebted to the French company; and having received a considerable quantity of wood from Hyder, the French factor agreed with him, that he should pay his debt in that commodity, which was much wanted at Pondicherry, for the entire rebuilding that town, lately destroyed by the English. The quantity sold to the French factor being arrived at Calicut, the English factor prevailed on the Raja of Coimbatoor to seize it, on pretence that the English company had a prior claim on the merchant: the Raja, who was guided by the English, adjudged, after hearing the parties, that the English factor should have the wood, which was accordingly carried by him to his factory: but on the appeal that the French commandant made to the Nabob himself, the Raja ordered the affair to remain in its then state, till the decision of the sovereign was known. He wrote at the same time in favour of the English; and the French factor, persuaded of the goodness of his cause, begged the commandant of Europeans to intercede in his favour. This officer having impartially informed Hyder of the difference between the factors, the Nabob made him this answer: "Neither you nor I are sufficiently informed to decide on this affair, especially as our attention is required to things of more consequence: but, that justice may be done, I have written to the Raja of Coimbatoor, to put the decision into the hands of the chiefs of the Portuguese, Danish, and Dutch factors; and whatever their judgment may be, to put it in execution."

In pursuance of this order, the delegated judges decided in favour of the French; but the English factor, to render the judgment illusory, caused all the wood to be sawed up, so that it was rendered unfit for any use, except to be burned: a piece of business that he could not have performed without the connivance of the Raja, whose duty it was to have placed a guard over the wood. The French factor, not being able to receive it in that state, wrote to the Nabob, informing him of this disgraceful manœuvre. On the account given by the French officer, Hyder immediately wrote to the Raja to repair to court with the utmost dispatch. The governor had no sooner received this order, than, suspecting the business, he sent for the English factor and the wood-merchant, and sent the latter to the French factory to offer payment of the sum due to the company. The French chief, bound to promote the welfare of his employers, could not refuse accepting a payment that was much more advantageous than the wood; and accordingly gave the merchant a discharge.

The Raja, furnished with this piece, departed to wait upon Hyder; who demanded, on seeing him, how the affair was terminated between the French and English? The Raja, without being disconcerted, answered with an affected laugh: "The English have lost their cause; but, as they had spoiled the wood without waiting for the judgment, I have forced them to pay the value in money; and the French have given the merchant an acquittance, which he has put into my hands." Hyder, who was not the dupe of his artifice, took this occasion to demand an account of the revenues and disbursements of the country he governed; and nominated commissioners to receive his accounts. Though the Raja did not seem abashed at the discourse of his sovereign, yet he retired extremely chagrined that his stratagem had been turned against himself. On inspecting his accounts, the committee condemned the governor to pay three or four lacs of rupees to the Nabob. To obtain either time or a mitigation of part of the sum, he complained for some days of the rigour of this judgment; which he affirmed would ruin him, as he protested he was not possessed of so large a sum. On his refusal, Hyder placed guards about his palace, to prevent water from being brought him, because, as a Bramin, he was obliged to wash himself many times in the day. This step forced him to open a secret repository of treasure in the very palace in which Hyder then resided, but which is the ordinary residence of the Raja.

A French surgeon, who had cured him of a secret disorder for the sum of one thousand rupees, half paid in hand, and the other half due, by a written promise to pay when the cure was completed, not being able to obtain the latter five hundred, though the cure had long been made, thought the present instant favourable to his desire of being paid. Hyder having heard his complaint, said, "Do as I did: let no water come into his house till you are paid." "But I have no soldiers," replied the surgeon. "But you have friends that have," answered the Nabob. Upon which advice the surgeon collected a number of French soldiers, by promising them a part of the sum: they took possession of the palace-gate; and the water-carriers not daring to approach, the surgeon received payment of his note, to the great diversion of Hyder, who, notwithstanding what had passed, did not remove the Raja from his government.

Hyder Ali, though in the midst of the most brilliant of courts, had become uneasy and thoughtful since the departure of Maffous Khan for Hyderabad. This lord, after making the utmost dispatch to arrive at the court of Nizam, had dispatched letters which removed the suspense of Hyder, and confirmed the intelligence given by the

Irish officer. He sent word that the English, by means of the Divan* Rocun Dowla, had determined the Nizam to carry the war into Mysore; that all the friends of Hyder had in vain attempted to dissuade him from the design; and that, having given himself up entirely to the suggestions of his Divan, he had bestowed the command of his army on General Smith, who had brought a considerable corps of Europeans and Sepoys from Madras.

Upon the receipt of this authentic advice, Hyder determined to defer his expedition against Travancore till a more favourable opportunity, and to march to Seringapatam, the capital of Mysore, to be in readiness to meet his enemies. Hyder had been long absent from this kingdom, in which he first saw the light, and where his fortune first began to disclose itself. He was about to return, as one of the greatest sovereigns in India, to a kingdom he had left in the capacity of a subject; for the Dayvas, notwithstanding their great power, are only the first subjects of the king. It was the desire of Hyder to make his entrance with all the pomp and state his rank demanded, and his Savari was therefore very numerous and brilliant. His daily march was a kind of triumph.—The description we shall proceed to give will be so much the more agreeable to the reader, as it will convey an idea of the magnificence of the Asiatic processions.

Hyder left Coimbatoor with a fine army of about fifty thousand men; of which twenty thousand were cavalry, extremely well mounted, thirty thousand Sepoys, and four thousand Topasses, with their uniforms.

Every day of the march the cavalry lined the right side of the road by which the Nabob and his attendants were to pass. The

* Rocun Dowla was brother-in-law to Mohumud Ali Khan, whom the English had made Nabob of Arcot. The title of Divan signifies the Minister and Keeper of the great seal of the Suba.

prince was saluted by all the officers and the standards. When all the elephants on which the great men were mounted had defiled before one corps of the cavalry, that corps turned about to the left, and rode full speed to take their place at the other end of the line. Two regiments of hussars, and one of dragoons, which formed the whole of the European cavalry, took the post of honour, and were the first to salute the Nabob; after which they placed themselves at the head of the procession; they were preceded by five hundred couriers, well clothed, and mounted on dromedaries. Next marched two elephants bearing the great standards of the Savari, being gold embroidery on a blue ground; one representing the sun, and the other the moon and stars. After the two elephants marched that which carries the great timbals, called the grand tomtom; they continually sound during the time the Savari is in motion, and may be heard at the distance of more than a league; there is even something grand and majestic in the noise;—the orders of the general are communicated to all the army by means of these instruments. After this elephant came four others, carrying the music of the Savari, consisting of small timbals, hautbois, flutes, and trumpets, the performers being thirty-two in number. Five elephants, called elephants of war, succeeded the four: they carry towers, or a kind of octagon chair, of gold, on their backs, strongly fixed to the saddle of the elephant by straps and silver chains. In each of these chairs are six warriors, armed from head to foot in armour which is musket proof; their offensive arms being fusils, and a species of blunderbuss of a very large conical bore, that discharge a whole handful of balls at once. One of these elephants is intended for the Nabob, but he never makes use of it in any battle.

The procession of elephants was succeeded by two regiments of Caffres or Abyssinian horse. The men were completely armed, one regiment having their arms polished, and the other bronzed, and both had large plumes of red and black ostrich feathers on their helmets, which hung down their backs: they bore lances, the steel work of which was highly polished; and the harness of their horses was red, with black silk fringes. The cavalry was followed by a number of men on foot, habited like Caleros; that is to say, almost naked, with large silk scarfs and close drawers, reaching to the middle of the thigh: they carried long lances, ornamented with ostrich feathers and small bells, that were made to sound by the motion of their march. The Caleros were succeeded by a body of men carrying small banners, or flags of red ground, with flames of silver.

The lance-bearers usually follow the prince to the chase: they are habituated to traverse the mountains and forests: the bearers of small standards are sent as safeguards to towns, villages, and castles: the appearance of these colours is sufficient to prevent the soldiery from entering any place; but the magistrates must attend at the gates or barriers, to furnish the army, upon payment, with everything they may want.

After this crowd of people on foot came the nobility following the court, marching as they pleased, in order, though without distinction of rank; generals, bahadurs, and even princes, marched indiscriminately with simple volunteers. Nothing could be more brilliant than this troop; they were armed from head to foot, and mounted on the most beautiful horses; their arms were damasked and encrusted with gold and silver; many had their casques ornamented with white feathers, formed of pearls and precious stones; and great numbers had coats of mail, gilt and enamelled: the bridles of their horses were enriched with pearls and other valuable stones, and with plumes of feathers. The number of this troop varied every day, they being volunteers; but it was usually about six hundred. They all had auftabgeries,* variously enriched.

* The auftabgeries is a parasol, not horizontal but perpendicular, formed of a rich stuff, embroidered with gold or silver. It is carried by men on foot at the end of a long staff, covered with gold or silver.

The nobility were succeeded by eight esquires or huntsmen of the Nabob, mounted on superb horses, and followed by twelve grooms on foot, each leading one of the Nabob's horses, richly harnessed: the first of these horses was a present from the general of the Marattas to Hyder, and was extremely singular: he was of a mouse-grey colour, with a white mane as brilliant as silver, and so thick and long, that it reached to the ground; it was tied together with a riband; his tail was answerable in beauty to his mane: but the most remarkable circumstance was, that he had a natural covering of a clear bay colour, which depended as low as his midthigh, and which commencing at the withers, finished at a small distance from the crupper; on this mantle flowers were artificially painted; so that, though the horse was absolutely naked, it was necessary to be very near him, in order to perceive that he was not covered with a cloth of some kind.

After the led horses followed a troop of running footmen, with black staves headed with gold, who were succeeded by twelve ushers or Sauquedars on horseback, carrying gold and silver maces with small crowns at top. After these came the grand officers of the household, as the steward, the chief usher, the sword-bearer, etc.: they had each a large collar or chain of gold depending on their breast, as marks of their dignity. These officers preceded the grand almoner or Purzadah, who marched alone, mounted on an elephant covered with green. He was immediately before the Nabob himself, who rode on the white elephant of the queen of Canara, an animal formerly worshipped as an idol, but now in a state of slavery, having large silver rings on his feet, with chains of the same metal. This elephant, which is said to be equal in value to a thousand others, was far superior to them in height and magnitude; he was covered with yellow, a colour much affected by the emperor and the Subas. The pavilion in which the Nabob sat was covered with stuff of the same colour, and had no other ornament than four small globes of silver; except that on each side, by silver chains, hung small hatchets or axes, such as the Samorin has carried before him. It is the custom of the Indians to assume the marks of honour of those they have vanquished. The elephant bore on his head a kind of buckler of gold, that represented a sun: he was led by two conductors, the one ranked as captain of horse in the Nabob's guard, and the other was his usual keeper. In a small pavilion behind the Nabob was a valet, to supply him with betel; and on each side an attendant stood upright on the foot-step, holding by the pavilion with one hand, and having in the other a large chowry to disperse the flies, made of white peacock's feathers, which he caused to move circularly, and produced a singular effect at a distance. About two hundred elephants followed that of the Nabob, two and two: they were rode by only three persons, the master, the conductor, and an attendant in the small pavilion. The coverings and pavilions of these elephants were very different in colour and magnificence; some were bordered with gold and silver lace; many of the pavilions were wrought silver; and there were some even enriched with precious stones, as were those of the sons of Hyder, and some others. The young princes were on the left of their father, and Raza Saeb on his right, but their elephants were not more than half the size of that of the Nabob.

After all the elephants in procession, came what are in India called the honours, borne by five elephants. The first carried a mosque of gold, and of exquisite workmanship, covered with white satin, that was taken off when the procession came near any town or city; the second carried, at the extremity of a red staff, the head of a fish, whose scales were formed of jewels and enamel, and a long horse's tail depended from the same; the third carried a large flambeau of white wax in a chandelier of gold; the fourth bore two small pots of gold, called chambou, at the end of a large red staff; and, lastly, the fifth elephant carried a kind of round chair without a canopy, covered on the outside with ivory inlaid, and ornamented with gold.* After the honours followed two regiments of Abyssinians on horseback like the two first; and the procession was closed by two hundred Caffres on foot, clothed in scarlet, with silver collars, and armed with lances varnished black, and interspersed with silver gilding: all the train was inclosed between a double rank of men on foot, clothed in white silk, having lances in their hands about fourteen feet long, varnished black, and adorned with plates of silver, at the armed ends of which were small red streamers with silver flames: the lance-men marched at such a distance from each other as to inclose the whole by joining their lances.

This grand procession, on its march in the plain, had the most superb and striking effect.

Hyder was everywhere received with the most lively expressions of joy; the highest honours were rendered him, and the people crowded to see him, while their acclamations, of "Long live Hyder!" were incessantly reiterated. Every village, town, and city, was ornamented; triumphal arcs, and other edifices, were erected in various places, according to the riches of the inhabitants; the houses, and even the walls, of towns and fortresses were painted, or at least new white washed; governors, commandants, and other great men, came out in state with their retinues, preceded by musicians, singers, and dancers, known by the name of Bayaderes, to meet the sovereign; flowers and sweet water were dispersed in his passage, and the cannon were heard in all parts of the country. It was in this triumphant march that he met his brother-in-law, Mughdoom Ali Khan, at the distance of about a league from Seringapatam. This potentate was at the head of a numerous retinue mounted on elephants, and marched before Hyder to the island, where tents were magnificently dressed out near the

---

* All these honours are allegorical, and expressive of the virtues a sovereign ought to possess.

city walls; all the army encamped on the island, and the situation of the camp brought to every one's recollection the great danger Hyder had avoided in the time of Canero at the same place.

Hyder came into Mysore without any fear of the events that might arise in the war he supposed himself to be engaged in with the Suba of Decan: he perfectly knew the indolent and enervated character of that prince, and had no apprehensions from his army, which was defective in the essential articles of discipline, arms, and pay, and whose chiefs, being proprietors of their own troops, were his friends and partisans. From this last circumstance he was assured that General Smith could make no movements without his receiving advice of them. As he was abused by Mirza, his brother-in-law, who every day gave him reason to think the truce with the Marattas would be soon renewed, he went forward with cheerfulness, and in spirits; and arrived at Seringapatam with the conviction that he could easily parry every attempt of his enemies. But his astonishment was extreme, when Mughdoom Ali Khan informed him that there was reason to suspect the fidelity of Mirza Ali Khan; since he had learned that the army of the Marattas, to the number of 150,000 men, was on its march from Pona, with Madurao,* Nana of the Marattas, at their head, who was then beginning his first campaign; his march being directed

* Madurao was the son of Balagirao, a Bramin, who had rendered the post of a general of the Marattas hereditary in his family. This young man was then no more than eighteen years old, and possessed the most uncommon share of virtue and ability; his uncle Raguba caused him to be assassinated. Nana signifies father: it is a name of honour given to Balagirao by the Marattas, which now serves as a title to his descendants. The general being called Nana, the king has no authority, and only acts, like that of Mysore, in the ceremonies of religion.

towards Scirra, as Mirza could not but know, since he had envoys at Madurao's court.

To conceive the trouble and astonishment of Hyder at this news, it will be sufficient to know, that Mirza Ali Khan, his brother-in-law and cousin, was the most beloved by him of all his relations; he had educated him himself; and the young lord, endued with the most estimable qualities, had always appeared full of gratitude and tender attachment. The great confidence Hyder had reposed in his virtues induced him to think that he could not, in spite of his youth, place the important government of Scirra in better hands. The only precaution he took was that which he commonly used with all his governors, namely, to give him a minister, or principal secretary, whose fidelity he could depend on; and who had orders to give an accurate account of the conduct of his brother-in-law.

This man, who, like most courtiers, had concealed his ambition, and the bad principles that actuated him, conceived the hope of making his fortune by means of Mirza. He undertook to gain the confidence of the young prince by flattery, and by condescending to all his wishes, or, in other words, to all his weaknesses.

Mirza was young, generous, and addicted to pleasure, and dissipated the revenues of his government in his amusements, instead of reserving a part, according to the orders of Hyder. The Bramin, his secretary, so far from advising the Nabob, as he had engaged to do, or at least remonstrating to his young master, flattered him that he would have time to arrange his accounts, in case Hyder should demand them, and to amass a sum sufficient to cover the deficiency, before the Nabob, then engaged in the war on the coast of Malabar, would think of visiting Scirra. Mirza suffered himself to be persuaded by the adulation of his secretary; and, continuing his imprudent extravagance, reduced the finances of his government to the utmost disorder.

Hyder, who thought it proper to keep his brother-in-law in some fear, and concealed his project of making war on Travancore, wrote to Mirza, giving him commission to renew the truce with the Marattas; and at the same time acquainted him of his intention to repair to Seringapatam at the end of the year, and afterwards to Scirra. He likewise gave orders to take, out of the money in reserve at Scirra, a sum sufficient to obtain the renewal of the truce with the Marattas.

This letter, sufficiently perplexing to Mirza in every particular of its contents, gave him much anxiety and trouble: but the Bramin, finding the occasion favourable for averting the storm that threatened him still more than his master, addressed him thus: "If you have skill to seize the opportunity that Hyder presents to you, you will not only be out of all embarrassment, but may become an independent sovereign. Send me among the Marattas, under the pretence, and with a commission to renew the truce, and I will treat with Madurao, and the national council, in such a manner, that they will with pleasure acknowledge you sovereign of the country you command; and for a small tribute they will engage to defend you, as they desire nothing more than to diminish the power of Hyder, who has taken this very country from them."

The insinuations of the Bramin's ambition, the pleasure of being independent, the fear of Hyder's arrival, and, perhaps, more than anything else, that false shame which prevents young people from recanting an error, determined this prince to betray his trust. He suffered the Bramin to depart, giving him a commission to treat with the Marattas as he thought proper. This faithless minister found the Marattas very much disposed to listen to him. There was an English envoy at Pona,* who proposed to them to attack Hyder, at the same

* Pona is the second capital of the Maratta country, the residence of the general and the national council, and the place where the army annually assembles.

time that Nizam and the English attacked him on their side. The arrival of the envoy determined the grand national council to make war on the Nabob; but Madurao, though very young, possessed courage and greatness of soul, and would not consent to form any alliance with a traitor. "I will not," said he, "consent to make war upon Hyder, unless he refuses to pay the Chotay;* and, in that case, the Maratta army will be sufficient to compel him, without requiring an alliance with any one, much less with a traitor." In spite of the generous sentiments of this young man, it was not in his power to determine the general council; and he was obliged to conform to their decision.

The very day following that on which Mughdoom had apprised him of the infidelity of Mirza, Hyder received news of the arrival of the Marattas into the country of Scirra. It was in the highest degree

---

* The Chotay is the seventh part of the revenue of the Subaship of Decan and its dependencies, which Aurengzebe granted to the Marattas. It is not regularly paid; but the Marattas raise contributions in consequence of their claim, which are regulated according to their power, and the riches of the State that pays them. Hyder, who possesses considerable tracts of country, as Mysore, etc., that owe the Chotay, in virtue of Aurengzebe's gift, has never submitted to this payment; insisting, that no one has any right to compel the people to pay any tax or tribute, except for the good of the State, or by the right obtained by superior strength; that the Marattas being in this last case, he owed them nothing, because God had made him powerful enough to defend his subjects against them. He has, therefore, never made peace with that nation, but only truces for three years, sometimes by paying them a sum of money, and sometimes without paying anything, according to the fortune of war. It is certain that, in the treaties made between these powers, the Chotay is never mentioned.

afflicting to him, when he heard that his brother-in-law, to complete his ingratitude, had joined his enemies with the very army that was intrusted to his charge; and that he had engaged to admit the Marattas into Scirra, and every other fortress in his government.

An event so totally unexpected overthrew all the projects Hyder had formed, and reduced him to the most difficult plan of defence. For though, upon the false advice of Mirza, he had supposed the Marattas were ready to renew the truce, yet he had concluded that, at all events, he should have time to meet them on the other side of Scirra; and, by joining his army to that of Mirza, he might give them battle with Scirra, and the other strong places of that government, behind him, to which he might retire, if necessary: an event he hoped to see decided before the Nizam could arrive with his army on the frontier of Bangalore, where of necessity he must make his first attack on him. But his dominions being laid open by the treason of Mirza, he could neither meet the Marattas nor the combined armies of the Suba and the English; but was forced to wait for them under the cannon of Seringapatam, the capital of Mysore: for the country between that city and Scirra being a plain, without one good fortress, and his army much inferior to the Marattas in cavalry, he must have fought to a great disadvantage, as he must have run the risk of a total defeat, without being able to secure his country from pillage. The numerous Maratta cavalry, habituated to make incursions, and to subsist on the straw that covers the houses, would infallibly spread themselves over all Mysore, and might cut off his communication with the magazines of Seringapatam, and the mountains in its vicinity, which were the only resource to support his army; and again, the army of Nizam would probably hasten its march, on hearing of the operations of the Marattas; of which concatenation of circumstances, the probable result would be, that, finding himself between two armies, he might be forced to retire into Canara, and abandon Seringapatam, and the kingdom of Mysore, to his enemies.

The genius of Hyder, vast and fertile in resources, seems to have been formed to shine in critical and embarrassing situations of this nature. He immediately determined on a plan of action: he divided all his army into small parties, and dispersed them over all the country, with orders to all the chiefs to command and oblige all the inhabitants, as well of the country, as of the cities, towns, villages, and fortresses, to abandon their dwellings, and retire to Seringapatam, bringing with them all their property of any kind whatsoever. The troops were ordered, at the same time, to lay the whole country waste, without sparing anything but the trees; and to burn all forages, even to the straw that covered the houses. To facilitate the devastation, and the transport of goods, all the sutlers, valets, and other dependents on the army, were permitted to share the universal pillage; and they went forth on this expedition, attended by every beast of burthen belonging to the army or the city.

It is scarcely possible to form an idea of the promptitude with which this extraordinary order was carried into execution; and in how short a time one of the finest and most beautiful countries in the world was changed into a desert, for thirty leagues round Seringapatam. It is difficult to determine who were the readiest to shew their obedience, the inhabitants or the army: the former abandoned their houses, leaving nothing they could carry away, and they were succeeded by the troops, one party after another, who finished, by leaving absolutely nothing. Horsemen and soldiers were continually arriving at Seringapatam, carrying corn, rice, maize, and even wooden beds and earthen pots, no one choosing to return empty-handed; and what may seem still more surprising, all the inhabitants arrived cheerful and contented, some carrying their children, others their sick and infirm; the number of whom, in this happy climate, is always very small. As soon as any troop of people arrived, they were paid immediately the value of their effects, at so advantageous a price, that no dispute ever arose on the subject; and afterwards they were dispatched to an allotted part of the neighbouring mountains, where they were allowed a sufficient quantity of rice and other necessaries, at a price much below that which was given for what they sold at Seringapatam.*

To remove the surprise, that a whole people cheerfully abandoning their habitations must occasion, we only need observe, that all the lands are the property of the sovereign, the cultivator being no more than an annual tenant. The Indians of this country, even those who dwell in towns, have no other furniture than a bedstead, without covering or tester, whose bottom is composed of withy, and the bed-clothes of the richest is no more than a carpet; a few chests of paste-board to inclose their linen, some mats, and utensils of pottery, without tables or chairs, whose use is unknown to them, as well as three-fourths of the moveables which the Europeans employ; and, as their houses are built of brick or earth, with very little wood-work, all the damage that the most merciless enemy can do, is quickly repaired.

While the troops were employed in laying the country waste, the utmost diligence was used in completing the fortifications of the camp

---

* The moderate price of provisions in the valleys, where these inhabitants of the plain went to dwell for a time, ought not to be a matter of wonder, when the abundance at Coimbatoor is reflected on, and it is considered that, in the warm climates, nothing is required on the earth but water to insure good harvests. The rains are the most abundant in the mountainous countries, and the Indians have made vast basins at the feet of the mountains, which preserve great quantities of water, more than sufficient for all the purposes of agriculture. Hyder, instead of receiving his revenues in money like the other Indian princes, receives them in provisions, which he disposes of as well to his own advantage as that of his people.

which, on the left, terminated against the city ramparts, and on the right at a redoubt situated at the extremity of the canal, that, with the river Caveri, forms the island on which the city is built. By this position, the back part of the camp was secured from every attack by the canal, which is very broad and deep, with steep banks: the front of the camp was defended by nine large redoubts, mounting twenty-four, thirty-three, and thirty-six pounders, that commanded the whole plain. About 300 toises before these, on the banks of the river, were seven other redoubts, flanking those before mentioned, each mounting six or eight pieces of cannon, and served by five hundred men. All these redoubts had ditches before them, planted with palisades; and as the river was everywhere fordable, and hard at bottom, twenty thousand coltrops were forged, to be laid as soon as the enemy appeared disposed to the attack. About one hundred pieces of cannon from the town ramparts, and fifty that were in a fortified pagoda situated on a very steep hill on the other side of the river, opposite the part of the island farthest from the city, would have flanked those who might have been disposed to attack the first line of redoubts; and the same artillery would have rendered the attack of the second line still more difficult.

In this camp, defended by three hundred pieces of cannon, it was, that Hyder waited the approach of his enemies; and, as his cavalry would have been of no use to him, he divided it into two parties; the principal of which was given to Mughdoom, who was sent to meet the Nizam in the country of Bangalore, where he made the same devastation as had been made in the plains near Seringapatam. As that country is interspersed with woods and mountains, and contains many very defensible fortresses, it was not so entirely abandoned: this circumstance furnished Mughdoom with better opportunities of harassing the army of Nizam, and carrying off the foragers, who were of necessity much spread abroad on account of the waste situation of the country.

The command of the rest of the cavalry, a small body of infantry, and all the irregular troops, was given to Meer Fizoolla Khan,* ancient Nabob of Colar, and principal general of Hyder, with orders to repair to the kingdom of Bisnagar, and defend the passes in the mountains which separate that kingdom from Canara, and to prevent the Marattas from penetrating, by joining his force to the military establishment of that country. He had instructions to assist Bassapatam, the capital of Bisnagar, if the Marattas should attack it, and to harass the rear of their army, if they should advance towards Seringapatam.

While Hyder was busied in these preparations, to which he was compelled by one of the most critical situations it is possible for a great monarch to find himself in, he rode out every day on horseback, without many attendants, and affected to shew himself often to the army and citizens. His countenance was not then enlivened with that gaiety that usually distinguishes him, because his mind was occupied with the danger that threatened him, and he has not acquired the habit of disguising his thoughts; on the contrary, a kind of mild languor or sadness appeared in his looks, that would have interested even his

---

* Meer Fizoola Khan is a Mogol nobleman of a very ancient house. All his family is attached to Hyder. His brother was Bucshee, or minister of war: he is a man of a very handsome figure and appearance, as fair as an European, very intelligent, of a most amiable and generous character, but more inclined to expense than his fortune allows: he would be an extremely proper person to be sent on an embassy to Europe. Hyder has a great regard and esteem for him; and his prodigality is one of the qualities that have procured him the confidence of that Nabob, who, like Cæsar, is of opinion, *that they who love mirth and pleasure, are not the men who engage in conspiracies.*

enemies in his misfortunes; his tent was open at all times, and he never was easier of access than at this juncture.

Though every kind of assembly and amusement was forbade, he instructed his generals concerning the means he thought proper to use in his defence, with an air and manner not in the least expressive of embarrassment.

The Europeans of his army, who interested themselves with an anxious eagerness in the success of the prince, were impatient to know the post he would assign to them, in case of an attack; for Hyder did not make public his order of battle, and caused the guards of every post to be changed daily, though, according to the news, the enemy was on the point of arriving. To satisfy their impatience, their commandant, with two other officers, waited upon Hyder, and acquainted him that, as he had always conferred upon the Europeans the honour of the most important post, they were come to request that he would put the defence of the first line of redoubts into their hands.* The prince immediately answered, "I had already determined to appoint "you to the post you request; and the demand you make, on an "occasion when my enemies are innumerable, is so much the more "agreeable to me, as it is a new mark of your affection: take the "command, plant your colours† in the centre redoubt; and you may

* The Topasses, commanded by European officers, were esteemed of this number, and the hussars and dragoons also served in defence of the redoubts.

† We have already observed that all the commandant generals have a set of colours before their tent; that of the European commandant was distinguished by a cannon with a ball in its chase, which denoted his post as chief of the artillery, and two streamers above, as marks of his degrees in the cavalry and infantry.

"be assured of being powerfully seconded, for I myself will command "the second line, and engage to send you the necessary succours. "I am very much oppressed with the treason of Mirza, whom I have "always treated as my favourite child; and I have had no reason to "expect so numerous a combination of enemies, who, so far from being "provoked, have been loaded by me with benefits; but, notwithstanding "their number, I do not despair. It is the power of God that has "raised me, and I possess nothing but through him: as long as he "supports me, I shall look down on my enemies; and if he should "forsake me, I must submit with resignation to his pleasure."

The fidelity of the commandants of the fortresses of Mark Scirra and Maggheri, gave Hyder all the time his preparations required; for these officers, when they learned that the Governor-General had joined his army to that of the Marattas under Madurao, refused to obey him; but the general, desirous of possessing the whole country, thought proper to besiege these places, which held out longer than was expected, particularly the fortress of Maggheri, into which a battalion of grenadier Sepoys had thrown themselves voluntarily, simply on the requisition of the governor of the place, while they were employed in laying the country waste: they made a journey of fourteen leagues without once stopping, for fear of being too late. When the fortress had capitulated, Madurao was desirous of seeing those grenadiers, whose formation had made so much noise in India: he was astonished to find these brave troops dirty and ill equipped. "I am surprised," said he, "that so powerful a prince as your master "pays so little attention to such brave men." Their commandant replied, "Desirous of the honour of fighting against you, we hastened "away without any necessaries but the clothes on our backs; and we "have marched a day and a night without eating or drinking." "I "am charmed at your spirit," returned Madurao, "and should be "concerned that your master, who sent you out well clothed, should "see you return in such a state;" and immediately ordered them two complete changes of clothes, adding,* that "Though the terms of "the capitulation require you to leave your arms and your colours, "yet I return your colours as a mark of esteem for your master, and "a recompense due to your valour." Thus it was that war was carried on by men we are so ready to think barbarous.

After thus displaying the merit of the Indians, it would be unjust to pass over in silence the spirited action of one hundred European cannoneers of different nations. They had marched, like the others, against the Marattas, supposing they were to fight them; but when they saw Mirza joined his army to theirs, they perceived the perfidy of the governor; and, repairing to their general, "Do you imagine," said one of their officers, "that we will fight against Hyder, whose "pay we have so long received? No, our intention is to fight for "him, and not against him. Adieu." At the same time they departed, leaving all their baggage, having no other arms but their sabres, because the cannoneers in Hyder's army do no other service than that of the artillery. They arrived at Hyder's camp, without having found any opposition; for Mirza, no doubt ashamed of his treason, gave orders not to oppose their departure. Hyder received them with great pleasure, and gave the officers bracelets of gold, and money to the soldiers, paying them likewise the value of their baggage, upon their own estimation. This daring act of fidelity was perhaps the effect of the disgrace inflicted on the Europeans who adhered to Canero.

General Smith and Rocun Dowla were soon advised of the junction of Mirza with the Marattas, and announced it to Nizam

* In the Indian capitulations the garrisons are never made prisoners of war; but all the arms, colours, and ammunition belong to the victors, and the baggage of individuals is spared.

as a certain presage of the ruin of Hyder. This news frustrated all the efforts and intrigues of Hyder's friends in the court of that Suba; and perhaps those very friends, convinced that his ruin was inevitable, might grow cool to his interests. The Suba being always in want of money to support his expensive pleasures, General Smith found it not difficult to persuade him to hasten his march, without stopping to make any siege, lest the Marattas should take Seringapatam, and seize the greatest part of the spoils. This forced march, and the time consumed by Madurao in his two sieges, were the causes that both armies arrived together near Cenapatam, about seven leagues from Seringapatam.

The absolute solitude and desert face of the country, which the enemies perceived in their approach to the capital of Mysore; the daily loss of their foraging parties, attacked by different bodies of Hyder's horse; and the impossibility of obtaining any advice concerning the situation and force of Hyder's army, gave the different chiefs of the armies to understand that the brilliant hopes they had indulged, of sharing the dominions and treasures of Hyder, were not likely to be realised.

As soon as the two armies were joined, different corps of horse appeared in the plain of Seringapatam. Many advanced so near as to reconnoitre the town, and the redoubts in which Hyder's colours were displayed; as they met with no interruption from Hyder, they rode about the plain, and viewed everything at their ease. The same ceremony was performed the following day; but on the third, at nine in the morning, the plain was covered with the cavalry of both armies, with the chiefs at their head on their elephants: this cavalry was followed by a body of infantry, who brought forward about fifty large cannon, that arrived about noon. The view was grand and striking: the number of horses was above one hundred thousand; and there were more than two hundred elephants.

General Smith, at the head of a large body of cavalry, among whom were distinguished various chiefs, though neither Nizam nor Madurao were seen, advanced to reconnoitre the camp. When this cavalry appeared disposed to advance no farther, a signal was given from the redoubt in which Hyder was, and the fire poured at once from all the redoubts, from the fortress at the head of the bridge,* and from the mountain: this last did no great mischief, but terrified Nizam and his army, and convinced General Smith that the project of attacking Hyder in his camp was impracticable, especially for an army whose chief strength lay in cavalry. Towards the evening they who commanded this vast multitude of men retired, together with their soldiers, in much disorder, to their respective camps.

The following day, a council was held with Nizam, at which the chiefs of both armies assisted. Every one being desirous of putting his own opinion in practice, no determination was settled on, though General Smith gave the only good advice, which was, to separate the two armies, and make feints, to draw Hyder out of his camp; but, notwithstanding the propriety of this idea, every one was dissatisfied with it, because it showed too plainly, that their elevated expectations were ill-founded, and required great abatements to reduce them to probability.

The Maratta chiefs having returned to their camp, no more councils were held; but the two camps remained in the same situation, many messengers passing between them. The Marattas traversed the country, as well as different corps of Nizam's army: they frequently met the cavalry of Hyder, which almost always had the

* This fortress is situated in a bend of the river. It is a good Indian fortification, to which Hyder has added a glacis and covered way, planted with palisades. The chief difficulty of the attack arises from the figure of the place, which, forming a crescent, would enfilade the trench of the enemy.

advantage; Mughdoom especially, who is an excellent officer, had the most decided success. Forages every day became more scarce, and the capture of the foragers, of horses, elephants, camels, and oxen, continued to such a degree, that they at last could not be sold at Bangalore at any rate. At length the provisions of rice brought by the merchants were exhausted, and the price of this indispensable article, as well as of every other necessary, increased every day. Hyder, who was informed of everything as it happened, remained at ease in his camp, where everything was in such great abundance, that subsistence cost scarcely anything. The inhabitants, supposing everything would fetch a great price, had laid in vast stores; every soldier had a hole in the earth near his tent filled with rice; the river afforded fish in abundance: and every kind of country provisions came from the mountains and valleys in the night, attended by a numerous escort of infantry, after four hours travel through a road intersected by hedges and ditches, where the cavalry would have had no opportunity of shining.

The Marattas, under the pretence of being nearer to the forages, withdrew from Cenapatam, and encamped on the Caveri, at five leagues from Seringapatam. It appears that they must have conferred with Hyder previous to the movement; for two days after the change of their camp the truce was concluded on; and on receiving six lacks of rupees in hand, and six payable in six months, they engaged to retire out of his country, and to restore Scirra: but the rest of the district intrusted to Mirza was abandoned to them, and they suffered that governor to remain in possession of it, on the condition of paying a small tribute; for the security of which they retained the fortress of Maggheri: the money was no sooner counted, than the Marattas raised their camp, and departed, taking the road to Scirra.

This news gave the alarm in the camp of Nizam, and that sovereign, more alarmed than the rest, was exceedingly embarrassed.

Hyder, who knew his character, and judged it a proper occasion to impress him with still more terror, recalled his army from the kingdom of Bisnagar, marched his troops out of the island, and encamped in the plain on the road to Cenapatam. This manœuvre produced its whole effect on the timid and enervated prince, and disposed him to listen to the suggestions of Basalutjung, his brother, Mahfouz Khan, and other friends of Hyder: and there is no doubt, but he would have proceeded in direct opposition to his Divan, if that minister, seeing the impossibility of encouraging his master, had not been the first to give him the direct advice to treat with Hyder; and offered to undertake the negociation himself, as a business that he was confident might be concluded with the greatest facility. To remove General Smith, and the greatest part of the English forces, he informed that commander, that since, in the present situation of things, provisions, and succours could only be had from the country of Arcot, it was necessary that the English should get possession of certain places belonging to Hyder, to secure a free passage for the convoys that might be sent from Madras and the other places dependent on the English and Mohumed Ali.

The English general had not been blind to the disposition that prevailed of treating with Hyder; but he was happy at an opportunity of approaching his frontiers, to place himself out of the reach of the perfidy it was probable he might experience, and to remove himself from a country in which he might be shut up, and obliged to surrender, with all his army, if Nizam chose to deliver him up to Hyder. He wrote an account to Madras of what had passed, and at the same time expressed his suspicions of Nizam and his minister; he proposed to make the best treaty they could with Hyder, for fear the English should find themselves charged singly with a war so much the more burthensome as it would be in their own country; and, after having taken leave of Nizam, who loaded him with caresses from the satisfaction he had of seeing him depart, he set off, leaving, however, to the faith of Nizam, two hundred Europeans, one thousand Sepoys, and some pieces of cannon.

While the government of Madras received the dispatches of General Smith, Mohumud Ali received others from Rocun Daulla, his brother-in-law, which gave him the most positive assurances that Nizam would continue the war against Hyder till he had forced him to yield at least all the country of Bangalore, and all Malleam, or the Carnatic; that is to say, the valleys of Coimbatoor, Ceylon, Kisnagari, etc.: and while he magnified the forces of the Suba beyond the truth, he diminished those of Hyder, who, he said, were incapable of presenting themselves before the army of his invincible sovereign. The council of Madras, persuaded by Mohumed Ali, paid no regard to the advice of General Smith, but ordered him to attack the places of Hyder, and to agree with Nizam in everything, promising to supply him amply with provisions, ammunition, money, and even troops, if necessary. At the same time that this unprincipled Divan wrote thus to Mohumed Ali, he dispatched his other brother, Mahfouz Khan, to Hyder, to offer to meet him at Seringapatam, and to assure him, that he was disposed to do everything that might be agreeable to him, as Mahfouz Khan would explain to him. Hyder, on receipt of Rocun Daulla's letter, in order to give some confidence to Nizam, caused his army to return to its ancient camp, and wrote to the Divan that he would be received as became a person of his rank and character: it was likewise permitted to the merchants of his camp, and the country people, to carry provisions to the army of Nizam. When this Suba had read the letter of Hyder, he ordered a cessation of arms, which was likewise ordered on the side of Hyder; and the Divan set out for Hyder's camp. Hyder received him, and, after a short conversation, retired, and Rocun Daulla having seen the grand retinue of Hyder, returned to his own camp. The day following, the Divan came to have audience of Hyder in great ceremony; and, to lose less time in going and coming, he came and encamped between the two lines of redoubts: both parties being desirous of concluding, the treaty was made in a few days. It was agreed that Tippoo Sultaun, the son of Hyder, should marry the daughter of Mahfouz Khan, who, as eldest son of Unvurudeen Khan, was the lawful Nabob of Arcot; that Mahfouz Khan should give up all his right to his future son-in-law; that the two Subas should join their forces to reduce Mohumed Ali Khan, and those who took his part; that, during the time the two armies acted in conjunction, Hyder should pay six lacs of rupees per month to the Nizam, and should have the sole right of putting garrisons in the several fortresses of the nabobship of Arcot, the command of which should be given to Mughdoom Ali Khan, brother-in-law of Hyder, who should govern the country in the names of his nephew, Tippoo Sultaun, and Mahfouz Khan; that the former should enjoy the whole revenue of that nabobship, for which Mughdoom should account, after deducting the charge of supporting the troops and administering the government.

To unite all the claims in the person of Tippoo Sultaun, Raza Ali Khan, son of Chanda Saeb, likewise yielded up to the young prince all his pretensions as well to the nabobship of Arcot as to Trichnopoli and Madura; and Hyder and Tippoo Sultaun, on their part, engaged to give him all the country of Tanjore, after deposing the Raja as a punishment for the murder of Chanda Saeb, father of Raza; the country of Tanjore was understood as intended to be held by him under the same vassalage to the Nabob of Arcot as it had therefore been held by the former Rajas; and finally, the two Subas engaged not to separate, but to exert all their forces to carry this treaty into effect.

Previous to the ratification of the treaty which Mahfouz Khan undertook to prepare, the retinue of Tippoo Sultaun was got ready; it was composed of six thousand of the best infantry, of which three thousand were grenadier Sepoys or Topasses, and four thousand chosen cavalry, with three hundred Europeans, and a regiment of hussars; he likewise had the greatest part of his father's Savari. Mahfouz Khan having brought the ratification, Rocun Daulla departed, loaded with presents, and Mahfouz Khan accompanied him.

It will hardly be credited that Hyder, at the moment of parting with his son, was in the greatest perplexity and concern, and expressed it to his friends. "I am afraid," said he, "of the perfidious and cruel Nizam; he has assassinated his own brother, will he spare my son? or, at least, have I not reason to conclude that he will detain him, and compel me, by the apprehension of my son's danger, either to pay him a large sum, or to make great concessions to him? For, in short, I trust my son in the hands of a wretch to whom nothing is sacred." This discourse, and many other actions of his, prove that one of the greatest weaknesses of Hyder is his extreme affection for his children and all his relations. However, on the assurances made by Raza Saeb and Meer Fesoulla Khan (who were charged to accompany his son, and who protested they would themselves perish before the least accident should happen to the young prince), he suffered him to depart, being likewise much encouraged by reflecting on the bravery of the troops and the nobility that attended him.

This little army arrived by a single march at Cenapatam. The whole army of Nizam, and especially the English officers as well as soldiers, were extremely surprised at their appearance. Though they had heard of Hyder's army, yet they could not conceive how Indian troops, who have always been ill-disciplined, could march in such good order, and perform their evolutions with such rapidity and exactness. The beauty of their arms and clothing was equally uncommon and strange to them; and they were astonished at the pomp of the Savari. The troops were no sooner encamped than the officers came to visit those of Hyder, and continually spoke with admiration of the excellence of the troops.

The following day Tippoo Sultaun received a visit from Busalutjung, brother of Nizam: he was accompanied by Rocun Daulla and the principal lords of the court. The succeeding day the son of Hyder repaired with all his retinue to the tent of the Suba, who rendered him the highest honours, and the voluntary cession of Arcot by Mahfouz Khan and Raza Saeb, the only legitimate pretenders to that territory, left no doubt concerning the rights of the son of Hyder Ali Khan. The Nizam dismissed the few remaining English troops, acquainting them that the alliance he had contracted with Hyder Ali Khan having terminated their differences he had no farther occasion for their services; and that he should write to the governor and council of Madras, to which place they might retire.

As soon as Hyder was informed that his son was acknowledged Nabob of Arcot, he wrote to his Vakeel, Menagi Pundit, resident at Madras, transmitting to him a memorial to be presented to the governor. The substance of the memorial was, that Nizam Daulla and Hyder Ali Khan, being well informed that Mohumed Ali Khan,* by his continual usurpations and intrigues, was the author of all the troubles that had so long agitated Hindostan, had resolved to make war upon him, till they had deprived him of all the territory he possessed to the exclusion of the proper and legitimate heirs; that in consequence they thought proper to warn the English against affording him any assistance; and required them to withdraw their troops out of any garrisons they might possess in the Nabobship of Arcot, or any of the countries usurped by Mahomed; that nevertheless, as it was known that these places were pledges for sums due to them from Mohumed Ali, Hyder Ali offered to reimburse them in any sums lawfully due, among which he could not reckon those sums that were

* Hyder was not ignorant that Mohumed Ali was no more than the agent of the English; but he acted in this manner to retort their own politics upon themselves.

dispensed for the purposes of dispossessing the Nabobs of Vellore, Vandevachi, and other rightful proprietors, of their territories; but, on the contrary, he expected that these last should be indemnified from all the losses they had sustained.

It may be easily conceived that a memorial, or manifesto, totally new and uncommon in India, and declaratory of a war against the English, of which they were to bear the whole expense, must have caused the utmost astonishment to that people. This declaration was directed against the possessions of the English, Mohumed Ali Khan being a Nabob merely nominal, without troops or money, and the slave of the English.

It was the policy of the English in India to traverse the designs of the smallest potentate, who might wish to enlarge his dominions, for fear he might arrive to a capability of making head against them: their administration had long been alarmed at the rapid conquests of Hyder, and the sudden elevation of his power. In consequence of Nizam Doulla's having ceded to them four northern provinces, they had engaged to furnish twelve hundred Europeans, and a corps of Sepoys, to the army of that Suba: General Smith, commander of this body of troops, was ordered to inspire Nizam with jealousy of the conquests of Hyder, and to confer with Rocun Daulla concerning the projected war; offering the Suba all the English forces, and fixing his attention on the immense treasures Hyder had found in the kingdom of Canara and the coast of Malabar; treasures which they affirmed could not but fall into his hands, as it was impossible for Hyder to stand against the united forces of the Suba and the English.

The English government did not at that time indulge the hope of plundering Hyder entirely, but they expected to stop the course of his conquests, and oblige him to abandon the coast of Malabar, among the inhabitants of which they proposed to excite a revolt. By this means their intention was to compel Hyder to yield, either to them or to Mohumed Ali Khan, all the country dependant on Mysore that lies beyond the great *Gates*, or mountains; which, according to them, ought to be the natural bounds of his dominions. They proposed to leave him in possession of all the rest of his dominions, in the persuasion that it was of advantage to the security and tranquillity of their possessions, that so warlike and powerful a prince as Hyder should be between them and the Marattas.*

But at all events, whether the hopes of the English respecting the war with Hyder were rational or not, it is certain that when they learned that the Marattas had declared war against him, and Mirza, his brother-in-law, had joined them, their expectations were unbounded, and they devoured by anticipation the treasures of Hyder.

The council of Madras, who till then had envied the brilliant fortune of the Calcutta administration in the enjoyment of an immense territorial revenue, flattered themselves in a short time to realize their chimerical hopes, and to equal them in splendour and importance. Their letters to the Court of Directors were filled with brilliant projects, that promised no less than the possession of all the coast from Cape Rama to Cape Comorin: the Court of Directors were thrown into a kind of delirium by their admiration of the profound policy of their servants; and every one being anxious to possess a

* That it may not be thought that the author of these Memoirs expresses his own idea rather than those of the princes, governors, and generals he speaks of, he thinks it proper to observe, that these pretensions are collected from a conference between himself and the governor (Boschier) of Madras, together with Colonel Call, first in council, and chief engineer, in which they attempted to persuade him, that it was the interest of Hyder to make this cession, in order to insure the protection and assistance of the English.

large share of the Company's stock, the price rose to £275 *per Cent.* in the year 1768, though it afterwards fell at once to £220, on the news of the excursion of Hyder's cavalry to the gates of Madras; a fall which, to the present time, has been constantly increasing.

Hyder Ali Khan having by his address destroyed the formidable alliance on which the English company formed such pleasing dreams, because they knew so little of the character and power of their allies, and still less of the enemy whose ruin they meditated, it became incumbent on the council of Madras to justify themselves: for this purpose they could find no better pretence than to attribute the defeat of their projects, and the war that threatened them in the county of Arcot, to the intrigues of the French

The despotism exercised in India by the English, against other European nations, was such, that there was nothing they hesitated to do against any power, whether native or European: they never pardoned other nations the crime of fulfilling their engagements, of whatever nature they might be, with any sovereign, though they themselves sold muskets and cannon to every Indian power; seven-eighths of Hyder's arms being of English make. Their cruelty towards their prisoners, and the barbarity with which they destroyed Pondicherry, had reduced the greatest part of the French to misery. The unhappy situation they found themselves in after the establishment of the peace, compelled great numbers of them to seek employment and subsistence from Hyder and other princes. When any of these unfortunate people fell into the hands of the English, a dungeon was the lightest punishment they were to expect. To accomplish their purposes they employed, as will be shewn in the course of these Memoirs, promises, menaces, and even forgery, to cause them to enter into their service.

So far from the French government having had any concern in this war, declared by Hyder, it is certain that no correspondence with respect to that Nabob's operations ever existed, either between him and them, or with any officer of Hyder's army, till after the conclusion of the treaty between Hyder and Nizam;—truth obliges me to make this last exception. The correspondence began by two letters, one from Hyder, and the other from Raza Saeb, which these personages charged the commandant of Europeans to forward to the governor of Pondicherry. Here follows the substance of the letters.

Hyder complained in his letter, that the English, without provocation, and after receiving many favours, had projected his ruin; and by every species of intrigue had formed a league with the Suba of Decan, and the Marattas, against him; that they had attacked his places, without any other inducement than a desire to rob others of their property; but that he had dissolved the league made against him, by forming an alliance with Nizam Daulla, for the purpose of making war against the English and Mohumed Ali Khan, the promoter of their unjust aggression.

He observed, that by having formerly assisted the French against the same enemy, and having saved Pondicherry, he had every reason to hope that the French would return him the same good office in so just a war: that he was not ignorant of the peace then (1767) subsisting between the French and the English; but that, while the orders of the French king were expected, he might send concealed succours, for which Hyder would be very thankful, and pay any price that might be charged for the service to be done: that, in short, he referred to the letter of the French commandant, on whom he had a perfect reliance, and whose proposals on Hyder's part might be credited as if signed by himself, and to whom he might address himself on any subject that required secrecy.

Raza Saeb wrote, that his family had always been attached to the French since their first establishment in India: that in consequence of his inviolable attachment, his father had lost his life, his mother was prisoner at Madras, and he himself had lost everything: that an opportunity now presented itself of repairing his fortune in some measure, by the assistance of his friends: that he hoped to find his most ancient allies, the French, disposed to assist him against those who had unjustly robbed him, and were the cause of all his misfortunes: he concluded his letter, like Hyder, by referring to the French officer for details, having, as he affirmed, the most unbounded confidence in him.

These letters were secretly carried to Pondicherry by the Persian writer of the commandant, a man deserving the most absolute confidence, and who had been long attached to the French nation, having been employed by M. Lally at Pondicherry, where his residence had been for above thirty years, and where his wife and children then were: the letters were put into the stock of a pistol, which this man wore at his girdle, walking on foot, and leading an ox loaded with several wares of the country, like a petty merchant or pedlar.

To answer the trust these two princes reposed in him, and to fulfil his duty to his king and country, the commandant despatched a letter, together with those of the Nabobs.

After confirming the resolution taken by the two Subas to carry on the war on the coast of Coromandel, he gave an exact detail of the forces of Hyder, and those of Nizam; and, to shew that he spoke with a knowledge of the business, he likewise gave an account of the English forces. He demonstrated that it was impossible for the English to secure themselves from loss in this war, because their former successes in India arose from their wars being carried on near the sea-coast, or on the banks of the Ganges, which gave them a facility of conveying stores and ammunition by sea, and receiving other assistance from their vessels; whereas, in their contest with Hyder, they would be deprived of those advantages, the war being to be carried on in a country remote from the sea, without one navigable river; where the fortresses are spread at great distances from each other; and where every advantage would depend upon cavalry, of which the English were entirely destitute: that the army of Hyder was totally unlike those of the other Indian powers, the duty being performed with regularity: and that, if the English placed any dependance on night attacks, surprises, or treason on the part of his generals, they would find themselves mistaken: that he himself, being intrusted with the safety and preservation of the army, could, with the most absolute confidence, promise to insure it from any surprise; and that the treasons so frequent in the other Indian armies could not take place in Hyder's, because the generals had no property in their troops, all the officers, horsemen, and soldiers, having but one master: and, concluding that Hyder would have the advantage, he advised that an exact and absolute neutrality would not be the most prudent mode of action, because it would of necessity displease both parties.* But the medium he advised was, to send some small succours to Hyder, promising to send more; the performance of which promise might be delayed at pleasure, by throwing the excuse on contrary winds, that prevented the arrival of shipping. As the force at Pondicherry was but small, no great force could be sent from thence, but it would be sufficient to send some officers and good gunners, who might join the army as deserters, without embroiling the nation, whose interest it was to see the power of the English in India depressed. The officer added, that as a faithful subject of his king, and from the daring character of Hyder when he is attended with victory, he judged it proper to advise the governor to fortify Pondicherry as early as possible, were it only by clearing the ditches, raising the ramparts

---

* Hyder and Raza Saeb requested succours, as a return for their former services; and Mohumed Ali demanded that the French should support him, as Nabob of Arcot, acknowledged by the treaty of Fontainebleau.

with dry earth or the ruins of the old works,* and mounting a few cannon on the bastions; because, if Hyder should approach Pondicherry, and perceive it without defence, he might lay aside the respect due to the French colours, and take all the artillery, and other matters he might be in need of, as payment of his due for the succours formerly granted the French: at the same time the officer assured the governor, that if any violence or want of respect for the king's standard should be shewn, he might depend upon the co-operation of about eight hundred Europeans, who were in Hyder's army. The letter was concluded, by advising the governor to purchase rice and provisions for Pondicherry, by taking advantage of the abundance then in the country, and the fear the inhabitants were in of being plundered by the Indian armies; because the resolution was taken to lay the whole country waste by the cavalry and irregular troops as was really done afterwards (the French governor profited by the advice, and was in consequence able, during the whole war, to keep the price of rice at Pondicherry at less than half its value at Madras): and, lastly, the officer added, that to forward the good disposition of Hyder and his allies, it would be proper to send M. B——, or some other person esteemed by Hyder, on an embassy, to compliment the two Subas.

The receipt of these despatches gave the governor infinite pleasure, as they dispelled his fears concerning Hyder, whom he justly considered as the natural ally of France. But, from experience, having a very low opinion of the bravery of Indian troops when they fight against Europeans, he could not adopt the ideas of the French commandant of Hyder's army: besides which, the Company's instructions,

---

* The new fortifications of Pondicherry were then scarcely begun; but the governor, immediately on the receipt of this letter, gave the place an appearance of being in a state of defence.

then subsisting, were so precise in commanding him to avoid every subject of contention whatsoever, and particularly with the English, that he thought himself obliged to answer these letters in a manner very different from what had been expected.

His letter to Hyder began by felicitations on the glory he had acquired by his conquests, and the glorious peace he had made with his numerous enemies, who were become his allies: he observed that it was with concern he heard that war, which is always ruinous to nations, was about to commence on the coast of Coromandel: that he wished the Nabob every kind of prosperity, and would not fail to send an embassy to compliment him when he came near Pondicherry; but that he was exceedingly concerned at its being out of his power to dispose of any troops against the English, because the two nations were at peace, which he could not infringe without new orders from the king his master, to whom he would write without delay: and, lastly, he referred to the French commandant, who had forwarded the Nabob's letters, and who, he said, would explain such matters as required detail.

The letter to Raza Saeb was to the same purport. In answer to the officer's letter, the governor advised him, that, by despatching the letters of the two Nabobs, he had subjected him to the risk of breaking with the English; that he earnestly begged he would spare him the consequences of such a correspondence, as he could not render a greater service to his country, in the then situation of the French in India, without troops, and without fortifications: that, in the mean time, he would not fail to represent his compliance to this request in its true light to the minister, and the East India Company; and he might depend on his informing them of the services he had rendered them by the important advices contained in his letter: that, from his own unhappy experience of the pusillanimity of the Indians, when they combat with Europeans, he had reason to fear that the future war would not turn out to the advantage of the two Subas: that he could not, in any manner, afford assistance either to Hyder or Raza Saeb, his orders being too precise in directing to give no subject of complaint to the English, or to Mohumed Ali: that he begged he would explain these reasons to the two princes who had written to him, softening his refusal as he judged best: and, more especially, he begged him to write no more directly to him, but that he should be glad to hear news of his negociation by a letter in cyphers, which he might send by way of M——.

There is no room to reproach this governor for his faithful and strict obedience to his orders. It is to be wished they had been less precise, as he might then have profited by this opportunity, that the ministry could not possibly foresee: by a correspondence with Hyder, he might have animated him to a war against the English, that would have been ruinous to their Company; and, by answering the wishes of that prince in a very slight degree, might have prevented certain events that impeded his progress, and which obliged him to make peace, and reserve himself for another opportunity of enforcing his son's just pretensions to the Nabobship of Arcot.

This governor gave advice to the minister and the Company of the approaching invasion of the coast of Coromandel by the combined armies of the two Subas: and at the same time he communicated his fears for the event of the war, which he considered as necessarily productive of the ruin of Hyder: who would, he said, have been a very useful ally, if the French officer (commandant of Europeans), wanting experience, had not carried him to this extremity, but had reserved him for the time of war between England and France;—an expression dictated by the European prejudice, which leads us to imagine that the inhabitants of the other parts of the world have not received from nature the same portion of reason and judgment as ourselves, to determine for themselves according to their own interest, rather than to follow the most specious reasoning that can be offered to the contrary. It is to be presumed that, on the simple exposition of the facts, or from the copy of the French officer's letter, the ministry had taken those resolutions, upon receiving the news of the invasion, which were not determined on till the end of 1769;—resolutions that would have been fatal to the English empire in India, if the differences relative to the Falkland Islands had not been made up.

Hyder, after having determined to make a descent on the coast of Coromandel with Nizam Daulla, took every precaution to prevent interruption from other parts: he was sensible of the importance of the war he was engaged in, and which was to be transacted with enemies so much the more to be feared, as they knew how to fight. By the advice of his European commandant, he gave up the idea of forming a corps of European infantry, on account of the impossibility of making them sufficiently numerous to face a single English regiment: he therefore determined to incorporate all his European soldiers either among his hussars or dragoons, or among his artillery, except such as were made officers of the grenadier Sepoys or Topasses; which was the corps of infantry destined to face the English troops. The artillery of his army was likewise considerably augmented; and he took proper measures to have always an immense quantity of ammunition, such as it was impossible for any European army to convey after them, or indeed for any other army that was not perfectly assured of its rear.

The Indian armies have great quantities of baggage, carried by oxen and camels. Besides the baggage of the army, it is followed by a great number of merchants and workmen of every kind, who have many beasts of burthen. Hyder gave orders that all these, not excepting those of the sovereign, should carry a ball, from twelve to six-and-thirty pounds, for which the proprietor of the beast should be answerable.

A horde, consisting of a kind of Bohemians, very numerous in India, of unknown origin, inhabitants of the woods (whom the prejudices of India have forbidden to dwell in walled towns, because it is said they eat every kind of animal or reptile,) was permitted by Hyder, who is above prejudice, to follow the army, and sell milk, wood, and every thing their industry could procure. These men undertook to convey a considerable part of the powder, by means of their little carriages drawn by buffaloes: to assist them in procuring a subsistence, part of them were taken into pay as pioneers, and were of the greatest utility in sieges and the construction of intrenchments, or repairing of roads, as well by carrying earth as by making gabions and fascines.

The harness of all the cannon and artillery was doubled; and, that nothing might retard their march, every piece of eighteen pounds or upwards was provided with an elephant.* The ammunition waggons carried two hundred charges of powder, and an immense number of cartridges for the musketry. Every battalion of grenadier Sepoys had two four-pounders in its suit.

While these different preparations were making, Hyder arranged

---

* It can hardly be imagined how useful these elephants are, nor with what skill and intelligence they do their work. When a piece of artillery is drawn up a hill, the elephant is behind it, and sustains it with his foot, while the oxen pause to take breath: if the piece is going down a hill, the elephant retains it by a rope fastened to his trunk: if the tackle gets entangled, or if a piece oversets, or sticks fast, he assists the oxen according to the circumstances. An officer of reputation, then major of artillery, but now (1782) resident at Paris, affirms, that he has seen the elephant of a piece of cannon (out of patience to see that the oxen did not draw, in spite of the whips of the drivers) cut a branch of a tree, and beat those animals till they acted as he thought proper. When the piece is brought before the battery, the elephant himself places it in the embrasure without any assistance.

every affair relative to his dominions, so as to be out of apprehension of any unexpected event happening in his absence.

The truce with the Marattas, and his alliance with Nizam, delivered him from the fear of any foreign enemy, and permitted him to employ his whole force against them, by depriving them of the means to create disturbances by their intrigues. He restored their dominions to the different Nayre princes, on condition of an annual tribute, which he proposed to demand, or to let accumulate, according to the situation of his affairs; and withdraw all his troops from the coast of Malabar.

The French commandant at Mahé, and the Dutch at Cochin, employed themselves with effect, to terminate the difference between Hyder and the Nayre princes; and to their efforts it is that the coast of Malabar is indebted for peace.

An important discovery, totally unexpected by Hyder, and which was made soon after the conclusion of the truce with the Marattas, occasioned an event that has induced many persons in India to speak against Hyder.

It was discovered, that Nand Raja, ancient regent of Mysore, whom Hyder called his brother, had joined with the Marattas and the English in the general conspiracy against him. Nand Raja then resided at Mysore, a fortress two leagues distant from Seringapatam; the capital of the lands he held *en appanage*. Hyder was exceedingly embarrassed when he discovered this treachery: the great age of the prince made it improper to propose his marching against the English: to leave him in his residence, and to give the government of the kingdom of Mysore to another, would have excited his complaints, might have furnished him with an occasion to excite new troubles.

The pretence made use of by those who irritated Nand Raja against Hyder was, that this last, after having conquered the kingdom of Canara, and fixed his residence at Nagar, ought not to have given the regency of Mysore to any one but Nand Raja; but without considering the advanced age and incapacity of Nand Raja, which alone would have prevented him from taking that step, he was restrained by his promise to the old dowager Dayva, who had always been the mortal enemy of her brother-in-law, and was apprehensive of being subjected to his power. Hyder, in gratitude for the services rendered him by that lady, could not consent to displease her in this respect; but as she was the object of the pleasantry of all the court, on account of the irregularity of her manners, it was whispered that Hyder made the old lady believe that Nand Raja demanded the government for the purpose of punishing her for the little respect she bore to the laws, and the name of her deceased husband; by which means he obtained large sums of her, either in the way of gift or loan; giving her likewise to understand that he was distressed for money to pay for the Maratta truce, and his alliance with Nizam. Thus it was that Hyder, from motives of interest rather than policy, took a pleasure in fomenting the discord between the brother and sister-in-law. An opportunity presented itself of doing this on the occasion of the death of the king of Mysore. Nand Raja wrote to solicit the title of king for the younger son, in preference to the elder, who, he affirmed, was weak, and incapable of the office; but his letter availed little with Hyder, who was solicited by the widow Dayva in favour of the elder. He wrote, in answer to both, that not being able at that time to attend anything but the war with the revolted Nayres, he had given orders to Mughdoom Ali Khan, to place on the throne that prince of the late king's sons whom he might think the most worthy to reign: he wrote, secretly, by the same courier, to Mughdoom, to place the youngest on the throne. This proceeding, which, as may be readily imagined, excited the complaints of the widow Dayva, and of most part of the nobility of the kingdom, gave Hyder an opportunity, on his arrival at Seringapatam, to make a parade of his equity, by giving the throne to the eldest. The whole business drew an additional sum from the old lady, and created many enemies to Nand Raja, and, perhaps, to Mughdoom, who readily assisted in all these artifices, through his unbounded attachment to his brother-in-law.

It not being practicable either to give Nand Raja the government of the kingdom, or to remove him out of it, and still less prudent to leave him discontented in the absence of Hyder, a council was held on the business; the general advice was to secure his person, at least during the absence of the Nabob, and in the mean time to remove from him a Bramin, his brother-in-law, who gave him bad advice; but to this Hyder opposed the written promise he had made to Raja, *never to make any attempt on his liberty, property, or life*, besides the difficulty of arresting that prince in his residence at the Mysore, a place capable of standing a siege, and where Nand Raja had upwards of two thousand troops, forming, it must be confessed, the whole of his little army.

This affair being of such a nature as to require a speedy determination, it was agreed, that Hyder should go the following morning in grand ceremony to Mysore, to make an honourable visit to Nand Raja, and invite him to come and encamp with his little army in the island of Seringapatam, in order to make his public entry into the capital in quality of viceroy, as Hyder was desirous of investing him with that dignity before his departure; the visit was accordingly made, and Nand Raja, at the height of his wishes, arrived with his family in the island, under the power of Hyder, who, that very day, under pretence of exercising his troops in their evolutions, invested the little camp, and enclosed it in the night by detachments of infantry, who were ordered to suffer no one to pass them, without first conducting him to the Nabob, to be questioned by him. As it had been difficult to persuade Hyder to secure the old man, it was easy for Nand Raja to perceive that he was under guard, which put him into such a rage against the Nabob, that he carried his views to an excess that might have been fatal to any other prince but Hyder.

The unfortunate Raja sent a messenger to the Persian writer, named Meer Saeb, secretary to the French officer, and who had been charged with the letters to the governor of Pondicherry; his pretence was to enquire whether he could not procure from Pondicherry some crude salt of tartar and other European drugs; the Raja being a chemist, or rather alchemist, who had worked many years to discover the transmutation of metals. The Persian being alone with Nand Raja and the Bramin, the former proposed to him to acquaint his master, that if he would assassinate Hyder, he (Nand Raja) would deposit the value of eight lacs of rupees in gold, silver, precious stones, and elephants; the irritated old man being determined to strip himself of all his property rather than not satisfy his vengence against his supposed enemy: the project, he observed, was easy to be put in execution, because the Nabob, on his return from the excursion he made every two days, passed the night by the light of flambeaux before the camp of the Europeans; and nothing could prevent their seizing this instant, and shooting him by an aim taken from the inside of one of the tents. The writer, according to his own account, not daring to shew the horror this proposition made in his mind, promised to speak on the subject to his master, and give an answer the following day to a Bramin, who was shewn to him; and who promised to wait at the gate of a small pagoda indicated to him. The writer made haste to inform his master of the interview he had had with the Rajah, and the abominable commission he was charged with: the officer, after recovering from the indignation this base proposition naturally produced, ordered him to keep the whole a profound secret.* Fortunately, this officer had been one of the council,

* The writer was not exact in his obedience, for he communicated the whole to Mirza Ali Nuki, who had been commandant of Sepoys at Pondicherry under Messrs. Lally and Leyrit, a man of great merit, esteemed by Hyder, and much attached to the French: he did not fail to acquaint the French officer of the indiscretion of his secretary.

in which the affair of Nand Raja had been discussed; he knew, consequently, that on that very day the Nabob was to decide whether Nand Raja should be arrested, and to direct in what manner it should be done. The storm that was ready to burst on the head of Hyder, did not permit the commandant to defer any longer the waiting upon him; he therefore went with a determination either to conceal or relate what had come to his knowledge, according to the disposition he might find Hyder in, with regard to arresting Nand Raja. When he came into the presence of the Nabob, that prince addressed him in private: "That old fool, Nand Raja," said he, "has sent for your Persian secretary to give him a commission to procure drugs from Pondicherry; has the man mentioned it to you?" "Certainly," replied the French officer, "he has given me an account of his interview, and I cannot but advise you, after what I have heard, not to delay a moment in arresting Nand Raja." "It is a decided step," returned Hyder; "everything is arranged for that purpose; he is to make his public entry the day after to-morrow into Seringapatam, at the head of his troops. The streets he passes through will be lined with grenadier Topasses, or Sepoys, and at the palace there will be placed an entire battalion: his troops will be arranged on the parade in readiness to relieve the posts as they are quitted by the grenadiers; Mughdoom has undertaken to disarm the troops and all his people; and leaving him only his women and a few domestics, will confine him in his own palace; and, since the old man is without abilities, and, no one can rely on him, everything will be performed without trouble, before the cannon of the palace salute Mughdoom, who will quit his government to-morrow. Send as many Europeans into the town as you can, as cannoneers: let them enter by small parties, and through the several gates, and unite, as if by curiosity, about the palace of Nand Raja. Do not go yourself, but command your officers to obey punctually the orders of Mughdoom, or his brother, Ismael Saeb."

The little attention paid by Hyder to the manner of the French officer when he insisted on arresting Nand Raja, shews how far he is from being inclined to suspect those who have gained his confidence.

This is not the only proof of the openness of his character, that Hyder has given the same officer: for that very night, after returning from the Durbar, being gone to rest, he was informed from the prince that the chief usher and sword-bearer of the Nabob desired to speak with him on an affair of the last importance, which they could communicate to him in bed, without his getting up. Being introduced, they said, "The guard, which, as you know, is placed round the camp of Nand Raja, stopped one of your people, a short time ago, coming from thence; and, though he said he belonged to you, it was thought proper to conduct him to the Nabob, because his orders on that head are very precise. The man, in passing by your guard, called for help, and the guard, knowing* him, took him out of the hands of his conductors, and set him free. The Nabob has therefore sent us to beg that you will send the man, that he may be known by those who arrested him: he has also charged us to give you his word, that as soon as it is certain that he is one of your people, he will send him back, for you to do what you think proper with him."

The officer, much astonished at this news, which he supposed to have some relation to the Persian writer, ordered inquiry to be made of the guard, concerning the man they had liberated: to which his valet-de-chambre answered, "He is a black Peon, whom I sent to the camp of Nand Raja before midnight, to procure some manna, as I was informed that a druggist of that camp had some. This Peon, having met an acquaintance, amused himself till after midnight, knowing that

---

* According to the privileges granted to the Europeans, all decisions respecting justice, among them and their dependents, are made by themselves.

he was not wanted: on his return he was arrested, which he supposed improper, on account of the protection of your bandalier he carried; he therefore called out as he passed the guard, and was set free." The officer ordered the Peon to be sent for, and put him into the hands of the prince's officers, by whom he was conducted into the presence. The guards immediately knew him, and Hyder was contented with asking him this question: "Did you come from Pondicherry with your master?" And on his replying in the affirmative, he sent him back, and the affair was thus terminated.

On the day appointed, Nand Raja, without any mistrust, made a pompous entrance into Seringapatam, at the head of his little army, the cannon firing, and the troops beating to arms, and saluting him. Being arrived at his palace, his attention was taken up by the compliments of the great men of the city, who were admitted by a few at a time, on a pretended account of not making too great a crowd. Mughdoom then entered the city, followed by a number of officers, and made a sign to the troops, not to pay him any honours: he went directly to the palace of Nand Raja, where every one supposed he was going to pay his respects, and dismounting, he caused the first company of the battalions of Sepoys who guarded the gate, to follow him. As soon as he came into the presence of Nand Raja, who came to meet him, he acquainted him that Hyder, being informed that he was surrounded by people who gave him bad advice, had sent him to remove them from about him: at the same time he commanded all present to leave the palace, which was done without uttering a word; the grenadiers followed them: and Mughdoom remaining with Nand Raja, his two sons, and some officers, the conversation was carried on with the greatest politeness. Mughdoom acquainted the two princes that they were to make the campaign; and that, instead of one father, they would find two in Hyder and himself. During the short conversation, the women and all the family of Mughdoom were announced. Mughdoom took his leave, carrying the two princes with him, to whom he represented, that it became their dignity to wait upon the Nabob, and give him an account of all that had passed. These young noblemen departed, accompanied by many of Mughdoom's officers; neither they nor Nand Raja expressing the least astonishment or chagrin. After their departure, Mughdoom spoke a word to Nand Raja's general, who ordered his troop to ground their arms, which was done with great silence. All the gates and windows of Nand Raja's palace, that looked towards the street, were afterwards walled up, except the principal entrance, which is no great disfigurement in an Indian palace, whose principal front lies towards the gardens. Then it was that Nand Raja, to the great satisfaction of the dowager Dayva, found himself shut up in his own palace. Hyder paid the arrears due to his troops, which, for the most part, enlisted among his own. On the valuation of the Raja's income, it was found to be equal to four lacks of rupees: two of which were allowed him for his own maintenance, and the other two were given to his sons, who made the campaign with a brilliant equipage, under the conduct of their father's old general, who appears to have been in intelligence with Hyder in the transaction just related.

All the preparations for the campaign being made, the two armies began their march; that of Nizam took the road of Oscota, and that of Hyder passed by the way of Bangalore.

When they had arrived, and encamped at the gates of this city, several councils were held, to determine on the operations, and take the necessary measures. Basalutjung, Rocun Daulla, and several other chiefs assisted at these councils. It was agreed, that the two armies should march always separate, but at such a distance as to assist each other in all their operations: that the army of Hyder should take the avant-garde till they had passed the mountains: and that, when they had entered the kingdom of Arcot, it should again be considered, whether it was best to act separately or conjointly.

Hitherto we have given no more than a superficial account of the different wars in which Hyder Ali Khan has been engaged against the Marattas, the English, and other enemies, who envied his success, or dreaded his power. The true reason why the former actions of this celebrated conqueror have not been given in a more ample manner in the present work, is that the Author, not having joined the army of the Nabob before the time of the war on the coast of Malabar, did not think it necessary to speak largely concerning military operations he could only know from the communications of others. Every person acquainted with subjects of this nature, must be sensible how very imperfect an idea of the particulars of any war can be gathered from the accounts of officers, who, engaged in their own duty, cannot have much opportunity to contemplate the general scene of action.

To display the character, the genius, and the talents of Hyder, with regard to the art of war, it would doubtless have been highly interesting to have described all the marches, sieges, and battles, in which he has exerted himself. But the curiosity of the reader will be amply satisfied by the details given of the facts that happened during the war between Hyder and the English. The Author will at least relate what he has seen, and clearly come to the knowledge of; with the assurance that this, of all the wars in which Hyder has been engaged, is the best adapted to make known the great abilities of that prince; because in this he had to contend with enemies who possessed the superior advantage of the military science and discipline. It will be easy to judge, from the war between the years 1767 and 1769, of the probable event of the present war, which commenced in 1779.

The war we are about to relate is so much the more interesting, as it forms an epoch in the history of the Europeans in India; since it is the first war the Europeans have finished by asking peace of the Indians.

Before we begin our account of the operations of this famous war, it will be proper to give a display of the forces of the respective combatants.

The possessions of Hyder in the year 1767, when he began the war against the English, consisted of the kingdom of Mysore; the country of Bangalore, that formerly composed part of Mysore; all the country called Malleam, or the Carnatic, in the charts, which words signify, in two different languages, the Country of the Mountains, and which comprehends all the vallies and mountains from Ambour to Madura, Travancore, and the coast of Malabar; the town of Scirra; the country of Ballapour; the little kingdom of Bisnagar; the kingdom of Canara, which extends from Cape Rama northwards along the frontier of Visapour; and lastly, the sovereignty of the coast of Malabar and the Maldive Islands, these countries being only tributaries. It may be seen, that the dominions of Hyder have the advantage of being connected together, and of being defended, on the part of the English, by mountains and narrow entrances. These countries contain, if popular report may be credited, above a thousand fortresses, of different magnitudes: however, as an eye-witness, I can affirm them to be very many. All the large fortresses or garrisons are guarded by the troops of the army, which are changed from time to time; and by garrison soldiers, who are a kind of militia, and serve for less pay than the regular troops. The smaller fortresses are maintained only by this latter order of military; and, in case of any alarm, the inhabitants of the mountains take arms, throw themselves into the forts, and defend them with obstinacy sufficient to require a siege. These fortresses, which seem to have been constructed to defend the country against the incursions of the Marattas, have trenches, and bastions or towers; many of them have their revetement of stone; but the greater part, especially in the flat country, have their embankments of red earth, which possesses the property of acquiring, in a short time, the hardness of bricks baked in the sun. They are all kept in the best repair, or at least have been, ever since they became the property of Hyder.

The dominions of this prince abound in rice, and every other necessary of life, as well as in cattle of every kind; that is to say, oxen, sheep, goats, and elephants. As to the horses and camels, they are for the most part brought out of other countries; and Hyder, by making a proper use of his money, is always provided with a great number of horses and elephants, the most useful animals in war. He has always a reserve of these in the villages, to the number of six hundred elephants, and twenty thousand horse. To be always provided with a supply of these very necessary animals, he never fails to purchase all that are offered to him, provided they be robust and strong, and the owners will part with them for the price he sets upon them, after a strict examination; and, as his offers are very equitable, dealers come to him from all parts, to present the finest of these animals for his inspection.

To all these means and inducements that might lead the prince to enter into a war with the English, we may add the assurance he had that the English, being almost without cavalry, could not prevent his army from being supplied with provisions from all parts of his dominions: and above all the immense treasures he possessed, which, joined to the considerable revenues of his kingdoms and states, put him in a situation to support with ease the most long and expensive war. In the year we speak of (1767) all the forces of Hyder Ali Khan were estimated at about one hundred and eighty or two hundred thousand men, of which twenty-five thousand were cavalry: but, as it was necessary to garrison all the fortresses, and leave some troops on the frontiers, the army he led against the English might be from fifty to fifty-five thousand men; of which eighteen thousand were cavalry, and about eight thousand Marattas, Pandaris, and others, that cannot be better compared than to the Cossacks who follow the Russian army, being fit for no service but to ravage the country, or rob the baggage of an army. The infantry consisted of twenty thousand Topasses, or

Sepoys, armed with sixteen thousand good firelocks, because all the officers, down to the corporals, have no muskets; the rest of the infantry were Carnates, or Calerots, armed with matchlocks and lances.

The number of Europeans was about seven hundred and fifty. They were divided into two companies of dragoons or hussars, two hundred and fifty cannoneers, and the officers and serjeants dispersed among the regiments of Grenadiers and Topasses.

There were likewise some troops, armed with arms either unknown or out of use at present in Europe, to the number of about three thousand men, mounted two and two on running camels, having each a firelock of a very great length, that threw a ball of about three ounces to a prodigious distance. These arms have an iron rest fixed to the barrel: and the soldiers, who are excellent marksmen, follow the cavalry, and plant themselves in covered places to flank the enemy, among whose cavalry they keep up a very destructive fire. This body of troops have the singular privilege of an ensign for every ten men; whether it be an honour, or a piece of policy to deceive the enemy into an opinion, from the number of standards, that they are opposed by a numerous corps of infantry. The troop is very ancient, being, according to all appearance, the first among the Indians that bore fire-arms. The same number of men, carried rockets of iron, which are boxes of plate-iron, in the form of fusees, and attached to direction rods: they are of various sizes, some containing more than one pound of powder or composition, and fly to the distance of a thousand yards. Many of these rockets are charged to burst: others are sharpened at the end; and others are pierced at the foremost end, being charged so that the wind acts strongly on the flame, and sets fire to the matters it may strike in its course. This implement is, on the whole, far more expensive than useful; which, I suppose, chiefly arises from the want of care and attention in making them up; however they have been sometimes productive of dreadful effects, by setting fire to* ammunition waggons. These rockets are very well adapted for setting fire to towns and villages in which the enemy have magazines. A body of cavalry, not used to this kind of instrument, would be quickly thrown into disorder by it; for the rockets falling at the feet of the horses, emit a flame resembling that of a forge furnace, which frightens them; and when they burst, they do considerable mischief. It is no small advantage, that they describe a curve line, and may therefore be thrown by people that are covered by a line of infantry. The English made use of them against the cavalry of Hyder; but as it was habituated to the fire by various exercises performed with paper rockets, the horses, instead of being frightened, marched fiercely over them.

A troop of Arabs, armed with bows and arrows, arrived at Seringapatam a short time before the departure of the army. The men were well-made, strong, and active; but, as Hyder did not suppose the arms they bore would have much effect on the enemy, he formed them into two companies; one clothed in red, which he joined to his Savari; and the other, in blue, he gave to the commandant of Europeans, to apply to any service he might think proper. They were very adroit in killing birds and game with their bows and arrows, which were large, and very much ornamented.

The army of Nizam Daulla, Suba of Decan, etc., was reckoned one hundred thousand strong; but he had not more than forty thousand fighting men, of which thirty thousand were cavalry, and ten thousand

---

* According to the relation given by the English of the battle gained by Hyder against the Colonels, Bailey and Fletcher, a rocket having set fire to an ammunition waggon, which in blowing up set fire to two others, the battle was lost; because Tippoo Sultaun, son of Hyder, with his cavalry, fell upon the English infantry, which the explosion had thrown into disorder.

infantry. Scarcely two thousand of the infantry were armed with firelocks; the rest had only that kind of musket that is called Cailletaux in India. The infantry was, however, commanded by a brave man, named Abderaman Khan, who had served under Messrs. Bourdonnaye and Buss. This last caused him to be promoted to the command he possessed. He was very sensible of the bad state of his troop, which was beside very ill paid.

The cavalry was good, but much better for show than service; every chief being proprietor and absolute master of his own troop. Following the army, for the most part, only as vassals of the empire, they were very little disposed to risk their life and their cattle in any war, except when animated by the desire of revenge, the hope of plunder, or some other passion.

These chiefs were the most powerful lords of Decan; such as Ram Schander, a Maratta, who bears the name of Alexander, his supposed or pretended ancestor; the three Nabobs of Sanour, Curpa, and Canour, etc.

The army was followed by a multitude of merchants, working tradesmen, women, and servants, which occasioned the camp to be vastly extended, and would have rendered it an easy matter for the English to surprise it, if Hyder had been possessed of less experience and vigilance. The army of the Suba, though capable of doing very little service in actual war, added vastly to the reputation of Hyder, and might have procured him many allies; but the well-founded suspicions he entertained against Rocun Daulla, and even against Nizam, obliged him to be on his guard against a stroke of perfidy, that would have been of more consequence to him than the loss of a battle. Besides, an indifference and coolness very soon arose between the two Subas, by reason of the continual wants of Nizam and all his chiefs; and Hyder was not disposed to comply with their repeated requests for money, lest he should by that means lose both his money and his allies. He moreover repented that he had not previously agreed that Nizam, after having given the investiture of the Nabobship of Arcot to his son, should return to his states. It will be seen in future that these allies very soon separated from each other.

The united army possessed a very considerable train of artillery, consisting of at least one hundred and ten pieces of large cannon. That of Hyder was more numerous, better provided with ammunition, better mounted, and served by good European cannoneers. The artillery of Nizam was all fine European brass cannon; and thirty, at least, were French pieces, cast in the reign of Louis XIV., being the remaining artillery of the squadron of M. de la Haye, which was lost in a hurricane in the road of Masulipatam: this port then belonged to the Subas of Decan, who recovered the cannon of the sunken vessels, which have come into the hands of Nizam Daulla. This beautiful artillery was ill provided with ammunition, badly mounted, and served by Lascars, or Indian gunners, who are virtually cowardly and unskilful.

Hyder likewise employed in this war a small army of six thousand men, returned from the coast of Malabar. He entrusted the command of this detachment to Maffous Khan, a man who he knew had no pretensions to military skill, but, in his opinion, able to cause the people of Madura, whose sovereign he was, to revolt. This able negociator and keen politician was, however, unfortunate in the attempt to become a warrior; for Colonel Beck, a German in the service of the English, pretending to fly before him, enticed him into the centre of Madura, and succeeded in taking him prisoner.

We do not reckon the fleet of Hyder among his forces: it was then composed of a ship purchased of the Danes, pierced for sixty guns, but furnished with no more than fifty; three others of thirty-two guns; eighteen palms, vessels both for rowing and sailing, and carrying fourteen guns; and about twenty large galliots, carrying eighty men, and two cannons. Three or four of the English company's frigates, that are always ready armed in the Indian sea, would have been sufficient to have dispersed this little fleet. An Englishman, whom Hyder had appointed his admiral, having carried the large vessel to Bombay to refit, it was seized and declared good prize as soon as the commencement of hostilities was known; an action that Hyder has always regarded as perfidious on the part of the English.

The power of the English in India was in its meridian in the year 1767. That nation possessed the whole of Bengal, the richest, the most fertile, and the most populous of all the provinces in the empire; the number of its inhabitants being estimated at nine millions when it fell into the hands of the English; but since reduced to six millions, at most, by their vexatious and barbarous government. Besides this province, they possessed all the coasts of Orixa and Coromandel, having no other limits inland than the gates or mountains; the large towns of Surat and Cambaya, the former of which is the most trading port of all India; the island of Bombay, and the country of Salsete, on the Maratta frontier; the forts of Tillicherry, Mondeli, and Anzingue, on the coast of Malabar; besides a number of factories and different establishments, such as are on the island of Sumatra, too remote to be of any advantage in the present war. The territorial revenues of all these possessions exceeded two hundred millions of French money,* as the Author of these Memoirs is well assured, having had in his hands the state of the English Company's affairs, which was given to the King of England and his Privy Council.

The forces of the English in India were more than ninety thousand men: namely, eight regiments of English infantry of one thousand men each, three on the establishment of Madras, three on that of Bengal, and two on that of Bombay, besides twelve hundred men forming the artillery companies on the several establishments, and one thousand or twelve hundred invalids in garrison at various

* In round numbers, about 8,700,000l. sterling.

places. The Indian troops consisted of sixty-four regiments of one thousand Sepoys each, of which thirty were on the establishment of Madras. Their cavalry might be estimated at about four thousand horse, twelve hundred only being on the Madras establishment. All this cavalry was Indian, except about four hundred Europeans. General Smith, after leaving the necessary garrisons, had at his disposal five thousand Europeans, two thousand five hundred Sepoys, two thousand five hundred horse, including two hundred Europeans; twelve hundred Indians, taught the English exercise, and commanded by European officers. The remainder of his army contained the cavalry of Mohumed Ali Khan, a troop not only much inferior in number to that of Hyder, but even unfit to face the cavalry of that sovereign, by reason of their want of discipline, and the bad state of the horses.

The English have never yet succeeded in the attempt to form a good troop of European horse in India. As they have sent a regiment of dragoons from England, it is probable that their arrival may place the affair on another footing. Though it may not immediately be conceived, the reason of the want of success in forming their intended troop of horse, consisted in the good discipline to which they were desirous of subjecting them.

The excellence of the English cavalry is sufficiently acknowledged in Europe; and its advantages consist less in the goodness of the horse than in the choice of the horsemen. The pay of a horseman in England is such as renders his situation very eligible; so that the sons of rich farmers and tradesmen are very desirous of entering into the service. This being the case, it is in the power of the officers to select handsome, well formed men, of good character, and to keep them in good discipline merely by the fear of being dismissed. The officers who were first entrusted with the formation of a body of cavalry in India, thought to establish and preserve the same discipline among them, without attending to the great difference of time, place, and persons. The recruits sent from England to India are in general libertines and people of bad character; and as the Company will not dismiss a soldier, all the punishment inflicted on a horseman is, to reduce him to serve in the infantry; so that a man is no sooner put among the cavalry than he is sent back again to his former station. The French have succeeded in forming very good cavalry in India, by attending more to their horsemanship, and less to their discipline and manners.

The English at Madras, in addition to all these troops, in number above thirty thousand,* had the disposition of the troops of Mohumed Ali Khan, with those of some Palleagars, and of Morao, a Maratta chief, which altogether might be about twenty thousand men. The whole army to be employed in the defence of Arcot was consequently at least fifty thousand men; and Hyder was likewise under the necessity of marching in person against eight thousand troops on the Bombay establishment, who attacked him at Mangalore, the centre of his kingdom of Canara.

General Smith had the advantage of possessing an army for the most part better disciplined, and more practised in their evolutions, than that of Hyder; with a numerous corps of Europeans, capable alone, as was generally believed before this war, of beating the twelve hundred thousand men which Mohumed Sha, emperor of the Mogols, opposed against Nadir Sha, king of Persia.† His artillery was served

---

* There is some error either in this number, or in the enumeration page 162, as they do not agree together.—T.

† This way of thinking among the Europeans was partly occasioned by the attack of the army of Nazerjung, above three hundred thousand strong, by eight hundred French, commanded by M. de la Touche. The courage of this small French army, and still more of their general, is not perhaps to be parallelled in any history, either ancient or modern.

by a sufficient number of officers and men, bred up in the service: in short, he had officers and engineers of every kind to second him, and was himself certainly much superior to Hyder in military knowledge. With all these advantages, and a superiority of double the number of firelocks, he was certain of gaining every battle, in which the nature of the place, or the post he might take, was such as to prevent the cavalry of Hyder from acting to advantage.

The advantages of General Smith over Hyder were balanced by very great disadvantages: namely, first, the inferiority of his cavalry, which obliged him to reduce the theatre of war as much as possible to the mountainous country: secondly, the impossibility of his preventing the cavalry from ravaging the country and cutting off his convoys: thirdly, the very great difficulty of procuring a sufficient number of oxen for the conveyance of his artillery, ammunition, and baggage; a difficulty of such importance, that it reduced him to the necessity of having an inferior train of artillery, and to spare his provisions and stores beyond what would otherwise have been necessary. But the greatest embarrassment he suffered consisted in his dependance on the Governor and Council of Madras; who, without having any well-founded knowledge of the forces of Hyder, either with respect to number or discipline—and who, at the same time ignorant of the nature of the country, were incessantly giving orders contrary to his views, and every rational principle of war; and even went so far as to reproach him for the ravages made by

---

But the success that attended their attempt on that glorious day which decided the fate of an empire is due to the policy of M. Dupleix, and the treachery of the chiefs and ministers of Nazerjung, in the same manner as the success of Nadir Sha originated in the intelligence he held with Nizam El Moulouc, the Grand Visir, and other chiefs of the Mogol army.

Hyder's cavalry, though in his advice to them previous to the commencement of the war, he had predicted this consequence to them. And as those gentlemen never lost sight of the occasions for enriching themselves, they supplied the army by means of contractors, with whom they were in league; treating the inhabitants of Madras in the most vexatious and odious manner, under pretence of furnishing the army with necessaries.*

---

* Two singular methods of plundering were invented upon this occasion. The first was, that instead of supplying the troops with arrack, an article easily procured over all the country, it was thought proper to give them rum; because it could be had only from Batavia, and consequently afforded means of enriching those who were concerned in procuring it. The second related to the supplying the army with beasts of carriage. As no one could be found who would engage to furnish the army with oxen for the artillery, baggage, etc., they took them by force from the inhabitants; but, instead of paying for them at the rate of six or eight pagodas, their real value, they took them on hire, at a pagoda per month. At the end of the first month, they paid the owner a pagoda; but on the expiration of the second, they informed him that his beast was dead. The ox thus obtained out of the hands of its proprietor, was passed to the account of the Company, as purchased at its full value; though, by this infamous manœuvre, it cost no more than a pagoda. If the proprietor had chosen to have a servant with his ox, he must have paid five rupees per month, instead of three and a half, which is the value of the pagoda of Madras. By the operation of this happy project the country was soon stripped of all its cattle—no one choosing to purchase any, for the purpose of seeing themselves robbed with impunity. In consequence of this, the greater part of the army necessaries were obliged to be carried by men.

Though we have spoken of the departure of General Smith to take possession of several places in the dominions of Hyder, we have not hitherto spoken of his operations; our intention being to unite all the military operations of this interesting war in one continued narration. The English General made several sieges during the time of the preparations and negociations of Hyder. He took Terpatoor, Vaniambari, and Singueman, without much difficulty; that is to say, each of these ill-fortified places held out some days. He likewise took Caveripatam, whose fortress did not yield till seventeen days after the trenches were opened; and he besieged Kisnagari, a fortress on a steep mountain, where he was obliged to raise the siege, after having made two assaults; in the last of which he lost twenty-four grenadiers, besides soldiers. This was the only place defended by an European officer.*

---

* The name of this officer was Constantin, a native of Andernac on the Rhine, in the electorate of Cologne. He came to India with Ficher's troop, in 1754; and married a Portuguese, by whom he had a very beautiful daughter: he was serjeant when M. Hughel commanded the Europeans in Hyder's army. The officers discovered that, together with his wife, he was in treaty with the Nabob about selling his daughter; they regarded this transaction as an infamous piece of business, that would disgrace all the Europeans in the army. M. Hughel sent for him, to inquire concerning the design laid to his charge, which he denied. A young officer in the army offered to espouse the girl, and the father received the proposal with gratitude. M. Hughel, in favour of the marriage, at the same time promoted the father: but that very night the parents sold their daughter to Hyder for fifty thousand rupees, and Hyder sent them into the country of Bangalore. Constantin has ever since that time lived at a distance from the army. After the brave defence of the fortress of Kisnagari,

It was during the siege of this place that the armies of Hyder and Nizam began to move towards the enemy. Kisnagari is twenty-two leagues from Bangalore, by the road that can be taken by an army; and, in order to arrive at this latter place, it is necessary to go through narrow passes, which are very easily defended.

Hyder directed his march so that, at the end of the second day, he found himself four leagues from the foot of the mountains; being opposite the pass of Vellore, which opens about four leagues from Caveripatam, a town and fortress on the Paler, seven leagues from the pass of Kisnagari, which was on the right, and about six leagues from the pass of Ventigheri, which is about two leagues and a half from Vaniambari. No precaution was taken to prevent the English general from being advised of the departure of the army from Bangalore; and consequently he was soon advised of that event, as well by his spies as by secret informers he paid in the army of Nizam.

General Smith, on receipt of this advice, raised the siege of Kisnagari, and posted himself to defend the pass of Vellore; and that with so much the more reason, as it was the only passage through which artillery could be conveyed; and being in the centre, with Caveripatam in his rear, he was better situated to repair to the defence of the pass Hyder might attempt; or to retire in safety, if necessary.

---

the inhabitants of the flat country brought their most valuable effects, and deposited them in the place for security: he opened the boxes and cabinets, taking out the richest property, to a vast amount, and escaped to Goa; from whence he went to Bombay, and afterwards to Europe. Hyder's French surgeon affirms, that the girl has since told him that she esteemed herself fortunate in being sold to the Nabob; as her father and mother might have made a more shameful traffic with her, if she had stayed with them.

Hyder convened a council of war, at which Rocun Daulla assisted. Its object was, to decide which of the three passes they should attempt to force; and in order that every one might form an opinion with sufficient knowledge of the business, he produced charts of the different passages, in which every particular was exactly delineated. The council decided, that as the English were posted with all their forces to guard the pass of Vellore, it was proper to issue forth by that of Ventigheri, the pass of Kisnagari being absolutely impracticable for artillery: and though the army of Nizam, by reason of its being encamped to the left of Hyder's forces, was nearer this pass, yet Hyder, according to the agreement, undertook to form the advanced guard with his army. In consequence, orders were given to march at two in the morning, in a single column, leaving all the baggage in the camp.

The Carnates, and other irregular troops, formed the head of the column; who were followed by all the Sepoys, each preceded by the grenadiers, and followed by the horse. The artillery came next, led by two thousand Topasses, their grenadiers, and the European cannoneers. And lastly, two companies of European cavalry closed the march, and completed the column. Hyder, at the head of two thousand horse, marched on the right flank of the column.

The English being informed of the order and direction of this march, moved to oppose Hyder, and to gain the pass of Ventigheri before him: a thing easily done, as they had but three leagues to pass over. But it was an unexpected manœuvre to them, when, after an hour's march, the Europeans, the grenadier Topasses, and successively the artillery and all the other Topasses, made a turn to the right, and marched for the pass of Vellore with the utmost celerity.

As this troop was supposed to have no other destination than to escort the artillery, it was contrived, in the course of the march, that there should be a considerable interval between them and the cavalry that preceded the Topasses, in order that this counter-march might be less perceived; the chief of the Europeans, who had the command of this part of the army, being alone entrusted with the secret.* The stratagem succeeded perfectly well. The hussars and dragoons passed full speed through the pass, which is long, narrow, and winding, but very even ground. They were followed by the European cannoneers, and the grenadier Topasses, who ran with great expedition, though they had already marched quickly over an interval of four leagues. General Smith had been careful to leave some of the infantry of Mohumed Ali, and a party of Indian horse, at the entrance of this pass; but a body of Hyder's cavalry, that had passed the strait of Kisnagari, having appeared in the plain, followed by the garrison of that fortress, the troops left by the English abandoned the pass, and retired with great haste to Caveripatam. At the instant the European commandant cleared the pass, he met Bahoud Khan,† com-

---

* When the army was commanded to hasten its march, on the news that the Europeans had taken possession of the pass of Vellore, a surgeon of the army, thinking to do wonders, took the opportunity of a Patimar going from Mahé to Pondicherry, to write to the governor of that place:—"We are in full march to descend to the "coast. Our commandant, who serves as a guide to the armies, has "forced a passage by the strait of Vellore." The Patimar having no reason to avoid the English army, General Smith took this paper from him, and sent it to the governor of Madras. It has since been used as an authentic piece to show the connection between the French governor and Hyder Ali Khan.

† Bahoud Khan was a Patane chief, that escaped the massacre, caused by Anaverdi Khan, of the Patanes in the service of the Nabob of Arcot. All his family perished; and himself and his brother escaped only on account of their youth. Their mother having retired with them to Pondicherry, M. Dupleix afterwards gave him a com-

mander of cavalry, who came himself to acquaint him that he found no opposition. On this news he gave orders to fire nine cannon, three and three; the signal agreed between him and Hyder that the pass was free. On this signal, the Nabob caused his whole army to march to the pass of Vellore, where he arrived himself, at the head of his cavalry, and saw the artillery advance, under the conduct of the Topasses.

General Smith was soon informed that Hyder's army was advancing through the pass of Vellore, and retired as quickly as possible to Caveripatam; where he did not think it expedient to stay, but leaving twelve hundred of his best Sepoys, some Topasses belonging to the artillery, and thirty European cannoneers, he retired to Tripatour, to be nearer assistance, and at hand to receive the convoys he expected from Madras, as well as to join a body of seven or eight thousand men, commanded by Colonel Wood, who was then employed in besieging the fortress of Ahtour, a very ill-fortified place, defended by Carnates; against which, however, he employed fifteen days, from the opening his trenches to the time of its surrender. General Smith, when he retired, left one hundred Indian horsemen, to bring him intelligence of the events that might happen in his absence.

The whole army and artillery of Hyder cleared through the pass in the course of the day, but the baggage and provisions came through in the night; so that the Europeans in the army, who had marched from daybreak till night, and were fatigued, as well by that as by hunting (the country abounding with game), were not very well

---

mission to raise a body of cavalry in the service of France; and he became commandant of the India cavalry. M. Dupleix employed and encouraged this Patane, who has exerted himself on all occasions to show his attachment to the French. He quitted the service of Nizam Ali Khan to pass into that of Hyder.

satisfied, at night, to be obliged to eat their game, roasted as well as they could, without bread or rice, to the great diversion of Hyder, who in vain advised them to wait for the cooks.

Hyder had no sooner passed the mountains with his cavalry, than he despatched his brother-in-law, Mughdoom, with four thousand horse, to pursue the English army, and invest Caveripatam.

This order was executed with so much diligence and address, that Caveripatam was invested, as well as all the avenues leading to the English camp at Tripatour, without it being possible for General Smith to receive any advice by the hundred horsemen left in the neighbourhood of Caveripatam, who were driven into the town. All the Hurkaras were interrupted, and the letters being carried to Hyder, convinced him that his suspicions of the correspondence between General Smith and many of the chiefs of Nizam's army, were but too well founded.

Mughdoom, after leaving the care of the investment of Caveripatam to another commander, hastened to the environs of Tripatour, and arrived during the night behind the small mountains or rocks that lie about a league from that place. General Smith, who arrived at his camp the second evening of his march, supposed the inactivity of Hyder to be the cause that he had received no news, either from the commander at Caveripatam, or his friends in Nizam's army. In this persuasion he permitted the servants, with the greatest part of the oxen belonging to the army, to go in search of forage the next morning. As soon as Mughdoom saw them dispersed in the plain, he detached some cavalry, who quickly threw them into terror and disorder. This was, of course, observed from the camp and fortress, and the piquets of cavalry, consisting of about one thousand horse, were despatched to chase the pillagers; who, according to their orders and usual custom, fled, on perceiving the enemy, and saved themselves by taking the road near which the ambuscade was. The English cavalry were no sooner within reach than Mughdoom fell upon them and, having put them to flight, pursued them with so much spirit, that a party being prevented from reaching the camp, and endeavouring to take refuge in the town, the cavalry of Mughdoom entered with them, and took the place, in spite of the fire from the fort. General Smith, who, on sight of the enemy's cavalry, had hastened to draw up his forces in order of battle, was apprehensive of being surrounded by the cavalry of both armies, and consequently of being obliged to cut his way through, in order to procure provisions and reinforcements; he therefore collected as many oxen, and as much baggage, as the circumstances would permit, and marched in three columns, his artillery and baggage forming the middle column; and, leaving the fortress of Tripatour, hastened to Singueman, situated at the beginning of a chain of mountains, transversal to the great mountains passing by Tirnmale and abutting at Gingi. He arrived in safety, though much harrassed by Mughdoom, who took many oxen loaded with baggage, and two hundred horsemen, with their horses, of which six only were Europeans.

This irruption of Mugdhoom, and the total want of every kind of advice respecting the operations of Hyder, ought to have given General Smith a very different opinion concerning the military skill and judgment of this Indian warrior, in comparison to those with whom he had hitherto fought: but, considering that Hyder could not come to him without besieging Caveripatam or Vaniambari, places whose garrisons might have interrupted his convoys, and being at Singueman, distant from Tirnmale only five leagues, by a road advantageous for infantry (besides possessing the advantage of his camp being defended by the fortress, a large tank or pond, and the river), he determined to wait the arrival of Colonel Wood; for which purpose he wrote to the council at Madras, to order the junction of the two armies.

Hyder, the evening after he had passed the strait of Vellore, encamped about a league and a half from Caveripatam, which was invested by his cavalry. He immediately repaired to a mountain at a small distance, from whence he could observe everything that passed in the town. It was easy to perceive, from the burning of the houses that would have favoured their approach to the fortress, that they intended to abandon the town, and retire into this last place. Hyder, in consequence, gave orders to the commandant of his artillery, to get everything in readiness for scaling the walls by the Caleros, and Carnates, and other irregular troops, to prevent the English from carrying their effects from the town to the fortress. This officer, who had brought thirty pieces of cannon behind the mountain, caused eight to be drawn across the plain, to the very edge of the ditch, in spite of the fire of three pieces of cannon the English had left on the ramparts of the town, after carrying the other pieces into the fortress, whose fire could not incommode them, because masked by the walls of the town. The English commandant was so far from expecting this attack, that, in order to see Hyder's horse more at his ease, he had seated himself with his officers in a tent on the ramparts, at a table covered with bottles. To engage his attention, the eight pieces of cannon, escorted by three battalions of grenadiers and some gunners, marched directly to the gate on the side remotest from the fortress; and, having placed them opposite the gate, they made their first discharge at the tent of the commandant, and immediately overthrew it: after which they directed them against the gate, and the towers that defended it. The troops that had escorted the artillery laid themselves flat on the earth behind the hedges and walls, and in the trenches of the gardens.

It was about two in the afternoon that this cannonade began. During this time, about ten thousand, and as many volunteers,* out

---

* When a place is intended to be assaulted by an Indian army, it is allowed to all those who are not upon duty, to go and risk their

of all the troops of the two armies, appeared scattered in the plain, and hiding themselves among the gardens and houses that had been abandoned. The English officers, who had never beheld a scene of this sort before, supposed that this multitude, arriving without muskets, had no other intention than to rob or to seek for garden stuff round the town. They imagined that the attack would be made at the breach, and that there would be sufficient time to retire into the fortress at the beginning of the night.

The town of Caveripatam is surrounded by an antique wall and rampart, with towers of hewn stone: the Paler washes part of its walls; but this river, which is very broad, was not then more than a foot deep; the rest of the walls was defended by a dry ditch of no great depth.

About three o'clock, the different chiefs of the troops destined for the attack having given notice that they were in readiness, two salvos of the eight pieces of cannon served as a signal; and on the second discharge, from eighteen to twenty thousand men issued from all parts, with loud shouts: some began to cross the river; others entered the ditch with wretched bamboo ladders; others again had only poles with hooks; and numbers had fastened hooks to their turban-cloths, which they threw on the ramparts, and attempted to scramble up; and lastly, another party were extremely busy chopping the gates with hatchets: the whole scene was very striking and laughable; and the activity of the assailants was vastly increased by the astonishment of the English, who made no resistance, but hastened to

---

lives in attempting to enter the place, to share the plunder. Great numbers, both of cavalry and infantry, go on these expeditions; and though the hussars and dragoons have thirty rupees, or £3 15*s*. per month, many of them went in hopes to plunder Hyder's unfortunate subjects, who are afterwards indemnified by him.

the fortress, though not with celerity enough to save fifty Sepoys, an Indian captain, and an European serjeant, who were cut off in their retreat: these were instantly stripped, as were also the inhabitants, who were but few in number, the more opulent having retired before the English besieged the place.

It was not without difficulty that the town was cleared of these pillagers, who were slain in the houses and streets by the cannon of the fortress.

In the night after the attack a battery of twenty pieces of cannon, of twenty-four pounds, was constructed, which announced itself at six in the morning by a full discharge, all the embrasures being unmasked at once. The construction of this battery was facilitated by a wall of earth belonging to a large house on an elevated ground, which the English had left standing after burning its roof. It is to be observed, that there is no trouble in Hyder's army to make platforms of wood for the batteries; the earth is sufficiently solid, and nothing is to be feared from rain during the fine season: the pieces are always mounted on their carriages, and consequently ready to be placed in battery; the carriages are very solid, and the fellies of the wheels very broad, so that they do not cut into the earth. It must likewise be owned, that in sieges of no great consequence, as well to satisfy the impatience of Hyder as to quiet the murmurs of the gunners and deceive the enemy, the pioneers often give the earth an appearance only of solidity: but, what will appear most astonishing and perhaps incredible, is, that the battery was partly constructed with the same gabions employed in the battery made use of by General Smith, which was still in good condition, and ready to have mounted cannon, if it had not been judged proper to place another to better advantage. The English commandant had raised two cavaliers of earth upon the bastions that fired on the battery, from whence he plunged with four small pieces of cannon, which killed and wounded many men, exclusive of those who suffered from the musketry, the battery not being more than seventy paces from the body of the place; but the officer of Hyder, who conducted the attack, recollecting that the ancient Flibustiers took places without any other firearms than their buccaneers, which are long muskets of a large calibre, caused about two hundred of them, with their guns, to place themselves in proper positions behind some ruins. We have already observed that they are excellent marksmen; and their fire was so well directed, that in less than an hour it silenced that of the ramparts and cavaliers: ten or twelve cannoneers and a number of Sepoys were killed at the first discharge; so that in a short time it became impossible for their officers to compel them to appear on the rampart: every discharge of a great gun from the place cost at least a cannoneer, who was either killed or rendered incapable of fighting. It was this destructive fire that,* according to the account of the English, compelled them to hoist the white flag at nine in the morning, after three hours cannonade at most, without any breach, except a few stones that began to be loosened. Hyder was so surprised that he could not persuade himself of the truth of the fact, but went out of his tent to a rising ground to see the flag: bestowing a disgraceful appellation on the English, he ordered the commanding officer, who had waited on him for instructions concerning the capitulation, to refuse nothing that might be demanded.

In consequence of this, Captain M—— obtained, that himself and his troops should march out with the honours of war; that the Europeans should retire to Madras by the way of Tripatour, Vellore, and Arcot; that the Sepoys should be at liberty to go where they pleased, or to enlist in the army of Hyder, which they almost all did, as well as the horsemen; that all the officers and soldiers should carry away

* This is exactly conformable to the account given by the English themselves.

what belonged to them; but that the arms, ammunition, stores, horses, and every thing belonging either to the king of England, the East India Company, or Mohumed Ali Khan, should be faithfully put into the hands of Hyder. Captain M——, observing the facility with which Hyder allowed all his demands, was not afraid to ask payment for the provisions, which he said he had purchased with his own money, and was not sure of being repaid by the governor of Madras: this proposition was so much the more absurd, as all these provisions had been taken by force from the inhabitants of the country, which, however, did not prevent the English administration from paying him the value; besides which, as a recompense for his brave defence, the command of the garrison of Madras was bestowed on him. This facility of Hyder to suffer the English to enjoy the fruit * of their rapines, has apparently served greatly to facilitate the capture of places.

Hyder having caused the English garrison to evacuate the place the day after the capture of Caveripatam, marched his army the following day about two in the morning; at noon he pitched his camp on the banks of the Paler, where the camp remaining under the guard of the irregular troops, the army passed the river, and resumed their march in several columns, with the cavalry at their head, followed by the grenadiers and artillery, the rest of the infantry forming the rear.

The army marched in this order till ten at night, at which time they rested about two hours in fields of carbi, a kind of pulse that

---

* It appears that, in the present war, Hyder finds much more difficulty in taking places; which perhaps may arise from the artillery being neither so numerous nor so well served, or from the presence of General Coote, who, after the former war, was sent to India as commissary, and caused some officers to be punished. This cannot, however, be decided so far from the scene of action.

horses and cattle are very desirous of, and which they were suffered to eat at pleasure. At midnight the moon rose, and the army proceeded; and at the break of day the hussars and European dragoons joined the cavalry of Mughdoom, that was dispersed in the woods at a small distance from the English camp. This cavalry had been seven days in the open air, without tents or baggage, and Mughdoom fared like the rest. It may be seen from this circumstance, how far Hyder's troops are from being infected with that want of hardiness the Indians have been so continually reproached with. The five thousand grenadiers, as well as the artillery that followed the cavalry, arrived at the same time, having traversed seventeen leagues in a march of twenty-eight hours, without taking more than four hours' rest: the fatigue these grenadiers had been subjected to, in the exercises and evolutions at their formation, had put them into a condition of making such long and extraordinary marches. The rest of the infantry remained in the fields of carbi, and did not begin their march till daybreak.

It may with justice be a subject of admiration, that so numerous a train of artillery, drawn by oxen, could follow the troops with such rapidity. This surprise will vanish, when it is known that the oxen of India are very strong, and that those who are practised in drawing almost always go on a full trot; it is also known how sure-footed this animal is: the elephants assisted in cases of need, and a multitude of pioneers, that went before the artillery, made the roads practicable and even easy.

General Smith, as we have already observed, supposed he might remain without molestation in his camp at Singueman till the arrival of Colonel Wood, being persuaded that Caveripatam would hold out at least as long against Hyder as it did against himself; but Hyder, who he believed to be at Caveripatam, was already close upon him with his cavalry, his artillery, and his best infantry. Mughdoom had distributed his cavalry and Caleros with such judgment, that they possessed all the avenues to the English camp. It was Hyder s project, when the rest of his infantry should arrive, to convey his forces to a small plain between Singueman and Tirnmale, and to take his post on the banks of a small river of considerable depth that General Smith would be under the necessity of passing in his way to Tirnmale. By this position, Hyder would have prevented the junction of the two English armies, which must have thrown General Smith into the utmost embarrassment; because it would have subjected him to the necessity of taking the road through Tripatour, Arni, and Arcot, and of traversing plains where he must have fought to disadvantage, on account of the numerous cavalry of his enemies.

But, contrary to expectation, Rocun Daulla arrived about ten in the morning, at the head of a large body of cavalry, announcing his arrival by the grand timbals, doubtless for the purpose of advising the English; besides which, after his junction with Hyder, he sent advice of the capture of Caveripatam, and the arrival of the army in the environs of the camp. This is confirmed beyond contradiction by the manœuvre of the English, who raised their camp a little before noon. On the advice of this, Hyder mounted all his cavalry, and the infantry repaired to arms. The hussars and dragoons having orders to issue out of the wood, and shew themselves to the English army, found them in full march in a single column, coasting the river, and covering their baggages: their cavalry was at the head and rear of the column, and appeared desirous of gaining a hill that was before them.

The European commandant, who had been at the head of the European cavalry to reconnoitre the English, gave advice of what he had observed, and of the apparent designs of the enemy. Hyder, in consequence, gave orders to his grenadiers, supported by his cavalry, to attack the English army; commanding the rest of his infantry likewise, who began to appear, to advance as quick as possible.

To judge of the disadvantages under which Hyder's army fought, it will be sufficient to consider how much his infantry must have been harrassed and fatigued by the prodigious march they had made without taking any repose. This did not, however, prevent the grenadiers from marching with such order and firmness to the attack, as astonished the English general.

The English army had gained the hill. It was composed of three thousand Europeans, ten thousand Sepoys, and two thousand horse: all the infantry was in a single line, the English being in the centre; except six hundred grenadiers, separated into two bodies, and closing the line with twenty-four pieces of cannon, that composed the whole of the English artillery. The artillery was placed in the centre and flanks of the line: every regiment had its own field-pieces. The cavalry, divided into two bodies, was at the front and rear of the baggage; it formed the two sides of a triangle, of which the infantry constituted the third; whose fire, as well as that of the artillery, would have flanked any cavalry that might have attacked them. The slope of the hill was gentle, but it was covered with underwood that impeded the march of those Indian battalions who approached to attack the English. Notwithstanding this obstacle, they advanced to the distance of twenty-five paces, and fought many hours without losing ground, in spite of the enemy's musketry and cannon; giving the rest of the infantry time to come up, though not with the same courage and ardour as the grenadiers; except eight or nine hundred volunteers from the different corps, who, led on by the European serjeants, attacked the left of the English line, and took two pieces of cannon. But a body of English, immediately sent to assist, repulsed them, and recovered the cannon, a little before night; which alone put an end to the firing on both sides: the two armies resting on the field, as if intending to continue the action. The disadvantages under which Hyder's infantry fought in this battle, and the good conduct of his grenadiers, must appear surprising to Europeans, who are accustomed to entertain a bad opinion of the bravery of the Indians: it appeared so to General Smith, who speaks in high terms of them, as well as of the European officers that commanded them. But to say the truth, this infantry was sustained by sixty pieces of large cannon, pointed by able gunners, who made great ravages among the English infantry, that was uncovered from head to foot; while the English artillery did little injury to Hyder's infantry, on account of the difficulty of aiming well in pointing downwards. This difference of advantage compensated, in some respect, for the advantage of position, and in the number of muskets, that were more than double those of the grenadiers, before they were joined by the rest of the infantry.

In this battle Hyder lost nine hundred of his grenadiers; a loss so much the more considerable, as they were brave men, accustomed to fatigue, and who never gave way. The Buckshee, or minister of war, who has the right of marching at the head of the infantry, though he does not command them, was killed by a cannon-ball; and the cavalry, which was of no use in this day's service, nevertheless lost some men and horses, the English artillery having good play among so numerous a troop.

It was perceived, about eleven at night, that the English retired in silence. Hyder gave orders to his troops not to attempt to molest them, the cavalry not being able to attack the English infantry in the night; and he was desirous of giving some repose to his infantry, who had distinguished themselves, and had need of rest.

Before day-break, the cavalry, headed by the hussars and dragoons, set out in pursuit of the English army, who had abandoned their baggage for the sake of carrying off their wounded. General Smith himself set the example: the dragoons finding part of his kitchen utensils, and two valuable trunks belonging to Major Bonjour, a Genevan officer, esteemed by the English, and who did the duty of major-general of their army—these baggages afforded the hussars and dragoons excellent plunder. In order more effectually to secure a conveyance for their wounded, the English threw their ammunition and stores into the river, from whence the Indians recovered the balls and sacks of rice; and, in order to conceal their loss, they buried their dead: but the night, and their haste, caused them to perform this duty with so little care, that the bodies were many of them partly uncovered. The avidity of the soldiers for plunder, when it is permitted, induced them to dig up the dead, in order to get the clothes they were wrapped in.

In spite of the haste employed by Hyder's cavalry in pursuit of the English, they gained Tirnmale, with no other loss than two small iron three-pounders they themselves left behind; and there was only one skirmish in sight of Tirnmale, between the grenadiers, who formed the rear-guard of the English, and the hussars and dragoons, one of whom only was wounded. Thus it was that General Smith escaped the risk he would have run, if Hyder, with his army, could have taken his post beyond the river, as he had projected.

All the irregular troops had been left in the camp at Paler; because this kind of troops being without discipline, it would have been difficult to have kept them out of sight of the English; and because the enemy's spies are generally of this body of troops.

Hyder, elated with the glory of having caused the English to fly before him, advanced, and encamped a league and a half from Tirnmale, in a place full of large rocks, and separated from Tirnmale by a plain; and, as he was encamped very near the enemy, to whose method of beating the Indians by attacks in the night he was no stranger, he took every precaution that could be required to secure his camp from any surprise.

A large opening between these rocks, that might have been taken for a work of art, and behind which his camp was situated, was fortified by a redoubt. All the heights were occupied by guards, whose sentinels continually called *Khuberdar!* which signifies *Take care of yourself!* Guards of cavalry and Caleros were despatched close to Tirnmale, with rockets to make signals; so that the English could make no movement to attack the camp of Hyder, without his being immediately advised. But General Smith had no intention to run any risk till Colonel Wood should join him with his army, which had been augmented, and was eight or nine thousand strong, exclusive of a body of Caleros from Tanjore.

Hyder, who ought to have sent a strong detachment, or the whole of his army, to prevent this junction, suffered it to take place, in spite of all the advice that was given him on the subject. He continued to keep his army collected, and to make war in a country where his cavalry was almost entirely useless; especially while General Smith remained in his camp at Tirnmale, situated between two mountains on which there are fortresses; having his van covered by the town, and a tank, where no force could arrive but through narrow passes, defended by retrenchments with artillery.

His hope was to draw his enemy out of their camp. For this purpose he caused his infantry to make a kind of parade every day; sometimes coming within reach of the artillery with all his troops, and at other times with his infantry alone. He lost his time so effectually, that Colonel Wood joined his forces to those of General Smith.

Notwithstanding this junction, which made the English army amount to above five-and-twenty thousand good troops, four thousand five hundred being Europeans, General Smith did not think proper to expose himself in the plain against Hyder; but, to give him an opportunity of attacking him in a country the most favourable to his infantry, he quitted his camp at Tirnmale, and marching to the left at daybreak, he pitched *another camp two leagues from Tirnmale, that his army might be less confined.*

Hyder, informed of the design of the English general, was desirous of laying a snare for him, that he communicated to no one, and which might have been attended with fatal consequences. The fact is this: the English army had to pass through a plain, bounded on all sides by woods and small eminences: Hyder gave orders, in the evening, to the chiefs of his artillery and infantry, to march into this plain at the dawn of day; entering it by a kind of valley that enlarged itself into the flat ground. He himself, in consequence of his project, departed at two in the morning with all his cavalry, which, by a very large circuit, he conducted into the close places that bordered the plain. They who commanded his infantry being apprized of his departure, began their march at the appointed hour; not doubting but they should either find the cavalry at the plain, or receive orders relative to their disposition. They were highly astonished, on their arrival, not to see a single horseman, nor any other troops whatsoever. In proportion as the entrance grew larger, the infantry extended their front, and drew themselves into order of battle. The plain, though to appearance even, was divided in two by a rising ground. Some officers, who went before, were astonished, on mounting the eminence, to find the English army drawn up in order of battle behind it. As there had been no orders given for attacking them, and no news had arrived of Hyder and his cavalry, a council, held hastily on the spot, decided that they should retire to the entrance of the valley, in order to post themselves more advantageously; while scouts were dispatched on all sides to obtain news, and the orders of the Nabob.

The English, who had been advised of the ambuscade prepared for them by Hyder, remained in order of battle till the beginning of the night, when they entered their new camp. The infantry and artillery of Hyder returned to theirs; and the prince returned very late in the night with his cavalry, much fatigued with having rode ten leagues in very bad ground, and without having taken any nourishment. Hyder supposed that General Smith was ignorant of the march of his cavalry; and would have been tempted to attack his infantry, who apparently were not supported by any horse; by which means he expected to find an opportunity of falling upon the English army with his horse. We may easily imagine that things would have been conducted in another manner, if he had communicated his project.

As Tippoo Sultaun, who was then about seventeen years of age, is now the right hand of his father, and is the person who had the most brilliant success against the English,—we think it proper to mention his conduct on this occasion. Hyder, who passionately loves his son, and is acquainted with his zeal and courage, was fearful respecting him on account of his very early age; for this reason, he usually entrusted him with the guard of the camp, when he supposed the day would prove too fatiguing or dangerous. The young prince, being charged with the care of the camp on the present occasion, was in great pain when the infantry returned, and the night closed in, without any news concerning his father and the cavalry. Two hours after dark, that is to say about eight o'clock, he sent for all the generals, gave them a short account of the state of affairs, and demanded their advice. The unanimous opinion was, that the English were too weak in cavalry to make any attempt against the Nabob: and that they could not come to attack the camp but by marching three leagues, and passing through straits where guards were placed. The prince replied to them, "As I have no orders from my father, I have need of your experience to direct my actions: I will wait here with patience and confidence according to your advice; and am much obliged to you for your attention and care." The whole company had not yet left the prince, when word was brought that Mughdoom, his uncle, second commander of the army, had entered the camp, having taken the van-guard with some horse.

Hyder, always indefatigable, advanced at dawn towards Tirnmale, with four thousand infantry and twenty pieces of cannon. The town was open to him; but while he was making the proper disposition to attack the fortresses, he learned that General Smith was in motion to attack him. This intelligence obliged him to return into his camp; not choosing to fight in a position where his cavalry would have been of no service to him.

He removed his camp the next day, because he could not reach that of the English but by narrow passes, or by marching above ten leagues; though the camps were not above four leagues asunder. After passing by the rear of Nizam Daulla's army, that had arrived two days before, and was encamped in a fine plain, he pitched his camp to the left hand of Nizam, but in advance, being then about four leagues from the English, with a plain before him, interspersed with some wood and a pond that covered the left of the English camp.

The very evening that Hyder had changed his camp, the English at the close of day struck their tents; the news of which was quickly carried to Hyder, and obliged him to keep his men to their arms all night. But the English contented themselves to pass the night in the open air; and at sun-rise they again set up their tents. This manœuvre was repeated, for no positive reason that can be deduced, the four following nights, in spite of the frequent showers they were exposed to; and Hyder, in consequence, fortified his camp with four large redoubts.

As the English camp was always surrounded with cavalry and light troops, as well on foot as on horseback, who had taken possession of all the passages, they could not receive provision and ammunition except from Tirnmale, where they had no other stores than rice. Their troops therefore suffered much, as Hyder was well instructed by the capture of patmars or couriers passing between the army and Madras, and likewise by the reports of individuals. The governor of Madras blamed General Smith for having given the soldiers their rations of arrack in money; saying that money being scarce, ought to be sparingly distributed, and that it would have been sufficient to have promised the men their due from the council of Madras. In a letter to the paymaster, he blamed him for having refused to pay the troops their money in lieu of arrack, at the orders of the general; observing, that no one in the army can refuse obedience to the general, who is alone reponsible for the consequences of his orders and dispositions. The governor likewise wrote to the doctor, who was commissary to the army, to continue to instruct him of all that passed, etc.

This knowledge of the inconvenience sustained by the English ought to have determined Hyder to continue the plan of investing the army, and ravaging the country. The English, impatient, no doubt, and desirous of extricating themselves out of their disagreeable situation, either by a night attack or by removing their camp, began to march about ten at night, after having struck their tents as usual. Hyder was soon informed of this unexpected march, by the repeated signals of rockets; and a short time after was apprized, that their course was directed to the camp of Nizam Daulla.

The news was extremely embarrassing to the Nabob. He had the best founded suspicions of a secret correspondence between Rocun Daulla and the English, and had sufficient reason to believe that Nizam himself had not the best intentions towards him. If Nizam was in concert with the English, his army, which was without defence on the side of his ally, was very much exposed to danger; and on the other hand, without considering the probability of actual treachery, if the English should attack Nizam, the little order that prevailed in his army might be dangerous to his own, where the fugitives would not fail to fly for shelter and protection. Having called a council in a small casemate where Hyder usually slept, at the head of his camp, it was resolved, that his army should be in readiness to march and intercept the English in their course to Nizam's army; which it was easy to do, as they had no more than a league and a half of ground to pass, whereas the English had near six: and that, in the mean time, the European commandant should march with all the irregular troops, and those dispersed in the country, to reach the front of the English army; and, by harrassing them, retard their march, so that they might not be able to reach Nizam's army before daylight.

It was about one in the morning when this officer learned that the English army was advanced about three leagues on their way. He immediately assembled the greater part of the chiefs of the Caleros and

Carnates, and commanded them to approach as near the English army as they could; extending themselves on their flank the whole length of the line, without fear of spreading themselves too much, and not to fire till within fifteen paces;—that they might fire at pleasure, though as quickly as possible, taking care every man to lie flat on the ground after making his discharge. This last piece of advice might have been spared; but it had its weight with them, as it was a tacit approbation of their manner of fighting. They very exactly obeyed their orders; their approach, and the great extent of ground they covered, which was known to the English by the matches of their muskets, stopped the march of the English, and obliged them to call into the column the small detached parties that were on their flank, no doubt for fear they should be surrounded. The fire of the Caleros having commenced, the English, who ought to have despised them, faced about and answered by platoons, which made much noise, and did little mischief for the space of more than two hours, the Caleros returning their fire to the best of their abilities. An hour and half before day-break, the English marched to their left, and pitched another camp that was nearer Tirnmale, which covered their right; the bank of a large pond was on their left, and before them a mountain of considerable height (where they placed a battalion of Sepoys) and surrounded with rocks and underwood, impracticable for cavalry.

After reconnoitring the English camp, Hyder raised his own, and took another station, that was within two leagues of theirs, and so situated as to prevent the enemy from attacking the army of Nizam, without first engaging his own.

By the new position of both armies, the numerous cavalry of the two Subas became still more useless and difficult to be supported; which induced Hyder to attend to a piece of advice that had long been given him,—to send a large detachment from his army to take Godelour, an English factory two leagues from Pondicherry; and to return by following the sea coast as far as Madras, whose environs they were to ravage and lay waste: a step that could not fail in obliging the council to recal the army for their own defence, which would have produced the greatest discredit and real prejudice to the Company's affairs.

This detachment was on the point of departing, commanded by the European officer who gave the advice, and was assured of taking Godelour, from his intimate acquaintance with the place: but an English emissary, introduced into the camp of Hyder, and who had acquired the confidence of Raza Saeb, ancient Nabob of Arcot, a man of a contracted understanding, and much given to suspicion and jealousy, took the advantage by means of this man, to make Hyder believe, that the whole was no more than a contrivance of the French officer to return to Pondicherry with his troop, being recalled (as it was insidiously affirmed) by the governor of that place.

If the answer of the governor of Pondicherry to the letters of the two Nabobs had been less precise, and had given some hope of assistance to them, as sound policy perhaps required, the imposture of the English emissary would have made no impression on the mind of Hyder; and the commerce of Pondicherry would, by the ruin of Godelour, have been benefitted by the loss of commerce the English would have sustained.

Hyder had so much regard for the French officer who was to have commanded the expedition against Godelour, that he had caused the Nizam to grant him a Jaghire, or immediate fief of the empire, without any vassalship to the Nabob of Arcot, all the country along the coast between the rivers of Alemparvy and Divicoty, and a line drawn from one river to the other, touching and including Paniroti. The Paravana or patent recited, that this gift was made in return for the great services rendered to the empire by the said officer; and that it was without any other obligation than that of maintaining two hundred Europeans for the guard of the country, whose revenue was estimated at eight lacks of rupees; with a promise of enlargement of the territory, if it should prove less. Hyder, and his son, as Nabob of Arcot, had confirmed and ratified this donation.

The French officer, who was firmly persuaded that the English and Mohumed Ali Khan would lose all the Nabobship of Arcot in this war, thought it expedient to profit by the favour of Hyder, by obtaining a gift that would be so useful to his country. He did not wait till conquest had put that Nabob in possession of the territory; presuming, perhaps with reason, that he might not then be so generous. The investiture, which ought to have been a secret in the cabinet, was made public by the secretaries of Rocun Daulla, Divan and keeper of the great seal, who came in ceremony to compliment the officer, and receive his present on the occasion. This gift excited the jealousy of Raza Saeb and some others, and was doubtless one of the inducements that led Hyder to suspect the French officer.

But, whatever may have been the cause, there is no doubt that Hyder was fearful of suffering his Europeans to approach too near Pondicherry. He, therefore, informed the French officer, that, as he could not then spare any infantry, it would be proper to defer the capture of Godelour till another opportunity; but that he would despatch a body of cavalry to destroy the country close up to the gates of Madras; "and as it is no more than a kind of course," said he, "and my son has never yet had any command, it will be "doing him a great pleasure to give him charge of this operation, at "the head of five thousand horse." It may, perhaps, seem surprising that Hyder should use so much address to make this officer acquiesce with a good grace in the substituting another general to the command of a detachment that had been promised him; but no prince can possess to greater advantage the art of softening his refusal; so that he never appears to deny anything. In consequence of this conference, the young prince departed with his detachment; and advanced with so much speed and secrecy towards Madras, that the governor, Mohumed Ali Khan and his son, together with Colonel Call, and almost all the council, very narrowly escaped being taken in the country-house at the Company's garden. Happily for them a small vessel, that by accident was opposite the garden, furnished them with the means of escaping, which otherwise would have been impossible. Their flight was so precipitate, that the governor did not stay for his hat and sword, which were taken by the soldiery, as well as the breakfast equipage; it being the custom at Madras to take the air every morning, and breakfast in the country. The governor and his company would infallibly have been made prisoners, if a domestic of their French emissary in Hyder's camp, sent expressly to apprise them of the incursion, had not arrived the very moment they were preparing to take their usual ride. The cavalry of Hyder arrived full speed, and cut off their return to Madras: Mohumed Ali Khan, who alone took the high road, escaped being taken only by the swiftness of his horse. If the governor had had the misfortune to have been taken, his own vanity and presumption would have been the cause: for his company had scarcely met, before a crowd of the country people ran past towards Fort St. George, crying *Maratta! Maratta!* the people of the coast never having, before the present war, experienced any incursions except from that nation. The governor and other English, instead of paying any attention to the cries of the fugitives, were much diverted with the circumstance. A second troop passing by, and some of the company observing that the business deserved attention, the governor answered, "The enemy's cavalry cannot "arrive here without first passing by fortresses where we have "garrisons, whose commandants would send me advice: the terror "of these people is certainly a panic; and to put an end to it, I "will order the Chaubuc to the next that comes to alarm us in "this manner." Everybody applauded his discourse, according to the established custom of crying *Amen* to what is said by men in power. But in the instant arrived a crowd from St. Thomas,* many of whom were wounded; they announced that the enemy were plundering that town. The whole company was seized with fear and had just time to save themselves by the sea-coast, in consequence of the advice so luckily given them.

While Tippoo Sultaun ravaged the environs of Madras, his father reconnoitred the English camp; which it was easy for him to do, without danger, from a plain on the top of a hill that commanded a view of the rocks and underwood we have described. The Nabob perceived that he could annoy a part of their camp with large cannon; and having taken his resolution, he caused his army to march the next day early, and conveying some large pieces of cannon to the top of the hill, he caused them to be pointed at the English

---

* The town of St. Thomas is supposed to belong to the Portuguese, and the colours of that nation are still displayed at the place. The bishop takes the title of governor. It is entirely open, and the English do not scruple to keep Sepoys in garrison there. The governor of Madras often sends for the bishop, as if he were at his orders; and his house and church are occasionally searched, without any respect of places. Having received orders from his court to expel the Jesuits, they have remained in their convent, under the protection of the English, preserving their habits, and exercising their functions, in spite of the interdiction. This poor bishop is so much the slave of the English, that, notwithstanding the ill-treatment he receives, they compel him to give a Portuguese passport to an English vessel that trades every year from Madras to the Manillas, where it is received by virtue of the false passport of the Portuguese governor, who is acknowledged by the English merely for their own convenience.

camp, where they carried admirably well, and occasioned a kind of disorder and haste in striking and removing tents, etc. Hyder, delighted at having thus insulted the English, caused all his artillery, even the very smallest pieces, to be drawn up the hill for the purpose of making a vain parade, though the greater part of the balls could never reach the English. He imagined he should give the enemy a high idea of his forces, and intimidate them by shewing them all this artillery, and the vivacity and spirit it was worked with; and, in order that his intention might be answered, he encouraged the soldiers himself, by giving abundance of gold and silver money to the cannoneers of those pieces that appeared to be best served:—all which was matter of derision and laughter to the English; and, in reality, answered no other purpose than that of frightening the feathered inhabitants of the underwood that grew on the hill-side.

While Hyder thus exercised his artillery, and kept his infantry in parade, his cavalry galloped about the plain to almost as little effect as the discharge of the greatest part of his artillery. Nizam, who did not think proper on this occasion to be an idle spectator, had marched with his army, nearly at the same time as his ally, and caused his cavalry to parade round the English camp; but about three in the afternoon, with his whole infantry, he attacked the Sepoys that General Smith had posted on the mountain. To defend themselves against this attack, the Sepoys were obliged to take positions that exposed them to the artillery of Hyder: seeing themselves obliged to give way, they made several signals to General Smith, who marched to their assistance with his whole army. It was near four in the evening when his columns were observed to march out. Hyder immediately caused his artillery and infantry to descend from the hill, and recalled his cavalry, in order to face the English with his whole force. His troops were scarcely drawn up, in order to march, before the whole infantry of Nizam was seen in the most precipitate flight and disorder; while his cavalry appeared to advance bravely and in good order against the English, followed by his artillery; but instead of extending itself in the plain, to the left of Hyder, the troop placed itself between the English and his army so as entirely to mask it from their sight. The English advanced along the banks of the pond near the mountain, marching on ground covered with stones and shrubs,* whose branches being very flexible, are no great inconvenience for infantry. They were formed into two columns, having their cavalry in their rear, and their artillery in front, which firing on the cavalry, caused them to give way, and in a short time put them to flight full speed by the shortest way, which happened to be through the camp of Hyder, across which they drove, spreading terror and disorder as they went. Hyder perceiving the flight of Nizam and all his army, found himself exceedingly embarrassed, as he had every reason to suspect some treachery: he was likewise apprehensive, that, while he fought with the English, his camp would be plundered by the fugitives; and the approach of night added to the trouble that employed his thoughts.

When the dispersion of Nizam's army had left the English army uncovered, it was seen advancing in one full line, with the cavalry in reserve. The artillery of Hyder, distributed along the front of his infantry, made a few discharges, which must have slain a number of the enemy; but as the ridiculous cannonade from the top of the hill had exhausted his ammunition, his great guns soon became useless to him; the cavalry that formed the two wings having received orders to charge, the right wing, where the hussars and dragoons were, made

---

* The shrub that grows in all this part of India, and in all the uncultivated lands, is of the greatest utility. Its wood, leaves, and flower, distil a kind of syrup, which the great heat, I imagine, prevents from forming into lumps, like honey. It is with this shrub that the distillers, who follow the Indian camps, make their arrack, by adding more or less sugar according to the season.

several charges, and advanced within pistol-shot, but could never stand against the fire of the English artillery and musketry. The left wing, for some unknown reason, made only one charge, and afterwards kept at a sufficient distance from the fire. Hyder seeing very little hope of beating the English, who had the advantage of artillery, and the night closing in being in favour of their infantry, yielded the field of battle, and retreated in good order; the Nabob himself forming the rear-guard at the head of his cavalry. He withdrew his army into their camp, without leaving the English any mark of their victory, except one of the iron three-pounders they themselves had lost before, whose oxen were killed, and might have been easily replaced by the oxen from the empty ammunition waggons, if Hyder would have consented. The English made no prisoners, except a Portuguese officer of the Topasses, who, being wounded, was given to be carried by four of his soldiers, and thrown by them into a ditch; and a Pandari, who was likewise wounded; all the other wounded were brought off. The number of killed in the army of the two Subas, did not exceed four hundred men. The English followed Hyder to his camp; but his situation between two mountains, a large pond, and two redoubts, between which they must have passed, prevented them from thinking of the attack. They contented themselves with firing some cannon across the pond, none of which reached the camp; and passed the night in the open air, a good cannon shot distant from the redoubts.

Upon the arrival of Hyder in his camp, he found it in confusion; the greater part of the servants and other people in the suite of the army, terrified at the flight of Nizam and his troops, having ran off, leaving the camp all standing. After placing his infantry in the redoubts, and behind a retrenchment hastily thrown up, he ordered all his heavy artillery and baggage to march; the execution of this order was attended with great difficulty. Hyder has a particular talent in choosing places where his camp can be in security, as well from the nature of the ground, as from the defences that art can add; in which particular he has gained the praises of General Smith, who himself possesses this talent in a superior degree. The continual wars of Hyder with the Marattas, who are far superior to him in cavalry, have no doubt obliged him to make it a particular study of the art of encamping in advantageous positions, which are without number in his dominions; all the country being intersected by mountains and valleys, and covered with towns, fortresses, ponds, and woods. But he has the fault of not projecting easy sorties to his camps; though the inconveniencies have been often represented to him, especially on the occasion of the retreat after the battle of Tirnmale; his camp having no other way out behind, but by a pass filled with rocks and underwood, through which was a winding, narrow road, scarcely practicable for a single carriage. This road was very soon choked up by the number of beasts of burthen, whose owners had anticipated the order for raising the camp. The pass was divided into two, one leading to the camp of Nizam: all the baggage marched at their own discretion; a considerable number took the right-hand road, and crossed the immense baggages of Nizam's army, that marched in the greatest disorder, intermixed with artillery. The consequence of all this disorder was, a stoppage that prevented the march of Hyder's artillery, in spite of all the pains that were taken to get forward by the light of more than a hundred torches;* for, as they compelled the loaded beasts to walk on the borders of the road, they fell and overthrew their burthens; which occasioned cries and a dreadful tumult, the noise being repeated by the mountains: so that nothing better could

* These torches must appear very extraordinary in Europe, on account of the many risks they must be productive of; but the Indians have not yet been induced to submit to reason with regard to their imprudent use of torches and fire.

be done than to despatch some troops to stop the march, and give orders for every one to remain where he was till morning. When the day appeared, regularity was soon restored, as Nizam's army was already in the plain. If General Smith had detached a small party of his infantry, by a circuit of two leagues, they might have entered the camp of Nizam; and by a few shots among the fugitives and conductors of baggage, they might have occasioned so much disorder, as would have rendered the consequences of the victory of the greatest importance; for, though he met with no molestation after his defeat, he left seven or eight pieces of large cannon in his camp:* Hyder caused the carriages to be repaired, and sent them to him with the harness. Even the silver plate, and other valuable effects of Nizam, were found in the roads.

Hyder, instead of imitating the cowardice of Nizam, appeared at day-break with his troops drawn up in order of battle, at the entrance of his camp: all his infantry being in the first line, and part of his cavalry in the second. In this position he made the English respect him. When his artillery and baggage had gained the plain, he retired with his army, himself forming the rear-guard with his grenadiers, who did not quit that post of honour to the cavalry, till after the whole army had reached the plain. The English, who followed them, durst not make any attack, but fired a few cannon, which slew four

* The English have published, that they took many pieces of cannon belonging to Nizam on the day of battle, which they afterwards returned when they made an accommodation with them. There are strong reasons for doubting this fact; because these pieces were not conducted in triumph to Madras, where they would have been exhibited, if it were for no other reason than because they were ornamented with fleurs-de-lis.

men, including a quarter-master of dragoons, who was struck by the last rebound of a ball.*

It will readily be supposed, that General Smith hastened to forward the news of this victory to Madras, which extricated the government of that settlement out of the most tormenting embarrassment. The unexpected incursion of Hyder's son had thrown them into the greatest consternation; the garrison of Fort St. George consisted only of two hundred Europeans, and six hundred Sepoys; so that the Black Town, which is properly the town of Madras, was at the discretion of Tippoo Sultaun, a youth of eighteen. This town contains a great number of inhabitants, not less than four hundred thousand, according to the English calculation; and their number was then vastly augmented by the fugitives from the country. Though it bears the name of the Black Town, it is inhabited by great numbers of Europeans of all nations, who have warehouses furnished with the richest products of every country. Among others, there is a large colony of very rich Armenians, possessed of immense riches; and great numbers of Guzerats, or wealthy bankers, dealers in pearls, precious stones, and coral: in short, this town is always one of the richest emporiums in the world.

The terror that spread itself among this immense population, when they saw the fugitives from the country enter, was so great, that they imagined the whole army of Hyder, headed by himself in person, was on the point of entering the town. Men, women, and children, all ran to take refuge in Fort St. George, abandoning their houses and

* The contrast of Hyder's army with that of Nizam, both in the battle and retreat, may serve to show what kind of armies those were that were beaten by a small number of Europeans; and likewise what the English and other Europeans, who flatter themselves with conquests in India, may expect in future.

all they possessed. As the governor, counsellors, commandant, etc., were not yet arrived, no one gave orders to shut the gates; so that in a short time the fort was crowded with a multitude of people, that filled the streets, the ditches, and even covered the glacis. The governor, on his arrival, could with difficulty force a passage to his house; where he entirely lost all fortitude, and remained two days with his head resting on a table, suffering Colonel Call, the chief engineer, and a man of abilities, to take the charge of everything. This gentleman did his utmost; but has since confessed, that if Hyder's son had entered the Black Town, and pursued the fugitives, nothing could have prevented his taking Fort St. George. But this young prince was without experience; and his cavalry having approached the Black Town by the road from St. Thomas, passed of necessity under the cannon of the fort, a few discharges of which served to impose on him. Tippoo Sultaun convened a council, where the advice of the grand almoner,* who had been sent with him in quality of Mentor, was, that it was not proper to run the risk of entering the Black Town: but that the orders of Hyder ought strictly to be followed, namely, to ravage the environs of Madras: and more particularly, not to hazard the life of the prince by exposing him to the cannon of Fort St. George, or any other fortress. Every one was obliged to submit to this opinion, which, it may be affirmed, was the cause of saving the English, and other inhabitants of Madras, the sum of more than one hundred millions of French money, that might have been lost to them by burning the Black Town, or forcing the governor

---

* The grand almoner was the friend of Hyder.—He will be mentioned in the portraits of the great men, and especially the friends and confidents of Hyder. Nothing can serve more effectually to display the true character of a prince, than accurate portraits of the people that enjoy his favour.

and council to accept of peace on the hardest terms, by threatening them with this consequence.

The Author of these Memoirs had advised Hyder to besiege and take the Black Town of Madras, and to burn it; though he did not imagine the thing to be so easy; yet his advice was partly the cause why he did not accompany the young prince, for fear of exposing him; and it is this advice alone that was the ground of the prosecutions of Governor B—— against him, as well as the foundation of a legal process, in which no other evidence was brought than that of the English spies, who affirmed that they heard him give it. But this proceeding, contrary to every notion of justice and the laws of nations, was an ordinary act of that despotism the English have arrogated and exercised in India.

Though the town of Madras suffered no damage, because Colonel Call, having armed all the Europeans he could collect, despatched some Sepoys and volunteers to defend the entrance of the Black Town, who prevented the pillagers from approaching; yet the damage sustained by the English was, nevertheless, very considerable. They have superb houses in the neighbourhood of Madras, richly furnished: and all the villages, which are very numerous and full of people, are inhabited by painters and manufacturers of every kind, who were all pillaged, or affirmed they were in order to take advantage of not restoring the works that were entrusted in their hands, or paid for in advance. An English merchant, named *Debonnaire*, of French extraction, was the only one of the inhabitants of Madras who did not suffer by the ravages made by Hyder's troops round that city: not by way of gratitude for the services he had done Maffous Khan, the friend of Hyder; but by the effect of chance, which led Chaki Shah, grand almoner of Hyder, and his real friend, to fix his residence in the country house of this merchant, which was situated at St. Thomas's Mount, a league and a half from Madras. On the appearance of Hyder's cavalry seen from the mount, the servants of Mr.

Debonnaire made their escape, with his children; leaving all the moveables and effects to the mercy of the enemy. The situation of the house was agreeable to Chaki Shah, who chose it for his residence during the time Tippoo Sultaun remained in the environs of Madras. On his entering the house, he told the gardeners that he was a man of peace, and that his presence would secure the house from insult. He forbade his people either to take or spoil the smallest thing; and having assured himself that his orders were not infringed, he inquired the name of the proprietor, and sent one of his gardeners, accompanied by one of his own people, to carry him his children's clothes, with fruits and herbs; assuring him that nothing in his house should be either damaged or stolen, but that he himself would overlook the gardeners, and see they did their duty; and would take care to send him the necessary produce of his garden every day, which he punctually performed. The young prince, in a visit to the grand almoner, was desirous of taking a microscope; but that nobleman would not consent, but wrote to Mr. Debonnaire to set a price upon the instrument; and it was not till he had received the merchant's second letter, that he consented to offer it as a present, on his part, to the prince.

The fugitives from the environs of Madras having spread themselves all over the coast, carried the news of the capture of that town by Hyder; and it came to Europe by the way of Pondicherry, Tranquebar, and the other European settlements. The caravans, and every possible conveyance, distributed this news with pleasure; for the jealousy and hatred that other nations have conceived against the English, smothered the account they themselves had given of their victory at Tirnmale. The consequence was, that the price of the Company's stock, at London, fell at once from 275 to 222. General Smith, to convey the news of his victory with readiness and expedition to Madras, despatched a courier mounted on a dromedary, who, instead of avoiding the troops of Hyder, addressed himself to them, to demand news of the Prince, saying, that he was charged by his father to inform him of the loss of the battle at Tirnmale, and to order him to rejoin him. By means of this stratagem he succeeded in gaining access to the town of Madras, though the Prince was not above half a league distant. The governor, on receipt of General Smith's letters, announced the victory to the people by one hundred and one guns; and distributed the most exaggerated accounts of the advantages gained over Hyder.

The young prince, astonished at so unexpected an event, consulted his council, who unanimously advised him to rejoin the armies of the Subas as early as possible; which he executed in good order, carrying with him four monks, and a priest, grand vicar of the Bishop of St. Thomas, who was then at Pondicherry. On the reputation of Hyder's lenity, these priests did not think proper to follow the example of the other inhabitants of St. Thomas, by abandoning their habitations. But as Hyder had recommended to his son to bring away some person of distinction, who might instruct him concerning the forces of the English, and the succours they expected from Europe or elsewhere—for want of more important personages, he engaged these monks to accompany him; and conducted them with all possible care and attention, though by a disagreeable carriage, having caused them to mount two and two on the backs of camels, a beast whose pace is very fatiguing. Their journey having lasted five days, they arrived worn out with fatigue, and in the most deplorable condition, especially the Jesuits, who wore their square bonnets, and who, to retain this head-dress, and at the same time to defend themselves from the heat of the sun, had been under the necessity of wrapping their heads in painted silks given them for that purpose.

The battle of Tirnmale happening in the month of November, which is in the rainy season in that part of India where the theatre of war then was, General Smith thought proper to send his army to quarters, as they had already suffered greatly. He distributed it into

Vellore, Arcot, Cangivaromarni, Gingi, etc., after having strongly garrisoned Tirnmale, Vaniambari, Ambour, and other advanced places.

The loss of the battle of Tirnmale, though of so little importance, spread itself over all Hindostan with the greatest rapidity, and was variously related, according to the dispositions of the narrators. Hyder was very little concerned at an event that he attributed solely to the fault of Nizam, whose alliance, instead of producing advantage, was a real burthen to him. Nizam, on his side, perceiving that the conquest of the country of Arcot was by no means so near a conclusion as he had flattered himself, was desirous of returning to his own dominions; but he was desirous first of extorting money from Hyder, as well as from the English and Mohumed Ali Khan. The different motives and intentions of the two Subas augmented the distrust that was between them; but, instead of its becoming apparent, they were both careful to redouble the public testimonials of mutual friendship. Nizam Daulla, on the return of Tippoo Sultaun, invited Hyder, and all the great men of his court, to a superb festival. He rendered the highest honours to that sovereign; and, among other things, caused him to sit on a kind of throne or sofa of massive gold, with cushions of cloth of gold, which he presented him with in the evening, when they parted. He likewise paid the highest respect and honour to Tippoo Sultaun, and bestowed honourable titles on several of the retinue*

* They who have charges in the palace that place them in the household, never sit before the sovereign, however high their dignity (as do the generals, and other persons of distinction), till a prince, the friend and equal of their master, gives them a title. Nizam gave a title to Hyder's high-steward; and Hyder returned the compliment, by giving an honourable title to the son of Nizam's nurse, who possessed an employ in his palace.

who were most in Hyder's favour. A few days after, Nizam was invited by Hyder in his turn; but, instead of causing him to sit on a throne of wrought gold, a sofa was prepared with sacks of star pagodas and gold mohurs, covered with fine carpets and cushions of velvet, with a gold ground—all which was likewise presented to him on his departure. It was agreed, at this last interview, that the two armies should separate, and that Nizam should return to his own dominions. This separation was not, however, to take place till after Hyder had taken possession of Vaniambari and Ambour, which he had resolved to besiege. It was likewise settled that Hyder should continue the war against Mohumed Ali Khan and the English; and that Nizam should attack the English on the side of Masulipatam, to oblige them to divide their forces.

To show the intimacy between Hyder and his family, as well as his manner of conducting himself with respect to his relations, it will not be amiss to describe an interview he had with his mother about this time. This lady, who in quality of queen-mother has the right of commanding in the seraglio or palace, having received information of the check her son had experienced, and which, no doubt, she supposed more considerable than it really was, departed from Hyder Nagar to see her son in the army, notwithstanding the inconvenience of travelling a hundred and fifty leagues in the rainy season. She made long journies, and arrived at the camp in a few days. When the Nabob, who had been apprized of the queen's departure, was informed of her approach, he left the camp with his whole army, in Savari, or parade. The army met the head of the queen's retinue at a league distance from the camp, at which time they halted; and Hyder and his sons advanced alone on horseback, till they had joined the palanquin of their mother, which was close, and covered with muslin. They inclined as low as they could on their horses; and, placing themselves on the right and left of the palanquin, the lady continued her journey, guarded by her son and grandsons, and followed by the whole retinue of Hyder. She passed through the middle of Hyder's army, who saluted her as if she had been the prince himself. The retinue of Hyder's mother consisted of about two hundred ladies, mounted on horses; they were enveloped in large pieces of thick muslin, which prevented even the smallest part of their clothes from being seen. They all went before the palanquin of the queen-mother, which was followed by eight carriages, covered with scarlet cloth, and drawn by large Persian oxen, There were likewise ten elephants, and a great number of camels and beasts of burthen. Some European horsemen preceded the women, and marched on one side. All the retinue was surrounded by about six hundred lancemen, having feathers and bells to their lances; and the horsemen who preceded and followed the retinue were about four hundred in number.

It is said that when this lady was conducted into her tent, Hyder inquired what could have induced her to make so long a journey, especially at a time when the continual rains rendered the roads almost impracticable; and that she answered—"I was desirous, my "son, of seeing how you bear the ill-fortune you have sustained." The prince having replied—"That if heaven should put him to no "greater trial, he should find no difficulty in supporting it." "Very "well, then," replied she, "since that is the case, I give thanks to "God, and shall immediately return, that I may be no impediment to "your operations." Two days after, this lady, having wished her son every kind of prosperity, departed, accompanied by her son and grandsons, to the place where they had met her.

The first place of encampment of Hyder's army, after the battle of Tirnmale, was at Singueman. After having rested two days, they passed the Paler, which was much swelled by the rains, and encamped in a plain five leagues distant from Caveripatam, and six from Vaniambari. It was in this camp that Tippoo Sultaun rejoined the army, that the Subas formed their last treaty, and that Hyder received the visit of his mother. The second day after the departure of that lady, the army marched towards Vaniambari: the cavalry and the greatest part of the infantry arrived in good time to reconnoitre the place, which was found susceptible of being approached by favour of the water, hedges, and trees, without the necessity of opening the trenches. For the purpose of the attack, a garden was chosen, in the midst of the inundation, upon a rising ground, on which was constructed, the same night, a battery of twelve pieces of cannon. As this place is not more than three-quarters of a league from the pass that leads to Vellore, a body of troops, with artillery, were sent to take possession of the same. The commandant of Europeans being slightly wounded, Hyder would not permit him to attend the works during the night, but insisted on his going to repose in his tent, while he himself undertook to superintend the workmen. In consequence of this determination, he passed the night in the battery, seated at the foot of a tree, in spite of the dampness and frequent rain—exposed to the balls and shot that killed many workmen and officers near him—and diverting every one by his pleasantries, till the return of the commandant permitted him to retire.

The battery began to fire about six in the morning, and though the service of the cannon was attended with much difficulty, the English fire was soon silenced, and Captain R——, commander of the place, displayed the white flag, and sent Mr. D——, his second in command, to treat about a capitulation. This gentleman, being conducted to the European commandant, demanded the same terms as had been granted to the garrison at Caveripatam. After much altercation, on the repeated orders of Hyder to refuse nothing, the required terms were granted, on condition that the commander of the place, and the other European officers and soldiers, should not serve against Hyder for the space of a year. When these conditions were agreed on, Mr. D——, much chagrined at not being treated so favourably as he desired, demanded that Hyder should affix his seal to the capitulation. Hyder, being advised that the conference was broken off, and the officer was about to return to his place, came forward, and seating himself by the European commandant, upon a cannon, addressed himself to the English deputy: "I am not," said he, "commander of the siege. You demand my seal: I have not my great "seal here; but to put an end to all difficulties, I give my small seal "into the hands of my commandant:" and pulling his ring from his finger, he gave it to the commanding officer of artillery, saying—"Make what use of this you think proper." The officer made an impression with it at the bottom of the capitulation; and this dispute of self-importance was thus, by the good sense of Hyder, put an end to.

The garrison of this place consisted of one thousand Sepoys and thirty Europeans: fourteen iron cannon, that had been dismounted for the most part by the cannon of the besiegers, composed all the artillery. Besides these cannon, that were found by the English in the place, two other pieces belonging to the regiment of Sepoys were taken. The place made no great resistance, though it was well provided with ammunition and stores, though there was no breach, and a sufficient number of workmen to repair the carriages: but we have already hinted at the reasons that induced the commandants of these places to make so little resistance.

After placing a good garrison in Vaniambari, the army marched towards Ambour, a place famous for the battle gained by the French, and the troops of Mouza Ferring and Chanda Saeb, against Unvurudeen Khan, father of Maffous Khan and Mohumed Ali Khan, who lost his life, at the age of eighty-two years, on the third day of the battle, after having repelled the enemy from his retrenchments for two successive days. This place, in which the English had amassed considerable quantities of ammunition and stores, together with artillery, muskets, uniforms, and tents, is composed of three different fortifications, inclosed the one within the other.

The first is the citadel, situated on a mountain of the most difficult access, on account of its steepness on all sides. This extensive fortress is capable of containing a numerous garrison, with all the necessary stores, not excepting even beasts of every kind: two very large basons, cut in the rock, contain much more water than it is possible to consume from one rainy season to another: and lastly, the ramparts are constructed with such strength and firmness, that for this reason, as well as the elevation of the mountain, very large cannon, and much time, would be required to make a breach.

At the foot of the citadel, and on the only accessible side, is a fort, which the English have strengthened by the addition of a palisaded covered way, and a glacis: and lastly, a town of considerable magnitude incloses the fort, defended by a brick wall, with round bastions, and a dry ditch. Half the town is covered from any attack by a large pond; at the end of which the English have constructed a redoubt, which closed the road that led between the pond and the river, and commanded the road on the other side between the river and a high mountain.

As soon as the army had encamped about a league distant from Vaniambari, on the banks of the river they had passed at Vaniambari, Hyder went, the very same evening, to reconnoitre the town, in spite of a very heavy rain, that was partly the cause of his being in great danger: for, having advanced to the border of the pond, he found himself unexpectedly opposed to the cannon of the redoubt, which was masked by trees, and the end of the bank of the pond. This artillery, which consisted of three large pieces, made a discharge that killed fifteen horses, and covered Hyder with blood, and the limbs of the unfortunate men that were slain. Notwithstanding this accident, Hyder continued to reconnoitre the approaches; and resolved to cross the river again with his army, to encamp on the other side of the town; where he should be in a position equally advantageous for the security of his camp, and for prosecuting the siege of Ambour, which would be blocked up by his camp on the side of Vellore and Sattgheri, and by the army of Nizam on the side of Vaniambari and Ventigheri.

In consequence of this resolution, the army traversed the river during the night, and passed under the fire of the redoubt before the break of day; so that a few stragglers among the valets and suttlers were the only persons that suffered.

Between the river that flows on the side where Hyder's army was encamped, and a chain of mountains that extend from Ambour to Sattgheri, is a plain about three leagues in length, and of an unequal breadth, from half to three-quarters of a league. One extremity of this is entirely shut up by the town of Ambour, the redoubt and the river. This part of the town, whose approach was much favoured by fields of a kind of millet, then very high, was judged capable of being taken by storm, without making any breach. Orders were consequently given to prepare ladders of bamboo: but as it was thought that the garrison, which was numerous, might make resistance, the grenadiers and best infantry were ordered to make the attack.

The order of attack being settled, the chiefs of each corps were conducted, in open day, to reconnoitre those places they were destined to march against; and at the close of the evening, after supper, the troops spread themselves in the plain, carrying their ladders, and posted themselves opposite that part of the town they were to assault; with orders to lie down, and wait in silence for the concerted signal. Cannon were likewise conducted into some deserted houses, that formed a village in the midst of a great number of trees, fronting the part nearest the river; from whence it was judged they might favour the attack, by enfilading the rampart. The English, who could not be ignorant of these preparations, as they were openly made, appeared very busy during the whole night; and kept a great firing on the village, whose houses they shot through and through, without killing more than one man. They continually threw out fire-pots and fusees, to discover the manœuvres of the assailants; but while the night lasted, Hyder's troops remained at their ease. At the break of day they advanced in good order from all parts, carrying their ladders, with drums beating and colours flying, till they came to the edge of the ditch, into which they descended. They mounted the walls and bastions so quickly, that Hyder's colours were hoisted on the ramparts immediately after, in spite of the cannon and musketry of the enemy, which was not very sharp; whether it be that the commandant of the place did not think proper to make a longer resistance, or whether the English had retired, supposing the escalade would not take place. Some men were at first seen on the bastions; but the cannon placed in the village, or perhaps their fears, drove them away: for the grenadiers in ascending found them abandoned, and immediately proceeded to plunder the town. Some of them having ventured to pursue the fugitives as far as the glacis of the fort, found themselves exposed to a cannonade that destroyed considerable numbers; others were slain in the streets by the cannon of the fort and citadel, which obliged them to stretch curtains across the streets, and to cut passages through the houses. Among those who were slain in this attack, was the brave and generous Caki Shah, Peerzadah, or grand almoner, who was running from house to house, according to his laudable custom, to prevent the soldiers from committing any act of cruelty.

Hyder himself formed the project of this attack by day; and conducted the left wing of his troops in person, on horseback, with his sabre drawn, to the edge of the ditch.

At the beginning of the night an English gunner, a deserter, gave information that the garrison of the fort would retreat into the citadel that night, and that they were employed in carrying off the most valuable effects, and destroying the rest. The commandant of Europeans proposed to Hyder, immediately to attack the fort with all the grenadiers; having the Europeans, as well horsemen as gunners, at their head. This being agreed to, every preparation for the attack was made in an hour; and at eight o'clock the troops sallied forth through the streets, and leaping into the covered way, scaled the fort, which the English made haste to abandon; however, they could not do this so quickly, but that twenty-five sepoys, an officer, and six Europeans were taken prisoners, two of the latter being wounded.

The English had thrown a large quantity of cartouches into a pond in the middle of the fort, and had caused a fire to be made in the *place d'armes* for the purpose of burning the uniforms, a considerable quantity of which were saved. The besiegers found eighteen brass cannon designed for field service, three thousand fire-locks, a great quantity of shot, bullets, and gun-flints, and a considerable stock of rice and flour. There were likewise store-houses filled with tents, chests, and effects belonging, or intended to be sold, to the army; which was very acceptable plunder for the soldiers; and might easily have been saved, as Captain C——, commandant of the place, was in a situation to have defended the fort a very long time, his garrison being numerous, and well provided both with artillery and ammunition.

The facility Hyder met with in taking all the English places he attacked, encouraged him to undertake the siege of Ambour; though he had received advice, that the English were marching from all parts to assemble at Vellore. Firm and determined in his smallest resolutions, he refused to follow the prudent advice that was given him, to repair immediately to Vellore; as he easily might in a single march, the distance from Ambour being only ten leagues. At this last place he would have been in the centre of the English quarters, which were dispersed for more than forty leagues round, and might have prevented them from uniting; a step of so much the more consequence, as the English at Madras had lately received a reinforcement of troops from Bengal, which the position of Hyder's army, at Vellore, would have prevented them from joining the other troops.

The difficulty of taking the citadel of Ambour, which we have described as being situated on a steep mountain, was rendered much greater to Hyder, by the circumstance of his being without either bombs or mortars. The ditches of the town, serving in some respects as trenches, favoured the approaches; and many guns were mounted in a short time, though with the loss of the best gunners, who were uncovered from head to foot, by reason of the elevation of the castle. Hyder allowed but one night for constructing the batteries, and consequently the parapet could not be made of the requisite height and thickness, till after the loss of many brave men. Cannon were planted on a mountain that overlooked the citadel; but the English, in two days, erected a bulwark on that part of the citadel exposed to the ricochet, or rolling shot of the cannon, which rendered them absolutely useless. The great distance between the two places prevented the firing in battery from the mountain; so that after seventeen days' siege, with the loss of many Europeans, and much powder and ball, the work was no more advanced than at first. In this state of affairs news arrived that the English army was assembled at Vellore, and was preparing to march and raise the siege.

On this intelligence Hyder took the resolution of anticipating the enemy, and retreated.

The redoubt we have spoken of being entirely cut off from all communication with the fort by the escalade of the city, its garrison, consisting of one hundred Sepoys, six European cannoneers,* and an English serjeant, who commanded, was obliged to surrender at discretion.

A number of irregular troops being introduced, at the close of the day, into the city and fort, who climbed up the sides of the mountain, and fired upon the guards—the cannon was drawn off under favour of

---

* It is to be observed, that in India there are not above three or four Europeans quartered to the largest guns, the rest being Indians.

this noise; and at midnight, an hour before the rising of the moon, all the troops quitted the trenches, and marched to join the rest of the army that had left their camp, at the beginning of night, and repaired to another on the road to Vaniambari.* On the following day the army marched, and encamped on the banks of the river of Vaniambari; its right wing bearing against that fortress, and its front directed towards Ambour.

This retreat of Hyder was the signal of Nizam's separation from him, that Suba retiring into the country of Curpa.

The same day that Hyder pitched his camp at Vaniambari, General Smith arrived at Ambour with his army, consisting of 28,000 men, of which 5,000 were English; for the Bengal reinforcement consisted of six hundred Europeans, and six thousand Sepoys, very much superior in appearance to the Sepoys of Madras, and esteemed by the English as the best infantry in India.

The English general allowed his troops a short time for repose, and left Ambour on the very evening of his arrival, directing his march to Vaniambari.

Hyder was so confident that the English would not come to seek him, that he did not take the usual precaution of despatching advanced

---

* A surprising phænomenon happened on the night of this retreat, which was at the end of December. The moon rose at one in the morning; and about three it was so extremely cold, that no one in the armies of the two Subas could remain either in bed or in his tent, though they were provided with carpets and cloth coverlids, but were obliged to light large fires and warm themselves, as in the time of the greatest frosts at Paris. The weather, during this great cold, was very serene, with little or no wind; and nothing similar to it happened on the night following. This event was so uncommon in that climate, that the most aged persons had never known or heard of the like.

guards of cavalry and light troops on the side of the enemy. There were no other than large bodies of cavalry on the other side of the river, about half a league from the camp; and two redoubts, raised about one hundred paces from the same bank, on an eminence, that served as posts for the advanced guards of infantry. Each of these redoubts mounted two pieces of cannon: and it was not till seven in the morning that the approach of the enemy was known by the cannon of the redoubts, that gave the signal of alarm; at the same instant that the arrival of the horsemen put the fact out of doubt.

That which induced Hyder to suppose the English would not pass Ambour, a town on his frontier, was, his having dispatched propositions of peace to the army and to Madras. The bearer of these proposals was an Englishman, formerly factor or consul at Carvac. As the chief preliminary was, that everything should remain *in statu quo* (an offer so much the more convenient, as neither party had any restitution to make; all the places formerly taken by the English being recaptured, and Hyder having evacuated the dominions of the English, or of Mohumed Ali Khan) he did not doubt of their being accepted. This mediator had promised to send advice, as early as possible, whether he had any hopes of succeeding in his mission. But General Smith, who had his instructions and his projects, did not think himself at liberty to suspend his operations, though he was of opinion that peace would be advantageous to his nation. The Englishman continued his journey to Madras, without sending back advice according to his instructions. On his arrival at Madras, he found the governor and council recovered of their fright, and elated with the hopes of success from certain intrigues they were carrying on. In this disposition they treated him as a young man, and derided his propositions; but the consequences gave them sufficient reason to repent.

On the news of the enemy's approach, Hyder put himself at the head of the piquets of cavalry, and passed the river; after giving orders to strike the camp, to draw up the infantry in order of battle, and to march the heavy artillery and baggage to Caveripatam; at the same time commanding his brother Mughdoom to follow him with all the cavalry.

The Nabob advanced as far as the redoubts. The enemy appeared in good order, coming forward in three columns of infantry: their whole cavalry formed the rear-guard in a single line, except two hundred English dragoons who rode before the columns.

The first care of this sovereign was to draw off the cannon of the redoubts, and to cause the advanced guards of infantry to rejoin the rest of the army; and as he observed that the enemy continued to advance, he himself repassed the river, leaving Mughdoom Ali Khan at the head of a large body of cavalry, and the commandant of Europeans at the head of the hussars and dragoons, with orders to observe the march of the enemy, and to harrass them even so far as to attack the head of their columns; with the intention of causing them to slacken or stop their march, that Hyder's army might have time to retire. This cavalry, with the dragoons and hussars at their head, hastened to attack the enemy's columns to the centre and the left, which appeared in a situation to come up with Hyder's army the soonest; because the column to the right was on an eminence, and could not pass the river without defiling, as the banks were very steep. The European cavalry were advancing full trot to attack the centre, when several cannon, discharged from the right-hand column on their flank, killed two horses; one of which was that of the commandant of Europeans, who falling, found himself immediately surrounded by the English dragoons, and abandoned by his own, through the treachery of the greater number, who, together with their officers, gave themselves up to the English. The French commandant, in falling, received a contusion on the buttock and thigh, that formed an abscess; in the cure of which he kept his bed three months at Madras. This desertion stopped the Indian cavalry, who returned; and General Smith ordered his army immediately to halt, suffering Hyder's army to retreat unmolested. A few shots were fired at some cavalry that came to reconnoitre his army, that remained on the same ground till evening, because his equipage could not arrive sooner; at which time he turned back, and encamped on the road to Ambour, about half a league distant from the river.

It is impossible to exceed the politeness and respect that General Smith shewed to his prisoner, the French commandant. He caused him to sleep in his own tent; and informed him, that the march of his army had no other purpose than that of favouring the desertion of the Europeans, which was expected to be much more considerable, in consequence of a plot that had long been carried on, and which they were apprehensive could be no longer concealed.*

The honour and integrity that the writer of these Memoirs has adhered to in the relation of the facts they contain, do not allow him to pass over in silence the odious plots that were made use of, in order to execute this infamous piece of treachery.

After the capture of Caveripatam, the permission was given to an adventurer,† a surgeon by profession, to retire to the coast of Coromandel, taking the advantage of going in company with some English officers, who had been taken in that place. This permission was, no doubt, a great indiscretion; but as the proverb says, we

---

* General Smith did not fire on this troop; and said, that in keeping the secret, he had forgot to give an order for that purpose to Colonel Linn, who commanded the column to the right.

† This man, whose name we conceal on account of his family, has, by his bad conduct, attracted the notice of government, and is now in confinement.

can never think of everything; aud there was, besides, a wish to get rid of a worthless man, from whom there was no reason to fear any thing. Nothing less than an unforeseen chain of circumstances could have given him the power of doing mischief.

This surgeon came to Hyder at Coimbatoor, where he announced himself as Chevalier de St. Louis, and ancient captain of artillery, travelling to Pondicherry. He found credit with the commandant of Hyder's Europeans, to whom he addressed himself; because he had been recommended to that officer by the chief of the French factory at Calicut, who, in forwarding European news, added, *These things may be depended on, as they come from good hands: I have them from M. le Chevalier de * * * * *, who is arrived from Europe by the caravans, and is on his way to Pondicherry*, &c. &c. This commandant did not indulge a doubt respecting the good qualities of the chevalier, who, together with the cross he had the audacity to bear, possessed likewise, to the misfortune of many, an engaging and seductive exterior. On this false appearance of candour and rectitude, the commandant of Europeans received him in the best manner, and presented him to Hyder, who gave him the command of a battalion of Sepoys, with appointments to the value of £50 per month. The man was absolutely without common necessaries; and the French commandant supplied him with lodging, subsistence, a carriage, and every thing becoming a gentleman. After these services, it may naturally be supposed that he would have felt the utmost gratitude and regard for his benefactor: but, on the contrary, his perfidy and want of principle were such, that in less than three months he was dismissed from all his employs. Being on the point of being reduced to beggary, he had the confidence to request permission to exercise his business as a surgeon. This request was made by the mediation of Hyder's surgeon, who had been a fellow-soldier with him in Lally's regiment, and had recollected him perfectly on his arrival; though, at the request of the other, he did not expose him. Our gentleman, thus becoming a surgeon, found himself to be a Chevalier de Christ,* by the assistance of a cross that served every purpose; it was, however, a real cross of St. Louis, that side being untouched on which are the sword and laurel crown, with the motto *Bellicæ virtutis præmium;* but on the other, the enamel that represents St. Louis was taken off, and a small cross substituted in its place. He affirmed, that he had caused this cross to be made in this manner when in Portugal, in order to give it a French appearance. However, he was forbade to wear it; but he adorned himself by an embroidery on his clothes, that was permitted him. A specimen of his usual tricks having procured him to be confined, he obtained his enlargement by means of his comrade, with leave to repair to the coast of Coromandel, in company of some English officers who were to return to Madras. Our adventurer spoke good English, and undertook to court the favour of Captain M*****, by a string of narrations to which that gentleman either gave credit, or pretended to do so. Among other things, he told him that all the Europeans in Hyder's service, who constituted his chief force, were much disgusted with the service they were engaged in, and still more with their commandant; and that if the government of Madras would employ him, he would engage to cause them all to desert; in the execution of which project, his friend, the surgeon of the Nabob, would engage to lend every assistance in his power.

The English officer, charmed at the discovery of a method of turning the attention of the Madras administration from the cowardly

* He affirmed, on the second day after his arrival, that he was a knight of this Portuguese order. The facility with which he conferred these dignities upon himself, and a long stay at Lisbon, whence the fear of hanging had induced him to make his escape, and a patent since affirmed to be forged, were the causes why this quality was not called in question.

defence he had made, presented our chevalier to Colonel Call, engineer in chief, and a man of great influence in the council. He had great abilities; but, considering the extent of his mind, he was blameable for attending more to the purpose or end he aimed at, than to the difficulties that might prevent his arriving at it. This colonel, who, like many others, was bigotted to the opinion that the Indians can do nothing without the help of the Europeans in their service, was delighted with the project of the chevalier; and presented him to the governor and Mohumed Ali Khan, by whom he was received as a guardian angel. Thus it was that this man, from being a surgeon driven out of Hyder's camp, suddenly found himself the friend and confidant of the governor and Mohumed Ali Khan. He was nobly entertained, and loaded with presents, in spite of the railleries of some Englishmen, who knew him from the reputation he had acquired by exhibiting his tricks at Bengal.

While the gentlemen at Madras were deliberating on the means of carrying their plot into execution, an ancient French officer, of the East India Company's troops of that nation, arrived there. He supposed himself to have been unjustly treated by that Company; and came to offer his services to the English against Hyder Ali Khan.

The project of the chevalier surgeon was communicated to him. He did not hesitate to undertake the task of carrying it into effect. His offer was accepted, with a promise of making him lieutenant-colonel, with the command of a corps in the pay of the English Company; the basis of which was to be composed of the deserters from Hyder.

To engage the confidence of the English government, this officer caused his trunks and valuable effects to be carried to the house of the governor, who placed them in his cabinet. Not to make himself suspected by Hyder, this new emissary repaired to Pondicherry, where he communicated in confidence to all his acquaintance his design of going into the service of that Nabob. A number of officers and young men offered to accompany him. He was careful to transmit their names to the governor of Madras; and left Pondicherry secretly, at the time he expected the complaints of the English governor would arrive. The French governor, on receipt of the letter of complaint, sent for those who were nominated, and demanded their word of honour, that they would not leave Pondicherry without his consent.

The informer, who had the utmost facility in making his journey, because the country he had to traverse was entirely under the government of the English, repaired to the camp of Colonel Wood in the environs of Ahtour. He remained there two days; when that army departing to join General Smith, he went to Ahtour, and declared himself to be French: guides and everything he demanded were consequently allowed to conduct him to Hyder's camp. He arrived, accompanied by a single servant: and affirmed, that having met the army of Colonel Wood, he had passed two days in the forests, at the risk of being devoured by tigers; and that he had made the journey from Pondicherry to Ahtour on foot.

The reputation he had acquired, probably in consequence of the virtues and talents his relations had exhibited in India, prejudiced the commandant of Hyder's Europeans in his favour. That officer thought himself happy in seeing him arrive, supposing that he had found a companion to share his labours; and consequently endeavoured to render him every mark of friendship and respect. The emissary at first seemed to meet the advances of the commandant with cordial regard. He waited afterwards on Raza Ali Khan, whom he had long known, and who reposed the utmost confidence in him on account of his family, which had always been highly attached to that prince's father. Raza Saeb undertook to introduce him to Hyder, who, to the surprise of all present, received him with evident marks of chagrin: which was so much the more strange, as that Nabob always received the commonest French soldier with pleasure. But he had been informed positively by Mughdoom, his brother-in-law, who had seen the officer at the head of the French cavalry, when he escorted the convoys from Gingi to Pondicherry, that the man was a coward. It was not possible to persuade Hyder to receive him with any mark of respect; as he had too much esteem and friendship for his brother-in-law not to give credit to his report. By this prevention he could not obtain the command of a company of hussars, that was without a captain and was commanded by a lieutenant who could neither write nor read. The European commandant, not having the least idea of its being possible that a man of family and reputation, as the newly arrived officer was, could deserve such a character, was firmly persuaded that Mughdoom Ali Khan had prejudiced Hyder against him without reason. To convince him of his esteem, he communicated to him, in confidence, the secret of the expedition against Godelour; believing that he could give him good advice, because he had lately arrived from Pondicherry, which is not more than two leagues distant from Godelour; and expecting that the success of the expedition would be productive of advantage to him. We have already shewn how he made use of Raza Saeb to frustrate this undertaking; and how he prevented the governor, and the major part of the council, from being made prisoners: for as he knew of the intended expedition of Tippoo Sultaun by means of Raza, who had an entire confidence in him, he sent off his servant among the Pandaris that Tippoo Sultaun took with him, because, having no other intention than that of ravaging the country, he could not take a set of men more capable of doing it. The battle of Tirnmalc happened a few days after the arrival of this English emissary; and the officers of cavalry, with the permission of their commandant, who attended his duty as general of the artillery, offered to place him at their head during the battle. But he refused, and kept constantly behind Hyder, who seeing him mounted on a horse of one of the hussars, as he knew by the harness, caused a horse to be presented to him that belonged to one of the Pandaris that had been slain, which was the greatest affront he could shew him.

When the army marched from Singueman to encamp between Caveripatam and Vaniambari, and had passed the Paler about three leagues from their new camp, the commandant remained with the artillery, on account of the passage being rendered difficult by the rains that had swelled the river. At this time Hyder sent to him, on account of a sedition among the hussars and dragoons, who refused the pay that was offered them as usual, insisting on being paid in silver rupees instead of gold pagodas; which would have made a difference of about five shillings a month in their favour. As this difficulty had never been made before, the commandant had not much trouble in persuading them to receive the money that was offered them; and taking occasion of the battle lately lost, in which their attack, and still less that of the other cavalry, was not supported so well as might have been expected, he reproached them for raising difficulties about their pay, without shewing any great readiness to deserve it. They who secretly excited them to murmur, were doubtless eager in urging them to resent this affront; for that very evening they went off in a body, with their regimentals and sabres, and repaired with offers of service to the camp of Ram Schander, a Maratta prince, who had received into his pay the Europeans that Hyder had formerly disgraced and cashiered. On the news of their departure, the commandant pursued them at the head of a body of grenadier Sepoys. Kan Schander, cautious of giving offence to Hyder, and probably informed that the Europeans were pursued, ordered them to quit his camp. Being then totally at a loss what steps to take, they waited for the commandant, grounded their arms at his command, and suffered themselves to be conducted back without resistance. They were kept bound and exposed to public view for some days; but at length were reinstated, apparently at the intercession of Hyder, who did not think it beneath him to pretend to speak in their favour. All this may not seem very prudent in Europe; but it is necessary to attend to the situation of Hyder and the commandant. Hyder esteemed the

Europeans perhaps far beyond their value, and the other existed only by their means. This sedition was thought to be a kind of business that would not be attended with any consequences; more especially as they did not know where to direct their steps, or to situate themselves better.

This affair happened some days before the capture of Vaniambari; and everything seemed quiet, when advices came to the Nabob from Vellore, and from St. Thomas, to the commandant, that some treachery was carrying on, and a desertion projecting, among the Europeans in Hyder's army. Not being able to build anything upon such general advice, and the agents being such as were least suspected, the commandant supposed he could do nothing better than to assemble all the Europeans, and to require an oath on the cross and the holy gospels, by which they should promise to serve Hyder Ali Khan with fidelity; to advise the prince and the commandant of everything they might hear to his prejudice; and not to quit his service without asking for permission. Before the oath was administered, every individual was asked whether he had received his pay, and was offered his dismission, if he requested it. This precaution was thought sufficient, and would have been so, if the government of Madras had not employed means to prevent its effect.

The English emissary found an excellent coadjutor in the surgeon, the friend of the Chevalier de Christ; for this man had a natural inclination for hazardous undertakings, and sought to render himself the subject of discourse at any rate.* He offered to undertake every

---

* To give an unequivocal proof of the character of this surgeon, it may be recollected, that in 1776 there appeared in the different journals a letter pretended to be written by a physician in Sweden, which announced that a man had been delivered of a child, or was at the point of delivery. The singular and ridiculous disputes on the

thing, on the assurance of being appointed surgeon-major in the English service. But the conspirators not succeeding with the soldiers, on account of the oath they had taken, wrote to Madras, informing their principals that it was necessary they should have the co-operation of two Jesuits then in Hyder's camp; and that it would be expedient to forward a letter from the governor of Pondicherry to those fathers, ordering the French to quit Hyder's service, by passing over to the army and through the country of the English, who would receive them, and suffer them to join their own standard at Pondicherry.

The Jesuits were in the most absolute state of dependence on the English; and having no other existence in India than they were pleased to grant, they thought themselves obliged to serve them according to the directions transmitted to them. They obtained passports from Hyder for their domestics passing to and from their houses at St. Thomas's, and by that means became the agents of the correspondence of the English with their emissaries. They were provided with a fictitious letter from the governor of Pondicherry, who had already written to Hyder in their favour, supposing them to

---

subject of this phenomenon, are fresh in the memory of every one. The true inventor of this tale was no other than our surgeon, who in 1766 transmitted from Coimbatoor to the Sieur de la G., first counsellor at Pondicherry, the history of this monstrous pregnancy; affirming that Hyder had employed him to act the part of midwife in the business. To his history were added the anatomy and description of the parts, entirely resembling that said to be from Sweden; and as the inventor is in a double capacity the favourite of Apollo, the god of medicine and poesy, he adjoined a poem on the wonders of nature, relative to the prodigy he announced. This history is too well known to admit of the least doubt of its truth.

be prisoners, though they received every kindness, and only waited a favourable opportunity to return. To perform the commission they had from the English, they privately shewed the Europeans the pretended letter, affirming that they were forbidden to shew it to the commandant; but that the governor had sent to them to excite the Christians to leave the service of a Mohumedan prince; at the same time that, as divines, they informed them that their oath given to an infidel was null, and ceased to be obligatory, by reason of the order of the king's representative. The producing a letter of this kind to the soldiers of Hyder cannot be denied, as the fact is notorious, and can be proved by many witnesses now in Paris. The letter was false, because the governor of Pondicherry could have no reason for concealing it from the commandant; on the contrary, that officer being in possession of letters entirely written in the governor's hand, it would have been in his power to have prevented any suspicion of its forgery, if it could have stood that test; and as the governor was not ignorant that a counsellor of Pondicherry had a correspondence in cypher with the commandant, by which all despatches were communicated to him, he would certainly have informed him of the contents of this letter, which was addressed to all the French in Hyder's army. The Jesuit fathers who served the English in this business, as well as the three Portuguese priests, were sent back in company with the English factor, who went to Madras with propositions of peace.

When the Portuguese priests arrived at Vellore, and saw the Jesuits give their letters to General Smith and the governor of the place, they were in the highest astonishment to find that those reverend fathers had charged themselves with a mission of such a nature; and so much the more, as the news they brought appeared to be not casual, but early and important. The priests never spoke of this event without trepidation and fear; protesting they were innocent, and totally ignorant of the intrigues and manœuvres carried on against a prince who had loaded them with favours. In fact, Hyder had given each of them, at parting, the sum of three hundred rupees to bear their travelling charges; a sum which is equivalent to thirty guineas; and if he had been so disposed, it was in his power to have inflicted on them the punishment the worthless Jesuits had so well deserved.

Hyder having retired to Caveripatam, General Smith took possession of Vaniambari, which had been left without a garrison; but he could no longer follow Hyder, because he was obliged to wait for the convoys of ammunition and stores that had a great distance to travel: and the difficulty of collecting a sufficient number of oxen for draught and carriage was such, that he was under the necessity of detaching a part of his army to bring forward the convoy. The capture of the stores and ammunition laid up at Ambour, was the cause of all these delays in General Smith's operations.

The government of Madras, according to their promises, formed a body of light troops, composed of cavalry and infantry, under the name of the foreign corps; of which their French emissary in the camp of Hyder was made commandant, and the Chevalier de Christ commissary. To put a finish to the relation of these detestable proceedings, we think it necessary to mention, in this place, the fate this new troop experienced in spite of the intrigues of the commissary, who employed not only subornation but assassination. To augment the foreign corps, he was always reduced to little or nothing; those who were sent to Pondicherry and elsewhere to enlist men, were discovered; almost all the horsemen deserted, and took refuge either at Pondicherry or with Hyder, who paid them for horses they brought, as if they had not stolen them from himself. The commandant of this unfortunate corps was punished, according to his deserts, by those very men whom he had served at the expense of his honour. An English court-martial declared him a coward, and unworthy to continue in the service; and condemned him to be degraded from his rank, and expelled from the army. We have already mentioned the fate of the Chevalier who first projected this scheme.

Nizam Ali Khan, who, as we have before observed, quitted Hyder, and departed for the country of Curpa, was no sooner arrived there, than his Divan and worthy minister Rocun Daulla wrote to Mohumed Ali Khan, his brother-in-law, to acquaint him that he had at length prevailed on Nizam to abandon Hyder; and that if he and the English desired it, he would repair to Madras, with full power to make such a treaty as they might wish for or expect.

The governor and council of Madras hastened to signify their desire of seeing him in their capital; and, in consequence, Rocun Daulla and Ram Schander, a Maratta prince, one of the principal confidants of Nizam, repaired with great pomp to Madras, where they made a magnificent entry, being saluted by the cannon, and the English troops lining the streets they passed through. They were every day entertained with new spectacles, and conducted to see the shipping, and everything that was deserving their attention: but what gave them the most satisfaction was, the valuable presents that were made them. Nizam had the least share; the presents sent to him were of inconsiderable value; but the deficiency was made up by promises of vast magnitude: and, on the other hand, these great and magnificent ministers signed a treaty, by which Nizam confirmed Mohumed Ali in the Nabobship of Arcot, and in all the country he possessed or might obtain. Nizam Ali likewise ratified the gift to the English of the four circars or provinces to the north of Masulipatam, as well as the gift of that great city.

Two counsellors of Madras afterwards departed, in quality of ambassadors, to Nizam Ali, who sent them back with the greatest honours, and loaded with presents for themselves and the governor. Thus it was that this Suba, who, twenty years before, held the destiny of India in his hands, became a kind of beggar among other powers, and daily lost that credit and consideration which gave him his superb titles.

Morarao, a Maratta, possessor of a small territory beyond Scirra, joined the English army, bringing with him about two thousand five hundred horse, and three thousand foot, the whole in bad order; but the English sought for succours from all parts.

General Smith, perfectly acquainted with the nature of the country, and the kind of war he was to carry on, endeavoured without success to prevail on the council at Madras to accept the offers of peace held out by Hyder. He therefore offered it as his opinion, that it would be more advantageous, instead of losing time in making sieges, to pursue and press Hyder's army as much as possible; and, if he could not be come up with, to besiege some place of consequence. He proposed, for the object of their efforts, Bangalore, the capital of a fine country. But the government of Madras, determined to conquer all the country on the exterior side of the grand Gates, obliged the general to divide his army into two parts, and to give the command of one part to Colonel Wood, for the purpose of besieging and taking all the small places that lie in the valleys, while General Smith was employed in keeping Hyder's army in employment.

General Smith having complied with these orders, the project appeared to be attended with the greatest success. Colonel Wood took a great number of places, and that with so much the more facility, as three-fourths of them had no other garrison than the militia of the country. These conquests wonderfully elated the governor and council, who, as the crowning stroke of their success, received the news that an armament of about eight thousand men from Bombay had landed at Mangalore, and taken that city; whose feeble garrison, not being assisted by the inhabitants, had made their escape. Hyder's vessels, being then at Goa, were not captured; but three hundred pieces of cannon were found in the place, including a quantity of very indifferent iron guns, designed for the shipping, and for the most part unserviceable: but this is of no consequence, as the number of guns is always a great ornament to a relation. The commandant of this army wrote word, that he intended, as early as possible, to march to Hyder Nagar, not imagining he should find any difficulty in penetrating so far, and still farther from indulging a doubt of taking it, together with the immense treasures Hyder had laid up in the place.

This important piece of news was announced to the people by one hundred and one cannon fired from Fort St. George; and the relation of the capture of Mangalore was spread into all the European settlements, and every other part of the country.

The news of the landing of the English at Mangalore had been instantly forwarded to Hyder: he was consequently under the necessity of hastening to oppose this army, that had taken footing in the centre of Canara, a kingdom lately subjected to him, and which he supposing, from its situation, to be out of the reach of insult, had not provided with any considerable number of troops.

The troops that had been left at Bisnagar, Scirra, and Seringapatam, received orders to march immediately for the kingdom of Canara. The son of Hyder had the advanced guard, at the head of three thousand cavalry; and Hyder himself marched with three thousand of his best grenadiers, part of his artillery, and about twelve hundred of his cavalry, leaving the rest of his army under the command of Mughdoom, with injunctions to harass the two English armies for the purpose of retarding their operations, but to hazard nothing.

General Smith, as soon as he was apprised of the departure of Hyder, proposed again the siege of Bangalore. The council, elated with the high expectations they had built on the news from Mangalore, were for once of his opinion: but as they regarded the siege of Bangalore as an affair of the greatest importance, it was resolved that Colonel Call, chief engineer, should have the direction; and to emancipate him from the orders to General Smith, it was ordered that there should be a committee in the army, composed of the Nabob Mohumed Ali Khan, Colonel Call, and Mr. Mackis; the two last being of the council. This committee were, conjointly with General Smith, to decide on all the operations; and in order that such grave personages might not have the mortification to fail in an enterprise of such importance for the English nation, it was determined that the greatest preparations should be made. In consequence, they were furnished with sixteen mortars of different calibres, thirty-three two-and-thirty pounders, fifty cannon, with a profusion of powder and ball, and every other ammunition: and since all these things had a tract of eighty leagues to pass over before they arrived at Bangalore, and the original difficulty of procuring oxen still remained, several stations were appointed to be waited at till everything was in sufficient forwardness to begin the siege. General Smith employed himself in securing a passage for the convoys, by the capture of a number of fortresses he found in his way. He even succeeded in taking one small place by stratagem. His scouts had taken an Hurkaru belonging to Mughdoom, who carried a letter, advising the commandant of that place, that at the close of the night he would receive a reinforcement of five hundred Sepoys; at the same time informing him, that he was in danger of being besieged. General Smith having an Hurkaru, who was perfectly acquainted with the court and army of Hyder, gave him the charge of this letter of Mughdoom, with orders to carry it to the commandant, and assure him of the arrival of the succours. The letter produced its desired effect. At the close of night they received a body of English Sepoys, who did not fail to take possession of the place.

Mughdoom being informed of this event had his revenge a few days after, and retook the place by another stratagem. He caused some Indian horsemen to appear on the plain, among whom were a number in blue uniforms, like the English dragoons. One of them was detached to advise the commandant of the place, in good English, that they were pursued by a large body of Hyder's cavalry, and that he was sent by the commanding officer of the detachment, to desire the gates might be kept open for their reception. This man was an English dragoon, who had newly deserted with his horse, which prevented any suspicion from arising. A large body of cavalry appeared, and the pretended English detachment came full speed into the place, took possession of one of the gates, and admitted the whole troop. The horsemen in blue were clothed with the habits of Hyder's cannoneers.

Colonel Wood besieging great numbers of places, according to his instructions, found himself very soon in a considerable embarrassment for want of troops. He accordingly wrote to the council at Madras for reinforcements, observing that his troops were dispersed in garrisoning the different places he had taken; adding, that if it was their pleasure that he should destroy these places instead of garrisoning them, it would be necessary to supply him with a large quantity of powder for that purpose. While he was in expectation of the answer of the council, he besieged Darmapuri, a place somewhat more considerable than those he had hitherto attacked. The commandant was a brave man, named Pinda Khan, highly esteemed by Hyder, and formerly in the service of the French. This active commander made a vigorous defence, and did not hoist the white flag till the breach was made, and the ditch filled. His deputies having waited on Colonel Wood, he offered them no other capitulation than that of surrendering at discretion. The deputies not being authorized to accept such hard terms without consulting the commandant, returned to the place, almost all the garrison being then on the rampart and in the breach. When they saw the deputies return, they crowded about them, to enquire what success they had met with; and at the same instant the English grenadiers leaped out of the trench, mounted the breach, followed by the Sepoys, who had been commanded for the assault, and all the garrison, the commandant, his son, and every officer, were inhumanly massacred, except twelve European cannoneers, who were saved by the English grenadiers. This assault was made while the white flag was on the breach. It is reported that Colonel Wood's army was enraged to find no plunder in all the places they had taken: for Hyder had commanded all the inhabitants of any place in danger of being besieged, to leave the same with all their effects; and had strictly forbidden the officers and soldiers from having any plate or valuable property, but only the small quantity of linen which is absolutely necessary in India. In this order he observed, that the Europeans make war on the Indians only in hopes of plunder; and that it was not proper to indulge their avidity.

It is not easy to determine why Colonel Wood and his officers did not repress the cruelty of the soldiers, since they avowed that the grenadiers made this attack without their orders.

To revenge the sufferers at Damapuri, Mughdoom afterwards massacred a considerable body of Sepoys in the plain of Ovilour: and as for Hyder, he conceived so violent a hatred for Colonel Wood, that he always afterwards endeavoured, in preference, to attack his army, and to lay snares for him; and it is probable that the consequences would have been very disagreeable to that gentleman if he had unfortunately fallen into the hands of Hyder.

After the capture of Damapuri, Colonel Wood joined his army to that of General Smith, according to the orders he had received from Madras. That general, after securing the passage of his convoys, marched towards Bangalore, and took several neighbouring places: among others were Colar and Oscota; and with the intention of making this last place the storehouse for the siege, he caused it to be fortified.

On his approach to Oscota, General Smith received a deputation from the inhabitants of Divanelli, who came to offer him a contribution. They informed him that the small town, and its fortress or castle, were the places that had the good fortune to see the birth of Hyder Ali Khan, a circumstance that had assured them of the favour of that prince, who had bestowed many privileges on the town and territory. General Smith replied that he should be the first in giving the example of respecting the birth-place of so great a sovereign; and granted safeguards as well for the town as the territory of Divanelli. He refused to accept their contribution, and strictly forbade any individual of his army from entering the place without his permission.

This proceeding augmented the esteem Hyder had long conceived for General Smith; and on this occasion that sovereign sent two superb horses, splendidly caparisoned, and the trappings studded with precious stones, to him, as a present he begged him to accept.

The commander of the army from Bombay, who supposed, after the capture of Mangalore, that nothing now remained, as he wrote to Madras, but to march to Hyder Nagar, found his expectations not a little abated, when he was informed that he had sixty leagues to travel in a country intersected by woods, mountains, and rivers, and more especially that the approach to Nagar would be attended with the greatest difficulty. He did not, however, give up his intention; but continued his preparations, though very slowly. His army was then encamped without the gates of Mangalore, in the greatest security.

The son of Hyder marched from Bangalore with all the ardour of a young man, who burns with a desire for glory. He quickly arrived in the kingdom of Canara, whose people, alarmed, but full of confidence in the son of their king, ran before him as the man on whom their safety depended. Animated by the acclamations of the people, the young prince continued his way to Mangalore, causing all the troops to follow him that he found in his way, and who assembled from all parts. His march was so rapid, and the fidelity of the Canarins was such, that he came in sight of the English camp before they had received any advice. He perceived the tumult and fear his sudden appearance had made. Without waiting for repose after his fatiguing march, he advanced, drove back the guards, attacked the army, totally routed and pursued them to the gates of Mangalore, where his cavalry entered pell-mell with the fugitives. Three thousand infantry, just come up, were astonished to find the English camp abandoned. They plundered the camp and the town of everything they found, which the prince allowed, to punish the inhabitants for refusing to assist in the defence of the city. The rout of this English army was so great, that very few had time to make their escape on board the ships, to which they communicated their fears. Their flight added to the ardour of Hyder's Europeans and Sepoys, who immediately embarked and took three transports.

In this manner was the whole English army taken, consisting of the general, forty-six officers, six hundred and eighty English troops, and above six thousand Sepoys, together with all their arms and baggage. This glorious event for Hyder happened the eighth day after the capture of Mangalore. It is difficult to conceive how a victory of this nature could be gained; or how, during the space of thirty days, the English general could neglect the taking possession of some advanced posts, which would have given him advice of the approach of the enemy.

Hyder arrived the evening after the victory; and his son had nothing to say but, with Cæsar, "*Veni, vidi, vici.*" It is said he wept for joy when he embraced his son. Some Portuguese merchants, established for several generations at Mangalore, entertained the opinion, that from the fortunate disembarkment of the English army, and the great successes that the English attributed to General Smith and Colonel Wood, it was probable that the English would conquer the greatest part of Hyder's dominions, or at least remain masters of Mangalore. They had therefore the imprudence to treat with the English general, and to contract with him for supplying the army with provisions. As soon as Hyder was informed of this circumstance, he caused these merchants to appear before him, with the chief of the Portuguese factory, and several Christian priests belonging to the three churches at Mangalore. He then demanded of the Portuguese chief and the priests, what punishment the Christians inflict on those who should presume to betray their sovereign, by giving assistance to his enemies. The Portuguese officer having without hesitation answered that such a crime deserved death, Hyder replied, "I do not "judge in that manner, for our laws are milder. Since they have "made themselves English by engaging to serve them, their property "shall be adjudged to belong to Englishmen; and themselves shall be "thrown into prison till I make peace with that nation." Hyder, after this decision, hastened to return to the kingdom of Bangalore, taking care to leave a strong garrison at Mangalore.

During Hyder's expedition and return, General Smith had sufficient time to receive his artillery and ammunition. Mohumed Ali, and the other commissioners of the council, were likewise arrived with a numerous suite, and with a new kind of luxury, unknown till then even in the armies of the Indians; this, however, consisted in nothing else than a number of large covered waggons, loaded with a provision of all sorts of wines. But, after all these preparations, it was discovered that the rice and provisions were in so small a quantity, that they could not possibly hold out the time the siege might probably last; while Hyder and his troops would not fail to recover part of the fortresses that were to secure the convoys from the country of Arcot. And it was, besides, impossible to send escorts strong enough to defend them against the army of Hyder; General Smith having need of all his troops, as well for the siege, as for the defence of Oscota, where his stores were deposited, and to keep an open communication between the two places.

Morarao proposed to make the siege of Little Ballapore, a strong fortress about ten leagues from Bangalore, and three leagues from the country of the Patane Nabobs; as he affirmed that, when they were masters of Ballapore, he could obtain, either from his own dominions, or from Sanour and the neighbouring countries, any quantity of rice or sheep that they might desire. This advice being approved of by the committee, General Smith left Oscota with his army, and every necessary for making the siege of Ballapore. He left a strong garrison in Oscota, where Mohumed Ali Khan, Colonel Call, and Mr. Mackis were to remain.

Hyder, who had followed General Smith, and continually harrassed him with his cavalry, and sometimes with his artillery, perceived that he could not prevent his opening his trenches before Ballapore: he therefore raised his camp, and marched for Oscota, where he arrived a little before day. As soon as dawn appeared, he attacked and carried the suburb of the place, which was defended by a single retrenchment of earth, and a ditch the English had made: he took a considerable number of soldiers and Sepoys the English had placed in an hospital there: and, desirous of intimidating Mohumed Ali Khan, whose pusillanimous character he was well apprised of, he ordered his troops to prepare ladders for scaling the ramparts of the place, himself animating and giving money to the workmen, and promising the highest rewards to his army if the town should be taken, and Mohumed Ali Khan made prisoner. The view of all these preparations, and the reports of some prisoners who were suffered to escape for that purpose, terrified Mohumed Ali Khan in such a manner, that, in spite of everything that Colonel Call could urge, it was decided that an order should be sent to General Smith, to raise the siege of Ballapore, which was already far advanced, and come to the relief of Oscota. The general, to whom the danger of Oscota had been magnified, was obliged to comply with this order, though so very prejudicial to his operations. Mohumed Ali Khan was encouraged by the return of General Smith; but was determined to run no more risk of falling into the hands of Hyder, but to return without delay to Madras. Colonel Call's colleague was of the same opinion; and General Smith alone not being a committee of the council, was obliged to follow them; and that more especially, as nothing less than his whole army was necessary to escort them. They were under the necessity, at their departure, of leaving at Oscota all that immense quantity of artillery and ammunition that was intended to overthrow Bangalore.

Hyder gave himself very little trouble to retake the number of places that were garrisoned by the English, but contented himself with following their army, and harrassing it; which he did in so vigorous a manner, that the terror of Mohumed Ali was not a little augmented.

It was during the time that General Smith marched against Ballapore, that Hyder had the satisfaction of beholding the return of his brother-in-law, Mirza Ali Khan, whose defection had so sensibly afflicted him. This young man, whether from the natural goodness of his heart, or from the contempt shown him by Madurao, the Maratta general, and the other chiefs of that nation,—was continually agitated by remorse for his past conduct; and had long reflected on the means of regaining the friendship of his brother-in-law. But when he saw him abandoned by Nizam, attacked by General Smith on the side of Bangalore, and obliged to hasten with his son to defend the centre of his dominions, attacked by another English army; when he reflected that all the misfortunes of his brother-in-law, the friend and protector of his youth, might with justice be attributed to his ingratitude, his remorse was too keen to admit of longer deliberation. He made levies of troops, quickly placed himself at the head of twenty thousand men, and traversing the kingdoms of Scirra and Mysore, arrived within two leagues of Hyder's camp. Attended by a few horsemen, he advanced to the outposts, where he announced his name, and requested to speak with Mughdoom. Mughdoom, astonished at so unexpected a message, hastened to meet him. "What has brought you here?" demanded Mughdoom with an earnest emotion, when he saw the young prince.—"Repentance," replied Mirza; "I come to repair as much as in my power the injury I have done to our brother. I bring a much better army than I deprived him of; and I offer my head to his mercy: bring me to him." It was in vain that Mughdoom represented that it would be proper to advise Hyder of his arrival.—"No," exclaimed Mirza; "bring me to my injured brother: I fear no consequences but those of not seeing him." Mughdoom told him to follow him, and they soon arrived at the tent of Hyder. The young prince threw himself at Hyder's feet, who raised him, and embracing him—"This is no surprise to me, Mirza," said Hyder; "I have long expected thee." The two armies joined; and every one esteemed this return of Mirza as a happy presage of the return of Hyder's good fortune.

Hyder, after following the army of General Smith as far as Vellore, changed entirely his manner of making war. He divided his cavalry into three bodies; of which he himself took one, and gave the command of the other two to Mughdoom and Mirza, his brothers-in-law: he kept no other troops but his grenadiers, his Caleros, and Carnates, which he likewise divided into three, between himself and his brothers-in-law, so as to form three flying camps. These light armies traversed the whole country, spreading terror and disorder everywhere, and throwing the council and all the English settlements into the greatest consternation. This was a subject of great pleasantry and satisfaction to all the other Europeans in India, most of whom they had insulted in the short period of their prosperity.* By their

* They had demanded that the French deserters, who had arrived at Pondicherry, should be given up, together with the horses they had stolen from Hyder.

They had threatened the government of Tranquebar; and had forced them to give up an emissary they had sent to entice away the men of their garrison.

quick movements the three armies seemed to be multiplied; and the news of their appearance arriving from all parts, it was impossible to determine which way to face; and General Smith's army made a number of useless movements, that harrassed his troops without finding the enemy.

The council determining to divide their army after the manner of Hyder, a body of troops under Colonel Frichman, a Swiss, who had never yet been engaged in service against the Nabob, was entirely cut off; he himself, as it is said, alone escaping by the swiftness of his horse. This colonel was marching in a plain, surrounded on three sides with wood: his army, at most about four thousand men, of which six hundred were Europeans, marched in a long column, when some horsemen appeared at the bottom of the plain. Several of the officers represented to the colonel, that Hyder's cavalry was habituated to make sudden attacks at full speed; and that it would be proper to close the column, and approach the wood, in order to support themselves against it. The colonel laughed at this advice: "Be easy," said he, "you shall see how I will serve these Negroes." The number of horsemen increasing, and no one daring to speak to the colonel, all on a sudden a cloud of dust appeared: the colonel then attempted to give his orders, but there was no time. Three thousand horsemen fell on his little army, and everything was in disorder in an instant. The colonel, in the general confusion, hastened to fly: he was pursued, and the goodness of his horse alone preserved him. Mughdoom, enraged at the massacre of Darmapuri, suffered his horsemen to act with unrestrained fury. Above fifty English officers were slain, or made prisoners. Captain R——,* who had surrendered Vaniambari, and

---

They had compelled the governor of Paliacate, a Duch fort, to deliver up a Frenchman who had taken refuge in that fortress, and had obtained their protection.

* A colonel of Sepoys ranks as captain of Europeans

had engaged not to serve for a year, was taken. It was more than ten months that he had signed the capitulation. He was, as it were, compelled by the governor of Madras to go with his garrison of Sepoys to garrison in Madura, and was on his march wlth Colonel Frichman. Mughdoom Ali Khan, on whom these reasons made no impression, having found him marching in the body of the army, caused him to be hung on a tree, after having refused the other officers the permission to ask his life of Hyder. All these events happened in 1768.

In 1769 Hyder, on his side, being employed following Colonel Wood, who commanded a body of eight thousand men, and in being very near Thiagar, succeeding in falling upon his rear-guard, and forced him to retire into a wood. This colonel was then endeavouring to throw a garrison into a place named Elvanisore. The commandant he had nominated was the captain who stood first in the order of seniority; a brave man, but subject to the vice of drinking to such an excess, as often to render him incapable of giving any orders; however, not to disgrace him, and with the persuasion that Hyder would never undertake the siege, Colonel Wood suffered him to possess the charge. It so happened, notwithstanding that the Prince came before the place with some cavalry, grenadiers, and cannon, without either the means or the intention of making a siege. The captain commandant, absolutely intoxicated, mounted his horse, caused the gate to be opened, and rode directly towards Hyder's troops, demanding to see his highness the Prince. Being conducted to the prince, he represented to him that he was governor of the place, and regarded it as an honour to be besieged by so great a sovereign; that he hoped to deserve his applause by making a brave defence; but that he and his garrison having neither wine nor arrack, he had come, in reliance on his great reputation, to beg he would either give or sell them a provision of both that they might be enabled by their brave defence to give him a new occasion of acquiring glory. Hyder, supposing him to be insane, and not believing him to be the governor of the place, promised to supply him with wine, presenting him with various sorts to taste; so that the captain in a short time was under the necessity of being carried to bed. While he slept off his wine, he was shewn to several people of the town, and they all knew him. On his waking he was informed, that, as he had entered their camp as a spy, it was a decided thing that he should be hanged; but that, if he was really governor of the place, he might give an order to surrender it to Hyder, it being left to his choice, either to give the order or to be hanged. The poor man obeyed, and signed the order; and, what is still more extraordinary, the commanding officer under him obeyed the order, and opened the gates. In this manner Hyder took a place, with a regiment of Sepoys, by the ignorance of him who obeyed the order, by the drunkenness of him who gave it, and still more by the imprudence of Colonel Wood. During the time these affairs were transacting, the son of Hyder and Mirza Fesoulia Khan, under whose command the greatest part of the infantry and artillery were, busied themselves in retaking those places the English had garrisoned; and in fact they retook them all, except Oscota, in which were a strong garrison, and a fine train of artillery, that Hyder hoped to obtain by a treaty of peace.

While the ravages, the success, and the rapid movements of the Nabob held the governor and council in perplexity, a vessel arrived from England with Mr. Dupré, ancient counsellor of Madras, and esteemed a man of great sense and understanding. He was sent out to take the government of that place on the first of January, 1769, and arrived early in March, 1770. He had orders for the governor and council of Madras to make peace on any terms.

The Company were weary of attending to the flattering hopes of conquests that were promised in the letters from Madras. Instead of the diamonds and treasures of Hyder, they saw nothing arrive from Madras but bills of exchange, drawn on them by the government of that place: they therefore thought it their interest to make peace with Hyder at any price, if for no other reason than to prevent the fall of their stock. But it is the great defect of all companies, that even their most essential deliberations cannot be kept secret. The resolution that any power takes to solicit peace, ought above all things to be concealed; and the axiom, *Si vis pacem, para bellum*, deserves the utmost attention. The Company's envoy signified and declared, that a messenger must be despatched to Hyder to request peace. The person charged with this mission received for answer, "I am coming to the gates of Madras, and I will there listen to the propositions the governor and council may have to make." This answer was taken for a declaration, that the Prince was determined to besiege the town. Preparations were consequently made, and orders given to the two armies to unite and encamp near Madras.

Hyder Ali Khan continuing his movements, came near Pondicherry and Godelour, and advanced as far as Collentz, seven leagues from Madras on the Pondicherry road. The English army prepared to defend the passage of the river of St. Thomas, when Hyder suddenly disappeared, and while all the world was at a loss to determine where he was, he all at once showed himself at the gates of Madras on the Paliacat side, and despatched a flag of truce to demand what propositions they had to make. The whole town was instantly in an alarm, the English army being a league and half on the other side. The council deputed Messrs. Dupré and Boschier, the one appointed governor for the year 1770, and the other brother to the then governor. They were received with great politeness. A suspension of arms was agreed on for the environs of Madras only. Hyder promised to establish his quarters on St. Thomas's mount; and on the 15th of April 1770, two treaties were signed to the following effect:

In the first, which is in the name of the king of England, it is agreed, that there shall be peace and friendship between George III.

king of Great Britain, etc.. and Hyder Ali Khan, Bahadoor, Suba of Scirra, etc., and their respective subjects; that all the prisoners shall be given up on both sides; and that there shall be an absolute liberty of commerce between the subjects, and in all the dominions of the two sovereigns, in the same manner as before the commencement of hostilities.

The second treaty between Hyder and Mohumed Ali implied, first, that Mohumed Ali should immediately evacuate the town and fortress of Oscota, which should remain in the same state as at the signing of the treaty; that all the artillery, arms, and ammunition whatsoever should be delivered to Hyder;* and the garrison should retire into the country of Arcot by the shortest road. Secondly, that Mohumed Ali should annually pay a tribute of six lacks of rupees, of which the first year's revenue should be paid down. Thirdly, that all the families of the princes, and other persons of distinction, formerly established in the country of Arcot, and then prisoners, should be set at large, and be at liberty to reside where they pleased.

The other articles of this treaty are not interesting.

The English Company engaged themselves for the performance of this, and promised to present Hyder Ali Khan with a fifty-gun ship,† instead of that which had been seized at Bombay, and was become unfit for service. The Company likewise engaged to supply Hyder with twelve hundred Europeans to serve in his army as often as he

---

* The state of the artillery and ammunition has been given in a former page. It may here be added, that six thousand firelocks were also found in the place.

† This ship was given in 1772 or 1773. It is said that it was a new ship, finely painted and gilt, with all its cannon of brass; but that it was built in such a manner, as to be unfit for any use but parade in a harbour.

should demand it. An engagement of the same nature was already subsisting between the Company and Nizam Daulla, Suba of Decan.

The council of Madras made the most superb presents to Hyder; and that prince, in return, presented them with much more valuable effects, both in gold and silver. The two treaties were made to save the honour of the king and English nation; and consequently the first treaty only was made public by authority. But as there is always an opposition wherever there is an English government, the second treaty was soon made public in England and elsewhere; with such annotations as the interests or opinions of individuals might lead them to make.

Colonel Call, the principal author of the last war, was one of those who most formally opposed the present treaty. General Smith, who had given his opinion for peace whenever Hyder proposed it, being persuaded that it might be concluded on with credit to his country, was, however, against the present peace. He urged, that it was out of the power of Hyder to do any future injury to the English, since it was in his power to prevent that Nabob from undertaking any siege: and he added, that there was no doubt but Hyder would be the first to give up a war he could not continue with any advantage; more especially as his truce with the Marattas expired at the end of the current year; and the prince was too intelligent not to be desirous of finishing the present war before he engaged in another. So that by holding out a short time longer, and refusing his propositions with the same haughtiness as they were made with, he would be forced to recur to those he had made after the siege of Ambour. To all these reasons he joined, that, in signing a shameful treaty with Hyder, they would dishonour the English name, that had never yet received a blemish in any of their wars with the Indians.

We shall finish the history of this war by describing a print, that shews, with considerable accuracy, the different sentiments of those who were then at the head of the Madras government.

There was fixed to the gate of Fort St. George, called the Royal Gate, a design, in which was seen Hyder Ali Khan seated under a canopy, upon a pile of cannon; Mr. Dupré and the other ambassador being on their knees before him. Hyder held in his right hand the nose* of Mr. Dupré, drawn in the form of an elephant's trunk, which he shook for the purpose of making him vomit guineas and pagodas, that were seen issuing from the mouth of this plenipotentiary. In the back ground appeared Fort St. George; and on one of the bastions, the governor and council were drawn on their knees, holding out their hands to the Nabob. On one side of the council, was a large mastiff growling at Hyder, the letters J. C. (for John Call) being marked on his collar; and behind the mastiff stood a little French dog, busily employed licking his posteriors. This last animal was adorned with a star, such as the Chevalier de Christ, Colonel Call's confidant, wore. At a distance were seen the English camp, and General Smith holding the treaty of peace in his hand, and breaking his sword.

By this peace, Hyder Ali Khan Bahadoor gloriously finished a war, which all India supposed would terminate in his ruin.

When Hyder quitted Madras, he marched by the way of Oscota and Bangalore, to dispose of all the artillery and ammunition which the garrison of the former place were commanded to deliver to him. After taking possession of the whole, he dispersed his troops into good quarters, that they might refresh themselves, and be of good service to him in the approaching war with the Marattas, which he knew to be inevitable.

The Marattas suppose they have a legitimate right to one-fifth part of the revenue of certain parts of Hindostan, by virtue of a gift made them by Aurungzebe. Hyder, as we have already observed,

---

* This gentleman is dignified with the nose of an enormous magnitude.

does not acknowledge this claim.* He gives money to the Marattas when the necessity of his affairs does not permit him to refuse it; but he never makes any other treaty with them than a truce for three years, not choosing to own the legitimacy of their demand; and the Marattas themselves are better satisfied with this mode of adjustment, than to continue the war at the risk of being forced to abandon their claim.

Madurao, who was not then arrived at his two-and-twentieth year, and already possessed all the qualities that form the hero, was far from wishing to consent to anything that could prejudice the honour and interests of his nation. He burned with the desire of opposing himself alone against Hyder. In consequence of the different sentiments of the two warriors, the greatest preparations were made on both sides; and the Marattas, as usual, came into the field in November, and approached Scirra in the month of December. They found Hyder Ali Khan encamped near that city; and in spite of all the ardour and courage of Madurao, the position of the prince appeared so respectable that he durst not attack him. But the Marattas being in possession of Maggheri and Mark Scirra, places acquired by the defection of Mirza, had the facility to spread themselves in the plain of Mysore. Hyder was obliged to follow them, and to encamp on the island of Seringapatam, which he had newly fortified, and put under the command of Mirr Fesoulla Khan, with a good body of infantry. As he returned from Scirra by Bisnagar, and kept near the mountains that cover the kingdom of Canara, he covered that kingdom, and could not be surrounded in his march to Seringapatam, though the Marattas harassed him continually.

Very early in the year 1770, Hyder arrived in the island, and was

---

* See page 119.

in perfect security from the Marattas. He suffered them to traverse the country, which he had not laid waste as he did when their nation had joined the English and Nizam Ali. He had no apprehension that the Marattas would employ themselves in sieges like the English; and he relied on the generosity of Madurao, whom he knew to be incapable of destroying for the sole pleasure of doing mischief; that general suffering his troops only to forage, and plunder the flat country, according to their custom.

The Maratta army was composed of two hundred thousand men, of which above one hundred thousand were cavalry. Against such an army Hyder risked much if he lost a battle, and could gain little by destroying a part of them. The Nabob therefore continued in his camp, notwithstanding many feints and temptations that were held out to him by the Maratta general. At length this young warrior pretended to retire, and take the road to the kingdom of Bangalore. Hyder thought he might with advantage follow the enemy in a country that was very favourable to his infantry, who were much superior to those of Madurao. He had already marched nine leagues, and hoped that very evening to gain a covered country, where it would be in his power to gain advantageous positions, as well for the purpose of harassing the Marattas in his turn, as for the easy subsistence of his army. But the Marattas having briskly returned, obliged him to encamp in a place, where indeed he was in no danger of being attacked, but where the enemy entirely invested him, and cut off his communication and means of subsistence from all sides; so that he was obliged to quit his camp, and retire towards Seringapatam. The Maratta army appeared to direct their care and attention to prevent him from following the road to the kingdom of Bangalore and the neighbouring mountains, while they left the road to Seringapatam free. Hyder choosing the night, as the most favourable to his infantry, deposited the greatest part of his artillery and baggage in a fortress, against which he had pitched his camp;* and at about eleven at night he began his march in a square battalion. His infantry was formed into two columns, and his cavalry at the head and rear closed the square, in the centre of which was the baggage, and the artillery at each end. This order of marching did not admit of much expedition; but he had already advanced more than three leagues by four in the morning, when it appeared that they were not pursued, and that probably the Maratta army was unapprised of their march. There were not then more than two leagues to be traversed, before they would arrive at a camp where they might safely remain till night; and one single night would have been sufficient to have brought them to Seringapatam. Every one supposed that nothing was to be feared, when a numerous corps of cavalry, consisting of about twelve thousand horse, appeared drawn up in order of battle, not behind them, as expected, but in front to oppose their march. Hyder ordered the march to be continued, making use of the artillery only to oblige the enemy's cavalry to give way. The cannonade appeared to succeed, and the army marched forward, though slowly; when at day-break the whole Maratta cavalry appeared, and in a short time surrounded Hyder's army. The enemy made several charges, which were well sustained and repulsed; but Mirza, who commanded the cavalry in the van, suffered himself to be hurried away by his eagerness to follow the enemy he had repulsed. He quickly attempted to return, for fear of leaving the infantry without defence; but the cavalry he pursued were close at his heels, and entered the battalion with him. In an instant everything is in the greatest disorder; the army is beaten and

* The Author of the present History was in India at the time of this event; but was not a witness of this stratagem of the Marattas. He gives the recital as he had it from an officer of distinction in Hyder's army on foot.

dispersed; Hyder Ali Khan is himself wounded, and many of his friends slain, and among others Ali Jami Khan, Nabob of Vendevachi. Almost all the troops threw down their arms. A single battalion of grenadier Topasses formed themselves into a close column, and made way by their fire to an eminence, where their commander* died of his wounds. This battalion was led to Seringapatam by a young officer, who was wounded in the shoulder, and was the only surviving officer of the corps.

Hyder, after running the greatest risks, arrived at his camp with the entire loss of his army, artillery, baggage, ammunition, and colours. As it is not customary in India to make prisoners of common soldiers, or even subaltern officers, the greatest part returned to him, though without horses or arms; but, by means of his resources, Hyder established his army, in a short time, in a better state than before. It will scarcely be credited that he purchased again of the Marattas themselves the greatest part of the arms and horses they had taken from him; but this arises from the nature of their government, which is purely feudal, every man having a right to dispose of his share of the plunder as he thinks proper.

Madurao, however, embraced this occasion to begin the formation of a body of Sepoys, with the muskets that fell to his share after the defeat of Hyder's army.

Many French officers lately arrived were present at this battle,

---

* He was a native of Westphalia, who had acquired almost all the languages of India. The Author of this History took him into his service as an interpreter. He was afterwards made captain of grenadier Topasses, at the formation of that body of troops. He died gloriously at the head of his battalion. His name was Lené.—The young officer is a Maltese; his name is Mammou. The Author introduced him to Hyder Ali Khan Bahadoor.

simply as volunteers: they were almost all wounded, and one was killed. M. Hughel, who had formerly served Hyder as commander of the French cavalry from Pondicherry, was wounded, and afterwards died at Tranquebar in consequence of his wounds.

There were likewise several English officers present: and among them Colonel Stewart, who arrested Lord Pigot, and who was reported to have been slain in the present war, in the first battle between Hyder and General Coote.

After this battle, Hyder kept constantly within his camp at Seringapatam; and the greater number of the Maratta chiefs having left the army, on account of their six months' service being expired, Madurao renewed the truce with Hyder, who was obliged to open his purse upon the occasion, though he had promised himself the contrary. This truce was made in July, 1771; but it was for no more than a year.

Mirza Ali Khan, who, as we have observed, was the cause of the loss of this battle, was taken prisoner, and conducted to Madurao, who addressed him thus: "Since you have made war upon us with the power we have given you, we should act properly if we were to take everything from you, and confine you for life; yet, however, if you will swear never to bear arms against the Marattas, I will restore your dominions and your liberty." Mirza took the oath without hesitation: and Madurao having set him at liberty, he departed to his small estate, where he made an absolute donation of all his property, dominions, and troops to his brother-in-law, Hyder; and a few days after became a Fakir, which, in Persian, signifies a mendicant, a man who voluntarily embraces poverty. This class of men make no vows, in which respect they differ from monks, who cannot quit their state; neither do they, like them, live in communities. He wrote to his brother-in-law the reasons that induced him to take this resolution, informing him that he saw no other means of preserving what he had consecrated to his service; and assuring him that if circumstances should in future point out occasions for him to be useful, he should always be ready, however dangerous the service. And, in fact, when Hyder is at war with any other enemies than the Marattas, Mirza takes arms and follows the camp, as he does in the present war against the English.

Hyder employed this short time in producing divisions among the Marattas; and from thence arose the catastrophe that deprived young Madurao of life, to the extreme grief of Hyder.

Raguba, uncle of Madurao, having performed the functions of general during the minority of his nephew, beheld himself, not without great pain, reduced to the state of an individual, after he had secured the dignity that devolved of course to his nephew. During his regency he had filled all India with his fame, and obliged the emperor of the Mogols to fly from Delhi, his capital, which he had destroyed and plundered in such a manner as perhaps never to recover its former splendour; while the emperor himself, by that event, became reduced to a mere phantom, possessing no more than the shadow of the power, the riches, and the grandeur of the ancient emperors.

Madurao, young, ambitious, and elated with his increasing reputation, disdained to listen to the counsels of his uncle Raguba and the other chiefs of his party, which induced the old general to contrive plots for his destruction. Madurao having determined to carry the war into the environs of Delhi, and on the Ganges, found much opposition in the national council: his opinion however prevailed, and he marched with a powerful army at the end of November, 1772, leaving a considerable force in the hands of a Maratta general, named Goupalrao, to carry on the war with Hyder Ali Khan. The army of this general was not at all comparable to that of Madurao when he made war in Mysore; he therefore suffered Hyder to recover Mark Scirra and Maggheri, which produced a suspicion that he was intimidated by the arms, or gained by the bribes, of that potentate.

Madurao did not meet with all the success in the north of Hindostan that he had expected, and marched his army back into the Maratta country. During his march there were many seditions among his troops, most probably in consequence of a plot contrived against the young prince: he was found assassinated in his tent in the year 1773, before his arrival at Poni, the usual residence of the general of the Marattas. As he left only one son, an infant, his uncle Raguba assumed the regency by his own proper authority. The cruel and unexpected death of the young Madurao, who was beloved by his soldiers, gave rise to suspicions among the principal chiefs that Raguba was either the author or accomplice of the assassination of his nephew. A conspiracy almost universal being formed against him, he attempted to collect and form an army of the troops in which he could place most confidence; but he had scarcely began his march against his enemies, when the greatest part of his soldiers left him. Perceiving himself abandoned, he had only time to take refuge among the English at Bombay, who received him with open arms, and promised him assistance. In return for this support, he thought proper to make a treaty, by which he granted very advantageous concessions to the English nation; and among others, never to demand the fifth part of the revenue of all the lands the English might possess in Hindostan.

On the news of this treaty being forwarded to the government at Bengal, General Goddard was despatched from the banks of the Ganges with an army of eight thousand men, twelve hundred being Europeans. With this force he crossed the peninsula, marching about six hundred leagues, in spite of all the petty princes whose dominions he traversed, and at length arrived at the banks of the Sindi or Indus. He found that the Marattas, after having surrounded the Bombay forces, commanded by the governor of that island, had forced him to capitulate; and that the governor had promised to abandon Raguba, to interfere no more in the affairs of the Maratta nation, and had annulled the treaty made with the fugitive general. This last event happened in 1774.

General Goddard, without waiting for any orders, declared the capitulation, as well as the consequent treaty signed by the governor of Bombay, to be null and void. Thus the war commenced again; and this general, who if he had belonged to any other power would have been criminated, had the good fortune to see his audacity crowned by many victories, which however finished by obliging him to act only on the defensive, his successes even destroying his army, and the Marattas seeming to multiply in consequence of their defeats; because they were defending their own homes, and their country is exceedingly populous.

Hyder, who, as we have before observed, had fomented the troubles that agitated the Maratta nation, took, at the beginning, the part of Raguba (which assuredly he would not have done, if he had had only that war to support). In consequence of this proceeding, after the defeat of the regent and the Bombay army, several Maratta chiefs, who supported the party of Raguba, and among them Goupalrao, were forced to throw themselves into his protection. He furnished them with troops, and taking advantage of the distraction of the Maratta nation, in consequence of the victories of General Goddard, he took a number of their strong places, which now form a second barrier beyond Scirra, Maggheri, and Mark Scirra. Though the greatest number of these places are of great strength, and advantageously posted, yet the most part were taken by simple blockade; which occasioned Hyder to employ several years in this war. He did not think proper to take more vigorous measures, for fear of obliging the Maratta nation to accommodate their difference with the English; which, however, was a very difficult thing to be brought about, on account of the horror and aversion that people had conceived against Raguba.

In the year 1775, Hyder profiting by the employment the English gave the Marattas in the defence of their own possessions, embraced the opportunity of sending a small army, under Cina Serrao, a Maratta lord, who had served him from his infancy, to punish the Samorin, and other princes of the Malabar coast. This prince refused to pay the tribute he had consented to give, when Hyder, in 1767, restored his dominions. The Samorin, fearing the anger of the Hyder, thought to secure himself by offering to become a vassal to the crown of France. The commandant at Mahé accepted the gift of the Samorin, and came with a few troops to take possession of the fortress of Calicut, where he hoisted the French standard. This was a most imprudent and inconsiderate step, for many reasons.

First, the commandant of Mahé had not forces sufficient to sustain the consequences of this act; the number of troops on the Mahé establishment being insufficient.

Secondly, he ought not to have made an agreement in the name of the French king, without first being authorised by the commandant general of the French establishments in India.

Thirdly, he could not but know that Hyder Ali Khan was reputed the natural ally of France; and that the Prince had claims on the whole country of the Nayres, by an authentic treaty, concluded by the mediation of his predecessor at Mahé.

Cinao Serrao, Hyder's general, paid all the respect to the French colours which his positive orders to take possession of Calicut permitted him to shew. But he gave advice to his master of all that had passed; and the latter having written to the commandant-general at Pondicherry, the commandant at Mahé was recalled, and Hyder's troops took possession of Calicut, which, as well as the rest of the Malabar coast, has ever since remained under the power of that prince.

Hyder being informed, in the month of August, 1778, that hostilities had commenced between England and France, made a truce of six years with the Marattas, by which they suffered him to retain all his conquests. The time required for the conclusion of this treaty, and the great distance between the Maratta frontier and the Nabobship of Arcot, did not permit Hyder to arrive in time to prevent the capture of Pondicherry, which surrendered in the month of October. The Prince not having arrived on the frontiers before the month of November, laid siege to Chiteldrough, whose lord being a vassal of Mysore, was encouraged by the promise of support from the English to refuse obedience to the orders of Hyder. This place surrendered at the beginning of January, 1779. During the siege, Hyder announced to all India the project he had formed of attacking the English. His principal invitation was to induce Nizam Daulla to attack them to the north of Masulipatam, in order to recover the four provinces they had extorted from him. The Suba promised to make the attack that was proposed to him; but, whether from timidity or the intrigues of the English, he did not keep his promise, but calmly suffered Hyder to bear all the dangers of the war, and to enjoy, without the participation of any other sovereign, the glory of being the liberator of India.

It is proper to mention here, that while the lion-hearted Hyder thus threw terror and dismay into the country of Payanghaut, the Nizam, under pretence of sickness, did not stir from his capital, and the Mahrattas also, after some movements, having by treaty obtained possession of the person of Raghoo (the usurper Raghoonauth) from the English of Bombay, remained where they were, and gave no assistance whatever to Hyder.

In the year 1780, Hyder Shah descended by the Ghaut or Pass of Chungum, and pitched his tents in the environs of Kilpauk, and from the same encampment detached his youngest son Kureem Shah, with the Kuzzak horse or cavalry, towards Muhmood Bundur, while he himself, with his army, marched on and took the small hill-fort of Turnamul. He then besieged the fort of Jeet Peeth, and gave orders to his conquering soldiers to attack the town. After the commandant,

Engd. on Steel by C. Morrish

KUREEM SHAH,

SON OF HYDER ALI KHAN.

who was a Sikh, named Gooroo Buksh, had held out with great spirit two or three days, he was killed at one of the gates of the fort, and the fort was therefore taken. From hence Hyder, after leaving a detachment at the fort of Dhobi Gurh, dispatched his son Tippoo, with a strong body of troops, to reduce Arni and Tumri; and then turning his victorious standards towards the capital of Arkat, encamped near Nimukpeeth and Ghalibpoora, and next invested the fort and town of Alumpunah, against which he ordered batteries to be raised. The chiefs in the fort, namely, Achna Pundit, a Brahmin (otherwise called Raijee Naib Souba, and who had also the title of Raja Beerbur, Bahadur, the founder or builder of the Alum Punah), and Nujeeb Khan Salar Jung, Bahadur, with 5000 regular infantry, 2000 horse, and 400 dismounted ashraf (that is, men of good families), held themselves in readiness to repel their enemies, and filled the capital with stores of provisions, arms, ammunitions, and materials for defence, and then arranged themselves for action. Two or three thousand ashraf or noblemen, inhabitants of the place, of all tribes, who rose in arms merely to defend their families and preserve their honour, were conciliated by a daily allowance, or subsistence, in money, and the show of a great deal of deference and respect, and the gates and bastions of Alum Punah also being confided to the inhabitants of the Muhlas, they fought desperately.

Kureem Shah, meanwhile, when he moved off to Mahmood Bundur, met with no resistance, and having by night marches arrived at the town, he surrounded, and, at the first assault, bravely took possession of it, and plundered the houses of all the wealthy merchants, bankers, and traders of bales on bales of merchandise, and bags on bags of gold and jewels. The next day, the whole of the wealth and commodities taken from all the merchants, who had expended millions of rupees in commissioning or procuring them from different parts of the world for the purpose of barter, were collected in one place. Amongst the rest was the whole of the property of a certain Muhammad Mokrim, a man of the Bohra tribe (the Bohras are a tribe of newly converted Mussulmans, residing mostly in the North Western provinces of India, they are chiefly merchants and traders), the chief of all the merchants, and the owner of three or four merchant ships, who about this time had purchased thirty-five young elephants of eight or nine years old, sixty taukun, or ponies of Manilla and Pegu, and also cloths of great value, and dresses of honour from the countries of Bengal, Bunares, China, Cashmere, Boorhanpoor, Mutchliputtun, etc. All these articles were taken, and laden on elephants, camels, bullocks, and carts, and with the merchant to whom they had belonged, and his dependants, as prisoners, were sent to Hyder.

The prince (Tippoo) after he had taken leave of his father, proceeded to Arni and encamped there, and gave orders to attack the fort. Budruzzuman Khan Bukshi accordingly raised a strong battery to the westward of the fort, and in one day fired a number of cannon-shot into the place. The killedar, or commandant, whose name was Hussain Ali Khan, who even in his dreams had never heard of battle or fighting, much less witnessed anything of the kind, lost all heart, and ornamenting himself with his unworthy arms, and taking the keys of the fort, he sought the presence of the khan above mentioned, and through his mediation was presented to the prince, and delivered up the keys as a paishkush to his servants. He then represented, that in the fort there were many houses inhabited by Syuds, or descendants of the prophet, and being in fear lest the Syudanian, their women, might be insulted or violated, he had given up the fort and its dependencies, but that otherwise he would have defended them as long as he had life. The prince, at hearing this foolish story, laughed outright, and having placed a garrison in the fort, Sidi Imam, an experienced officer, according to the orders of Hyder, was appointed its commandant. Taking with him the former killedar, the prince marched towards

Tumri, the chief of which also gave up his honour to save his life, and without a shot from either gun or musket surrendered the fort. Still advancing, therefore, Tippoo took possession of the small forts of Trivatoor, Gulwa, Kaveripauk, etc., and placing strong garrisons in each, returned to join his own army.

We can give no details of the operations of Hyder in the present war, having no other materials than the relations of the English; and on these we can place no dependance, because they are fabricated in India to deceive the English government, and afterwards arranged in Europe according to circumstances, and the necessity of imposing on the people. So that the only thing that bears the appearance of truth, is a letter from General Coote, in which we see that Hyder is master of the Company; that in November, 1781, he blockaded four places at once; that General Coote marched with his army from Madras to supply those places with provisions, without accomplishing his purpose as effectually as the necessity of the case demanded; that the difficulty of subsisting his army obliged him to bring it back into the environs of Madras; that in his marches his troops had always been harrassed by the cavalry and artillery of Hyder; that he had fought four obstinate battles with Hyder, and gained the field, without speaking of his having taken either prisoners, colours, or standards: to all which he adds, that he sends Colonel Crawford, who will explain the true state of affairs. It may be concluded from this letter, that the English are engaged in a most ruinous war, and that, with the assistance of the French, it may be hoped this prince will succeed in taking possession of the whole Nabobship of Arcot, to which his son has so just a title.

The direct news from Hyder's army gives an account of the capture of Chiteldrough, and the particulars of a council held before they entered the country of Arcot. It was deliberated whether he should attack the English, or wait till the landing of the French forces. The latter it seems was the general opinion, and even that of the European officers; but his son Tippoo Sultaun was of the contrary opinion, and remonstrated that the Prince had threatened so much to attack the English, that his reputation necessarily required him to proceed. Tippoo Sultaun spoke with so much spirit and animation, that he was joined by the whole council. It was this young prince who decided the battle that was attended with the deaths of Colonels Baillie and Fletcher, by taking advantage of the disorder the English army was thrown into by the blowing up of their ammunition waggons, to fall on them with his cavalry. The total defeat of a detachment commanded by Colonel Brawlie is likewise an exploit of Tippoo Sultaun; who having began, like Alexander, to gain battles at the age of eighteen, continues to march in the steps of that Grecian hero, whom he may one day resemble as well by the heroism of his actions as by the multiplicity of his conquests. As to Hyder, we may compare him to Philip of Macedon, who formed the troops that procured the numerous victories of his son, and subdued the Greeks his neighbours, who were the enemies that were the most difficult to conquer.

ADDENDA.

ADDENDA.

Hyder for a long time had laboured under the painful complaint of a cancer in his back, the violence of which had been much augmented by the fatigues of three successive campaigns, and in the month of November, the symptoms of his disorder increasing, he retired from the tumults of a camp to the city of Arcot, where, on the 6th of December, 1782 (the 1st of Mohurrem, A.H. 1197), he terminated his earthly career, aged 82 years, as appears by the statements of his family. His death was for several days kept a profound secret, and the body was privately sent away by night on the road to Sera. By their taking this route, it was probably the intention of his friends to have buried him near his father at Kolar: but, by direction of his successor, the body was conveyed to Seringapatam, and buried with much state, under a magnificent mausoleum, in the garden called Lall Bag.

Hyder Ali Khan was doubtless one of the greatest characters Asia has produced, and if his success cannot be compared with that of Tamerlane or Nadir Shah, it must be attributed more to the competitors with whom he had to contend, than to any want of ability on his part. Without the advantages of education, he acquired an extensive knowledge of the sciences of war and of politics; and by his superior talents, raised himself from a private station to the sovereignty of a powerful kingdom.

He administered justice with impartiality, and gave great

encouragement to agriculture and to commerce. He was indulgent to his subjects, but strict in the discipline of his army, severe in punishing offenders, and cruel to his enemies.

At the period of Hyder's decease, his dominions, exclusive of his conquests in the Carnatic, comprehended nearly 80,000 square miles. His territorial revenues amounted to two krore of rupees, or about two millions sterling; and notwithstanding his army consisted of at least 150,000 men, his treasury contained several millions in bullion and specie.

The day before his death, Hyder threw open the doors of his treasury, and gave all the soldiers of his army—every kutcheri or regiment separately—the amount of one month's pay, as a gift; and, at the same time, despatched two thousand horse to ravage the country of the Poligars, north of Arkat, and five thousand horse towards Madras, for the same purpose, and to alarm the people there. He next sent for some of his chief officers, and gave them strict orders for the regulation of their departments. He did not like great talkers (or makers of long speeches); the subject of conversation in his assemblies was generally relative to the order and regulation of kingdoms and empires, or to swords, muskets, jewels, horses, elephants, or invigorating medicines. His understanding was wonderful. He entertained, to a boundless extent, the pride of rank and station, and the noble desire to attempt great things; but of foolish pride, or vain glory, he had none; he had expelled them from his mind. He was a slave to the regulation of his working establishments or manufactories, and, if any one of the officers or overseers of the works was indolent or neglectful, he sent for him, and punished him according to his offence, telling him, at the same time, "We "gave charge to you of this work, relying on your honesty and "fidelity, why have you spoiled it?" All the operations or measures undertaken by Hyder's government, small or great, were superintended by himself in person; insomuch that even leather, the lining of bullock bags, or tent walls, and strands of rope, all passed under his inspection, and were then deposited in his stores. To horse dealers he gave presents of gold and raiment, besides the value of the horses he purchased; and so liberal was he, that if, on the road through his territories, any horse by chance died, he paid half the price of the horse, after the arrival of the tail and mane, with a certificate from the civil officers of the district. He was, however, the enemy of the indolent and luxurious, and the backs and sides of his negligent and extortionate servants were frequently softened by stripes of the whip. A man that had been removed from his place, after proof of neglect or mal-administration of his duties to government, or of extortion, extravagance, or oppression of God's people, and whose delinquencies were attested by official persons, was never restored to his office.

EXTRACTED FROM CHARLES STUART'S

CATALOGUE AND MEMOIRS

OF

TIPPOO SULTAUN,

PRINTED AT THE UNIVERSITY PRESS, CAMBRIDGE, IN THE YEAR 1809.

TIPPOO SULTAUN was born in the year 1740; his mother was the daughter of Nur Môinaddin, a person of respectable family, and who for several years was governor or lord of the Fort of Kuddapah. During this lady's pregnancy, she, in compliance with a custom frequent among the natives of India, paid a visit to a pir, or saint, to beg his blessing on her child, and prayers for her safe delivery, Her wishes being acceded to, the holy man informed her that her son should become a powerful monarch, and requested she would confer on him the name of Tipu: his commands were obeyed, and the boy, when born, named Futteh Ali, Tipu. His father, sensible of the disadvantages under which he himself laboured from want of education, procured for his son the most able masters in all the sciences cultivated by the Mohammedans, and enforced, by strict discipline, the attendance of the youth to his studies.

The princes and sons of gentlemen in the East are, from an early age, initiated into the martial exercises of riding, shooting, fencing, etc.

In addition to these, Tippoo, as he advanced in years, was instructed in the science of tactics, and attended by his father at all military reviews, in order to acquire a knowledge of the discipline and art of war, more especially as practised by Europeans. His first essay in a military capacity was during the years 1767 and 1768, when Hyder Ali invaded and overran the Carnatic. He at that time commanded a corps of cavalry, with which he committed many depredations, and laid waste the neighbourhood of Madras.

During the four years successful war in which Hyder was engaged with the Marattas, viz., from 1775 to 1779, it is probable Tippoo Sahib had many opportunities of acquiring experience, and of perfecting himself in the knowledge requisite for a general. He was at this period universally esteemed by the army, and the politicians anticipated the glories of his reign.

In the month of July, 1780, when the army of Hyder Ali rushed like a prodigious torrent into the Carnatic, Tippoo Sahib was entrusted with the command of the left division, consisting of 18,000 cavalry, 6,000 regular infantry, and twelve pieces of cannon, destined for the conquest of the northern Circars.

On the 6th of September, Tippoo, being reinforced by 8,000 horse, under the command of his uncle, Ali Riza, generally called Mir Sahib, attacked Colonel Bailey in the neighbourhood of Perimbakum, but, after a very severe contest of several hours, was obliged to retire, without having gained any other advantage than the plunder of his opponent's baggage.

In the subsequent engagement of the 10th of the same month, which terminated in the annihilation of the gallant English army, Tippoo Sahib is said to have taken an active part, and on the blowing up of Colonel Bailey's tumbrils, to have led on the body of cavalry which charged and penetrated the square. For this action he received much applause from his father who, from that period, considered his son as one of his most able generals.

Tippoo was present at the siege and capture of Arcot, the operations of which were conducted with much skill and vigour. He was afterwards actively employed in the sieges of Vellore, Permacoil, Chingleput, and Wandewash: and when, in the year 1781, Hyder Ali proceeded with the main body of the army to the southward, in order to attack Tritchinopoly, Tippoo was left with his division, to carry on the sieges of Vellore and Wandewash.

The victory gained by Sir Eyre Coote at Porto Novo, on the 1st of July, put a stop to the operations against these forts, and compelled the father and son to recruit their forces. Tippoo's next essay and greatest stroke of generalship was the attack and complete discomfiture of Colonel Braithwaite, on the 18th of February, 1782, on the banks of the river Kolerun.

A few months after this event, the English, having concluded a permanent peace with the Marattas, were enabled to employ some part of their forces to make a diversion in favour of the Carnatic. A respectable detachment was sent by sea from Bombay in the month of August, under the command of Colonel Humbertson, to attack the province of Malabar. The troops were landed near Calicut, and in a short time got possession of that city. Encouraged by this success, the Colonel quitted the coast, and directed his operations inland. He took the route of Paligatchery, and, advancing with caution, captured the Forts Paniany, Ramgari, and Mungarry Cottah, with several other strong places, commanding the roads through which the army was obliged to pass.

This measure was attended with all the success that could be expected, and rescued the fertile provinces of Tanjore and Malava from destruction, for, as soon as intelligence of Colonel Humbertson's operations reached Tippoo Sahib, he marched, with the division of the army, with incredible rapidity, to oppose the invaders. The English detachment arrived before Paligatchery on the 19th of October; but Colonel Humbertson, finding the place much stronger than he expected, and it being rumoured that a large force was advancing against him, very prudently determined to retreat. During the first day's march, he was pursued by the garrison, and a large party of Tippoo's cavalry who had preceded the army, and lost much of his baggage and provisions.

It was the intention of Tippoo to get between the English army and the coast, and thereby intercept their retreat, but, although his measures were conducted with great ability and celerity, the prudent precautions adopted by Colonel Humbertson defeated his projects, and the detachment returned safe to Paniany, on the 20th of November, having been pursued and considerably harassed by the enemy during the last two days' march.

Paniany is situated near the mouth of a considerable river, and on the sea shore, about forty miles south of Calicut. Here Colonel Macleod having arrived with a small reinforcement from Bombay, and being a senior officer to Colonel Humbertson, the command of the army devolved on him. He immediately posted the detachment in a strong situation near the sea, threw up redoubts on his flanks and along his front, and requested the commanding officer of His Majesty's ships, Juno and Pondicherry, to anchor the vessels as near the shore as possible, so as to cover the camp with their guns. Scarcely were these arrangements made, when the army of Tippoo, consisting of eight thousand regular infantry, six hundred Europeans, ten thousand cavalry, and an innumerable host of irregulars, encamped in their front, and for several days kept up a distant but ineffectual cannonade. At length Tippoo formed his infantry into three columns, one of which was headed by M. Lally with his Europeans, and made a regular and vigorous attack on the British lines. He was, however, everywhere repulsed and compelled to retreat, leaving two hundred of his men dead on the field.

The Prince acknowledged his defeat by crossing the Paniany river, and placing it as a barrier against his enemy. Several days passed

Engd. on Steel by C. Morrish

TIPPOO SULTAUN.

FROM AN ORIGINAL PAINTING PRESENTED BY LIEUT. COL. DOVETON

TO THE MOST NOBLE MARQUIS WELLESLEY.

without any further attempt on either side, when, on the night of the 11th of December, Tippoo, having received intelligence of the death of his father, suddenly broke up his camp, and proceeded, with all possible haste, to Seringapatam.

It is probable that Tippoo Sultaun reached Seringapatam about the 20th of December, 1782, and, without much display of pomp or ceremony, mounted the throne. After performing the funeral rites of his father (Tippoo Sultaun had a brother named Kurim Shah, he associated much with Fakirs or Derveishes, which conduct gave offence to Hyder, notwithstanding he was a great favourite of his father; he died long after these events, in 1832), and making the necessary arrangements in his government, Tippoo Sultaun returned to Arcot, and assumed the command of the army.

The capture of Onore by General Mathews, and repeated information of the progress of the English arms in the Bednore country and other places on the coast of Malabar, compelled Tippoo Sultaun most reluctantly to relinquish all his conquests and hopes in the Carnatic, and to proceed to the defence of his more valuable dominions. His troops commenced to file off by the Changarnah Pass early in March, 1783; and by the end of that month scarce a Mysorean was left in the Carnatic.

Tippoo Sultaun marched with the utmost celerity, and early in April appeared, with an innumerable army, in sight of Bednore. General Mathews, whose conduct seems to have been a series of errors and malversation, instead of taking post in the defiles of the mountains, which were strongly fortified both by nature and art, and whence he could, in case of necessity, have retreated to Onore, or other strong places on the coast, and where succours might have been conveyed to him by sea, allowed himself to be surrounded, in the defenceless city of Bednore, by the united armies of Mysore, commanded by their monarch in person. The British troops consisted of 600 Europeans and about 1,600 Sepoys; yet, with this diminutive force, the general had the rashness to encounter in the open field the host of Tippoo Sultaun, amounting to nearly 100,000 men; but in a very short period he was obliged to retreat with the loss of 500 of his best soldiers, and compelled to take refuge in the citadel, abandoning the city to the enemy.

The immense force of Tippoo Sultaun enabled him not only to surround the fort, but to send off a large detachment, which in a short time attacked and carried the posts at the head of the Ghats or passes; by which means he not only cut off all hopes of retreat from the garrison, but obtained free access to the low countries.

After seventeen days' hopeless defence, the unfortunate garrison of Bednore was reduced to the necessity of capitulating. The following were the terms agreed on:—

"The garrison to be allowed the honours of war, and to pile their "arms on the glacis. They were to retain all their private effects, "but to restore all public property. They were to be marched by the "shortest route to the sea-coast, and thence conveyed by shipping to "Bombay; and to be supplied, both on the march and passage, with "provisions and every other requisite. The general was to be allowed "a guard of one hundred of his own Sepoys, with their arms and "thirty-six rounds of ammunition."

On the 28th April, 1783, the troops having marched out of the fortress and piled their arms, were led about a mile from Bednore, where they encamped, being surrounded by several of the Mysore battalions. On the following morning, the general with his staff officers were ordered to wait on the prince, and after a short examination, were put into close confinement. Two days after, the field officers, captains, paymaster, and commissaries were sent for, and likewise detained.

The Bukhshy (paymaster) then came to the camp, where all the remaining officers were stripped and searched before him. Much money being found upon them, they were plundered of everything.

They were compelled to march for sixteen days under a burning sun, almost naked, and loaded with irons, to forts in the interior of the country, where they underwent the most grievous imprisonment. Though it is certain that the general suffered a violent death, the manner of it is not known.

The reasons assigned by Tippoo Sultaun for the infraction of the terms of capitulation and such cruel conduct, were embezzlement of the treasure found in Bednore by General Mathews, and the wanton behaviour of the troops on storming of some places in his country.

Immediately after the reduction of Bednore, Tippoo Sultaun marched with his immense army to Mangalore, the recovery of which, being the principal seaport in his dominions, became the first object of his wishes. The place was defended by the 42nd regiment of Highlanders and several battalions of Sepoys, under the command of Major Campbell, an officer of distinguished abilities; but the fortifications were neither well-planned nor in a complete state of repair. Notwithstanding the multitude of Tippoo Sultaun's troops, the chief burden of the siege fell upon the French auxiliaries, who alone managed the batteries; and owing to their exertions, early in the month of July, the works were so much ruined that the assault was daily expected. In this state of affairs accounts were received in camp of peace having been concluded between England and France; when, much to the honour of the French commander, M. de Bussy, and his troops, they declined to act any longer against the English. Tippoo Sultaun was exceedingly hurt at the conduct of France, in concluding a peace without his participation, but much more irritated against the troops who refused to comply with his orders. Sensible of the inefficiency of his own army to prosecute the siege with effect, and stung to the heart at the prospect of losing a place of so much consequence, and which he considered as just on the point of falling into his hands, he used every means, both of promises and threats, to prevail on the French to resume their operations, but in vain, and the detachment shortly after quitted the camp of Tippoo Sultaun, mutually dissatisfied with each other.

The siege of Mangalore was then converted into a blockade, and the garrison was at one period reduced to the greatest distress for want of provisions. Tippoo Sultaun entertained sanguine hopes of being master of the place in a few days, when the arrival of General Macleod, with a considerable reinforcement, and supplies of every kind, sent from Bombay by sea, put an end to his expectations. Negotiations for peace having commenced soon after, Tippoo Sultaun agreed to a suspension of arms; and early in the year 1784, Sir George Staunton, and two other ambassadors from Madras, arrived in camp, and on the 11th of March, a treaty of peace, stipulating the release of all prisoners, and the restitution of all places taken by either party during the war, was concluded. Mangalore, Onore, and all the other forts taken by the English, were in consequence given up. Previous to signing the treaty of peace with the English, Tippoo Sultaun had taken offence at the conduct of the Marattas; and being then at the head of a large and victorious army, he judged it a favourable opportunity to settle his litigations with that nation. He accordingly quitted the Malabar provinces, and passing by Bednore, entered the fertile district of Shanur, situated between the rivers Tumbudra and Kistnah. This country had been for many generations in possession of the ancestors of the Patan Nabob Abd al Hakim Khan, subject however to the payment of a chout, or fourth part of the revenue, to the Marattas. During the year 1777, Hyder Ali had invaded this country, and compelled the late chief of it to become also tributary to him, and to give his daughter in marriage to his son, Kurim Shah. Although thus nearly connected by marriage, the Nabob did not relish the visit of his brother-in-law the Sultaun, but quitting his capital, retired across the Kistnah into the Maratta dominions. As a punishment for this offence, Tippoo Sultaun ravaged the country, destroyed the palace and public buildings, and blew up or erased the fortress of Shanur Bankapur, which served as a citadel to the town.

From Shanur, Tippoo Sultaun proceeded to attack the forts of Darwar and Badamy, both of which he took. The possession of these fortresses gave him complete command of all the Maratta districts south of the Gutpurba and Kistnah rivers.

Flushed by this success, Tippoo Sultaun meditated crossing the Kistnah, and to carry his arms into the heart of the Maratta territories, when the Court of Puna, terrified by his approach, sent ambassadors to mollify his anger and to settle terms of peace. A treaty was concluded about the end of the year 1784, by which Tippoo Sultaun was allowed to retain all the countries then in his possession, excepting Shanur, which he agreed to restore to his brother-in-law on condition of paying a fourth part of their revenues to the Peshwa.

In the year 1785, Tippoo Sultaun forcibly took possession of the district of Adoni, the appanage of Mohabet Jung, nephew of the Nizam. He also seized the remaining territories of the Nabobs of Carnoul and Kuddapah, the greater part of which had been dismembered by his father in the years 1778 and 1779. In extent and revenue these acquisitions were not of much importance; but he thereby obtained possession of the fort of Imtiazghur, esteemed one of the strongest fortresses in Hindustan, and an object much coveted both by Hyder Ali and the Marattas.

He also ordered that provisions, sufficient for the consumption of 100,000 men for one year, should be collected and deposited in the granaries of Seringapatam, and that similar provisions should be made for all his other forts, according to their respective strength and importance.

During the years 1787 and 1788, the Sultaun marched with his troops towards the provinces of the Nairs, and Coorg district, and nominated his generals, M. Lally, Hussein Ali Khan Bukhshi, Meer

Mahomed, and Emam Khan, to attack their towns and forts, they having through the misconduct of their authorities, who had the management of the country, rebelled against the Sultaun. In the space of eight months some 80,000 persons, men and women, were made prisoners, with several chiefs, and many of their strongholds and towns were reduced. The Rajah of Coorg, after a captivity of four years, effected his escape. Shortly afterwards Mamooti Nair died, and Runga Nair became a convert to Mahommedanism, with the rest of the captives: he was named Sheikh Ahmud, and created a chief, or commander; and the above captive proselytes were placed under him, and were as a body called the "Ahumedi Risalah and Asud Eilahie."

He is also said to have carried away from the province of Malabar 70,000 Christians, and to have made Mussulmans of 100,000 Hindus. The conversion of the latter (by forcible circumcision and compelling them to eat beef), although involuntary and abhorred, effectually answered the purpose of the Sultaun, as these people, having lost their own cast, in order to retain any degree of respectability, were obliged to adopt that of their conquerors, and to educate their children in the Mohammedan religion. These being encouraged to enter the army, and obtaining promotion, many of them became zealots, and augmented the number of the faithful in the Sultaun's dominions.

Tippoo Sultaun's zeal for the conversion of his subjects was not, however, confined to the people of Malabar; he extended it to several of the inhabitants of Coimbatore, and to every other Hindu who incurred his displeasure, and had the misfortune to fall into his hands. It is said, that had it not been for the remonstrances of his mother, who was a very sensible woman, he would have compelled his favourite Dewan (prime minister) Purnea to have forsaken the religion of his forefathers.

It was probably about this time, that he issued an edict for the destruction of all the Hindu temples in his dominions, excepting those of Seringapatam and Mail Cotah. He also prohibited the sale of intoxicating liquors, and ordered that all the date and palm trees in his kingdom should be rooted up, and the cultivation of them in future prohibited; though by so doing he greatly decreased the amount of his revenue; but neither of these regulations were strictly enforced by his officers.

He resolved to destroy every monument of the former government; to which end he caused the ancient fort and city of Mysore to be razed, and removed the stones of the temples and palace to a neighbouring hill, where he laid the foundation of a new fort, which he named Nuzerbar. But, in the furiousness of his wrath, he spared not the works of the greatest public utility, in the destruction of the celebrated reservoir of Yadavi Nuddi, because it recorded the wisdom, riches, and power of the ancient Hindu sovereigns.

Immediately after signing the treaty with the English in the year 1784, Tippoo Sultaun had sent an embassy to France, to remonstrate against the conduct of that nation, in having made peace with his enemies, to enter into an offensive and defensive alliance, and to stimulate the court of Versailles to a speedy renewal of hostilities. For this purpose, the Sultaun selected Gholam Ali Khan, and two other learned and respectable persons of his court. But in order to conceal the real object of this mission, he furnished them also with letters and valuable presents for the Grand Signior (by whom they were highly treated and respected), and the King of England.

The ambassadors left India some time in the year 1784, and proceeded to Constantinople, but, meeting with obstacles which caused a considerable delay, they returned to Mysore in the end of 1786.

From the moment of Tippoo Sultaun's accession to the throne, until the day of his death, he never ceased to meditate on the means of subverting the British power in India; and as no method seemed so probable as that of uniting himself in strict alliance with the French, he was not a little disappointed at the return of his ambassadors; but imputing their failure in a great measure to the tedious route they had taken, and to the complicated business which had been assigned them, he determined on sending a splendid embassy direct to Paris. The persons selected on this occasion were Mohammed Derveish Khan, Akbar Ali Khan, and Mohammed Osman Khan. They embarked at Pondicherry, in a French vessel, on the 22nd of July, 1787, and landed at Toulon on the 9th of June in the following year; they were most graciously received by Louis the Sixteenth, who, at their public audience on the 10th of July, displayed all the pomp and grandeur of his court.

The ambassadors again had an audience of his Majesty on the 3rd of August, when they demanded, in the name of their master, the immediate assistance and active co-operation of the French nation, in expelling the English from Hindustan, in return for which, they promised an equal division of the spoils, and of all the territories that should be conquered by the united arms of France and Mysore.

However gratifying this embassy was to the court of Versailles, it was entirely out of the power of the unfortunate Louis to comply with the Sultaun's wishes. Pressed with the load of an enormous national debt, and alarmed by the symptoms of general discontent which soon after burst forth, he could only assure the ambassadors of his friendship for their master, and promises of future assistance, when delivered from his own cares and anxieties.

After remaining a few months in Paris, during which time they were hospitably and magnificently entertained, the ambassadors again embarked for India, and arrived at Seringapatam in the month of May, 1789. As they had not obtained the object of their mission, and, instead of a powerful army, had only brought the empty promises and compliments of the court of France, they were received very coldly by Tippoo Sultaun, who presumed that every circumstance ought to give way to his will, and whose only regard or attachment to the French proceeded from his hopes of their assistance, and his hatred to their common enemy, the English. He therefore scarcely deigned to ask the ambassadors any questions respecting their journey, the state of the countries they had visited, or the situation in which they had left his ally.

The ambassadors, much mortified at this treatment, very imprudently sought an innocent revenge, by relating and describing to their friends the magnificence of the court of France, the splendid cities, its extensive arsenals, its palaces and other public buildings, its numerous armies, and immense population, far superior to any kingdom then existing, or perhaps that ever had existed in the East. Tippoo Sultaun, who considered himself as one of the greatest sovereigns in the universe, could not bear the idea that there existed in the world, and especially among Christians, a monarchy superior to his own; and as the natives of the East generally consider the praises of a rival a reflection on themselves, he was much irritated at such sentiments being promulgated to his subjects; he, therefore, severely reprimanded the ambassadors, and forbid their ever again speaking of France.

Although Tippoo Sultaun had been disappointed in his expectations of assistance from France, his insatiable ambition and restless imagination would not allow him to remain quiet, but excited him, for the sake of getting possession of two petty forts, to risk the dangers of another war. These places were Cranganore and Jyacotta; they had been in possession of the Dutch for 150 years, when, in the year 1779, they were taken by surprise by Hyder Ali. On that nation uniting with him in the war which soon after followed, against the English, the forts were restored.

These places were situated on the northern boundary of Travancore, and were much coveted by the Rajah of that kingdom, one of the British allies, who made frequent offers to purchase them from the Dutch. This circumstance gave much offence to Tippoo Sultaun, who affirmed that as they stood in the territories of a chief (the Raja of Cochin) subject to him, they, in fact, belonged to the kingdom of Mysore.

In the year 1789 Tippoo Sultaun demanded these forts from the Dutch, who, alarmed at his threats, concluded a hasty bargain with the Raja, and put the Travancore troops in possession.

This proceeding highly incensed Tippoo Sultaun, who, in the month of June, 1789, marched with a considerable force towards Cranganore, with an avowed intention of recovering it. The Raja remonstrated, and solicited the interference and assistance of the English. This circumstance further irritated the mind of Tippoo Sultaun, who indignantly turned his arms against the territories of that chief, and upon the 29th of December made an attack on the lines or boundaries of Travancore (these lines commence nigh the sea, and extend along the north and east frontiers to the distance of nearly thirty miles. They were formed about the year 1762, and consist of a good rampart with a parapet defended at proper distances by bastions, and a ditch twenty feet wide by sixteen feet deep, in the middle of which is planted a thick bamboo hedge, forming altogether an excellent barrier. The remaining frontier of Travancore is either surrounded by mountain or sea), but was repulsed with considerable loss. Such conduct being an infraction of the Treaty of Mangolore, by which the security of the Raja's dominions were stipulated, was strongly resented by the English, who immediately sent some battalions of Sepoys to his assistance. This step, however, did not deter Tippoo Sultaun; for on the 6th of March, 1790, he repeated his attack, but was again foiled. He, in consequence, procured some heavy artillery, from Seringapatam, with which, having made an extensive breach, on the 15th of April, he again stormed and got possession of the whole extent of the lines.

The troops of the Raja retreated in good order towards the capital, whither Tippoo Sultaun did not think it expedient to pursue them, but proceeded immediately to the attack of Cranganore, which, after a short but vigorous siege, was compelled to surrender; Jyacotta, Parur, Curiapaly, and several other small forts, were also captured with little or no opposition. The northern district of Travancore being thus subjected, Tippoo Sultaun ordered the lines to be demolished, and laid waste the country with fire and sword.

This aggression being considered by the English as equivalent to a declaration of war, a considerable detachment was sent, under the command of Colonel Hartley, to the assistance of the Raja; and the troops, both of Bombay and Madras, were directed to take the field under the orders of their respective commanders-in-chief. Negociations for an alliance, offensive and defensive, were at the same time commenced with the Marattas and the Nizam, both of whom, convinced of the restless ambition of Tippoo Sultaun, eagerly embraced the alliance, and promised a zealous co-operation of all their forces.

The Sultaun, alarmed at this intelligence, withdrew his army from Travancore and returned to Seringapatam, whence he wrote to the Madras Government, desiring permission to send an Ambassador for the purpose of explaining the reasons and motives of his late conduct. This overture was rejected by General Medows, who, in a laconic reply, upbraided the Sultaun with a gross breach of faith, in not having delivered up all the British prisoners according to the articles of the treaty of 1784, and with having wantonly attacked a favoured ally of the British nation.

On the 15th of June 1790, the army under the command of General Medows, marched from Tritchinopoly, and having in a few days entered the Sultaun's territory, took possession of the Fort of Carur without resistance. Thence the general proceeded to Durapórum and Coimbatore, formerly the capital of an independent Raja, both of which yielded without opposition. A detachment under the command of Colonel Stuart, about the same time captured the forts of Dindigul and Paligatchery.

After placing garrisons and forming depôts in all these forts, it was the intention of General Medows to enter Mysore by the Gwzer Hatty Ghat (Elephant's Pass); and while the main body was employed in collecting grain at Coimbatore, Colonel Floyd was sent forward with his division to take possession of Sattimungulum, which he effected without difficulty. During these operations the only annoyance the English Army had met with, was from a corps of cavalry under the command of an officer named Syed Sahib, and some irregular horse, who occasionally plundered the baggage, and cut off a few stragglers.

As no intelligence had been received of the Sultaun's motion, it was supposed he was still in the neighbourhood of Seringapatam; when on the 13th of September, a reconnoitring party of Colonel Floyd's division fell in with the Sultaun's advanced guards. In a few hours his army, consisting of 40,000 men, with a numerous train of artillery, came up, and commenced a heavy cannonade on the British camp. The action continued the whole day, and numbers fell on both sides; but notwithstanding the Sultaun's great superiority he could not make any impression, and at night withdrew to some distance. Colonel Floyd having determined to retreat towards the main army, was, for want of cattle, obliged to leave great part of his artillery and baggage behind him. The detachment marched off early in the morning of the 14th of September, and was shortly after followed by the enemy. A distant cannonade was kept up during the whole of the day; but at four o'clock, the British troops having halted, a serious action took place, which lasted for three hours; at the end of which the Sultaun, despairing of success, drew off, and allowed the detachment to proceed unmolested to Velladi, which place they reached in safety the next day.

General Medows, on receiving intelligence of the approach of the Sultaun, anxious for the safety of Colonel Floyd's detachment, immediately hastened to his relief; but the guides, instead of taking the road to Sattimungulum, led him to Damiacotta, and the armies, in consequence, passed each other unperceived. The Sultaun, however, considering this march as a manœuvre of the British General to get between him and Seringapatam, fell back, and recrossed the Bavany river, on the northern bank of which he encamped in a strong position, while the British troops, having effected a junction, returned to Coimbatore.

The movements of the Sultaun's army were, in general, totally unknown in the English camp. He was enabled, by the great number and excellent state of his cattle, to march with great rapidity wherever he chose, while his irregular horse, always hovering about, seized and frequently murdered the persons employed to procure intelligence, and at the same time gave the Sultaun information whenever the British troops got under arms.

The government of Madras, finding that the force under General Medows was not of sufficient strength to effect anything of consequence against the Sultaun, resolved to re-inforce him by the addition of a considerable army under the command of Colonel Maxwell, originally formed for the protection of the Carnatic, but which had been lately employed in the reduction of the Bara Mahal district. Colonel Maxwell, in consequence, received orders to proceed towards Coimbatore, while General Medows moved to the northward in order to form a junction of the two armies. The Sultaun's scouts having brought him intelligence of these operations, he immediately marched to meet the Colonel, and having, by the celerity of his movements, outstripped General Medows for three successive days, cannonaded the army of the former and endeavoured to bring on a general engagement; but Colonel Maxwell being in expectation of the arrival of the grand army, contented himself with taking up a strong position and remaining entirely on the defensive. On the 19th of November, the Sultaun being informed of General Medow's approach, hastily decamped, and permitted the armies to join without further opposition at a place called Pulamputty, sixteen miles south of Kistnagurry.

The Sultaun, finding himself unable to oppose the united forces of the English, determined to adopt the plan of warfare pursued by his father, and instead of defending his own territories, to lay waste, with fire and sword, those of his enemy. In place, therefore, of returning to Mysore, he directed his march to the southward, with an intention of entering the Tanjore country and of making a sudden attack on Tritchinopoly; but on his arrival at the Colerun he was much chagrined to find that river so much swollen as to render the crossing of it, if not impracticable, at least imprudent whilst closely pursued by the English army, who might intercept his retreat. Disappointed in this quarter, he wheeled to the left, and taking his route through the middle of the Carnatic, burnt and destroyed all the villages on the road; and, about the middle of December, invested the fort of Thiagur; but that fortress being well garisoned, baffled all his attempts, and he was compelled, after seventeen days, to raise the siege. Thence he proceeded by the route of Trinomaly, Chittaput, and Wandewash, committing his usual depredations, imprisoning the Brahmins, and defiling the temples. He afterwards marched to Pondicherry, probably with expectation either of receiving some assistance from or of renewing his connections with the French; but the governor having pledged himself to observe a strict neutrality, he was disappointed in these hopes. He, however, had the good fortune to capture the fort of Permacoil in that neighbourhood.

During this campaign, Tippoo evinced considerable abilities, and by his conduct completely defeated the views of the English, who, instead of being masters of great part of Mysore as they had expected, found themselves attacked and annoyed in the very neighbourhood of Madras.

The arrival of Lord Cornwallis (Governor-General and Commander-in-Chief of all the forces in India) early in the year 1791, with considerable supplies of men and money from Bengal, added to the advance of the Maratta and Nizam's armies, quickly changed the face of affairs and compelled Tippoo to quit the Carnatic and return to the defence of his own territories.

On the 29th of January 1791, Lord Cornwallis assumed the command of the army at Velhout, and on the 5th of February marched for Vellore, where he arrived on the 11th of the same month. The Sultaun, expecting that the English army would enter Mysore by the Ambur or Ryacotta Passes, had drawn all his forces to these quarters; but Lord Cornwallis, on quitting Vellore, turned to the north, and, before the Sultaun was aware of his intentions, had got possession of the Mugley Pass and with little difficulty entered his country. The forts of Colar and Ouscotta surrendered to the British arms without resistance in sight of a large body of the Sultaun's cavalry, who had been hastily detached to lay waste the country and burn up all the fodder on the route which the English had taken.

On the 5th of March, Lord Cornwallis encamped before Bangalore, and on the following day the Sultaun arrived and took a position on the opposite side, placing the fort, as the object of contention, between the two armies. On this day, the British cavalry, being employed to reconnoitre, fell in with a division of the Sultaun's army, which they attacked, but, after a severe contest, were obliged to retreat with considerable loss. On the 7th, the Pettah, or town of Bangalore, was taken by assault, and many of the Mysoreans killed. During the assault, the Sultaun drew out his army and advanced some of his guns to cannonade the British camp, but with little success.

The batteries having played for nearly a fortnight on the fort, and a breach almost effected, the Sultaun attempted to postpone its fall by forcing the English to a general engagement. He, in consequence, drew out his army on the morning of the 17th, but, after a cannonade of some hours, again returned to his camp without effecting his purpose.

On the night of the 21st of March, the fort was taken by storm, the governor, with 1,000 of his best troops, were killed, and the remainder of the garrison made prisoners. On this event the Sultaun retired to some distance and wrote to Lord Cornwallis, requesting a truce, and begging permission to send an ambassador for the purpose of negociating a peace. But these overtures not being favorably received, he left the army under the command of one of his generals, to watch the motions of the English; and proceeded to Seringapatam, to prepare for the defence of his capital, for the fate of which he now began to be alarmed.

On the 28th, Lord Cornwallis marched from Bangalore to the north-east, with an intention of forming a junction with the troops of the Nizam, and of meeting a considerable convoy on its way from Ambur. During this day's march, the Sultaun's army kept in sight, but did not approach within reach of the guns. On the 13th of April, the English were joined by the army of the Nizam, consisting of 15,000 cavalry. It appears very extraordinary, that the Sultaun did not attempt to prevent this junction, as from the undisciplined state of the Nizam's troops, who more resembled a rabble than the army of a Prince, there is little doubt, that an attack on them would have proved successful.

Lord Cornwallis returned to Bangalore late in April, and on the 3rd of May commenced his march to Seringapatam; on the 12th, he encamped at Arakery, within sight of the Sultaun's capital.

The Sultaun had drawn up his army in a strong position on the northern side of the Kavery, covered in front by swamps and ravines. Here he was attacked early in the morning of the 15th, by Lord Cornwallis, and after a severe engagement, compelled to retreat under cover of the guns of the fort.

Some days previous to the arrival of the Madras army, the forces belonging to Bombay, under the command of General Abercromby, had arrived and taken post at Periapatam, a short distance to the westward of Seringapatam. It was Lord Cornwallis's intention to have formed a junction between the two armies; but the rains having set in, and the rivers considerably swollen, this measure was found to be impracticable. This circumstance, with several other obstacles which occurred, determined his Lordship to postpone his attack on the capital until another campaign. He in consequence directed General Abercromby to return with all expedition to Malabar. The want of cattle obliged the General to leave his battering train, and great part of his ammunition, behind him. He was also much harassed in his retreat by the Sultaun's cavalry, who plundered part of his baggage, took some prisoners, and killed several of his men. The gunpowder, having been all lodged in a celebrated Hindu temple in Puriapatam, was by order of the Sultaun set fire to, which not only destroyed the temple, but great part of the town.

The Sultaun's troops had so well obeyed his orders for the destruction of every kind of forage in the neighbourhood of the British camp, that scarce a blade of grass was to be found. The cavalry was half dismounted, and the cattle of Lord Cornwallis were daily dying by hundreds. His guards on the roads were also so diligent, that not a bullock load of grain could reach the camp; and all communication with the allies was so completely cut off, that no intelligence respecting the Maratta armies, under the command of Purseram Bao and Harripunt, who, long before this period, ought to have arrived at Seringapatam, could be obtained. Thus situated, Lord Cornwallis was compelled to destroy his battering train of artillery, throw his shot into the river, burn his carts and tumbrils, and on the 26th of May, commence his retreat towards Bangalore. On this occasion the guns of the ramparts fired a royal salute, Seringapatam was illuminated, and the courtiers congratulated the Sultaun, on having thus defeated the intentions of his enemies in a second campaign.

But the Sultaun, who had daily intelligence of the victorious approach of the Maratta armies, was sensible that, although the danger was suspended it was not averted. He therefore directed a letter to be written to Lord Cornwallis soliciting peace; and sent it out early on the morning of the 27th, accompanied by some presents. Unfortunately for the Sultaun, previous to the arrival of his envoy in the English camp, the Maratta army had arrived, bringing with them abundant supplies of every kind, and it appearing by the contents of the Sultaun's letter, that his object was to dissolve the confederacy, and to form a separate peace with the English, Lord Cornwallis returned his presents, with an answer, That he could not listen to any proposals, in which the allies were not included; but that, previous to commencement of any negociation, it was requisite he should deliver up, bonâ fide, the British prisoners of every description. The Sultaun positively denied having any prisoners in his possession; and finding he could not detach Lord Cornwallis from the general cause, resolved to try his efforts on the other confederates, and to brave the dangers of another compaign against the English.

The junction of the Marattas having restored plenty to the English camp, Lord Cornwallis was enabled to continue some time longer in the neighbourhood of Seringapatam; but as it was impossible immediately to replace the battering train and other stores, which had been destroyed, without which the siege could not be attempted, his Lordship resolved to employ his armies during the monsoon, in those districts of Mysore which had not yet felt the effects of the war; also to open a communication with the Carnatic, and to collect, at Bangalore, ample supplies of every kind for the prosecution of the ensuing campaign.

On the 6th of June the allied armies commenced their march, and taking a circuituous route by Nagmungall, Hulydurg, Outredurg, and Savendurg, arrived on the 7th of July, in the vicinity of Bangalore. Here the armies separated; the greater part of the Marattas proceeded towards Chittledurg, the Nizam's cavalry towards Gunjcotta, and the English to Bangalore.

The fort of Oussore was, about the middle of July, captured by a detachment from Lord Cornwallis's army, in which neighbourhood the English army remained the greater part of the month of August, and was here joined by a very numerous and valuable convoy from the Carnatic. During this period the Sultaun made another unsuccessful attempt to open a negociation. His ambassador on this occasion was named Apagy Rao, by birth a Maratta, but so much detested by his countrymen for having attached himself to the Sultaun, that he was obliged to solicit a guard of British troops to protect him from their fury. As it was useless to enter into any discussion with such a person, he was sent back to his master without obtaining an audience from Lord Cornwallis.

During the months of August, September, and October, numerous forts situated on the roads leading to the Carnatic and Hyderabad were captured by the English and their allies. The principal of these were Anchittydurgum, Oudeadurg, Ryacotta, and Nundydurg. The latter was taken by storm, after a siege of three weeks, although it had cost Hyder Ali three years to take it from the Marattas.

Whilst these operations were carrying on in the north-west quarter of Mysore, the Sultaun, having received intelligence that the district of Coimbatore, situated to the south of Seringapatam, was defended by a very inconsiderable force, sent a detachment to subdue it. His troops were at first repulsed, but being reinforced by an army under the command of Cummeraddin Khan, that General succeeded in taking prisoners Lieutenant Chalmers and the whole of his party, consisting of nearly 1000 irregular troops, and a company of regular Sepoys.

The Sultaun about this time marched with a very considerable force towards Bednore, in order to meet a valuable convoy coming thence. His approach caused some alarm to the Marattas, under Purseram Bao, who were besieging the fort of Chitteldurg; but the Sultaun, having effected his purpose, quietly returned to Seringapatam.

Lord Cornwallis having opened a free communication with the Carnatic and the territories of the Nizam, resolved to subdue the forts situated between Bangalore and Seringapatam. Of these Savendurg and Outradurg were the most important. Savendurg is so well fortified by nature and art, that it has been generally considered as impregnable. The atmosphere of the surrounding country, likewise, is conceived to be so extremely noxious (this is generally the case with the hill forts of India), that from this circumstance the fort has obtained the title of the Rock of Death. The Sultaun had such an opinion of its strength and unhealthiness, that when informed of the intentions of the English to attack it, he expressed his joy, asserting that half of the European troops would be destroyed in the attack, and the remainder would fall a sacrifice to the climate.

On the 10th of December, 1791, Lord Cornwallis approached this terrific fortress, and after a siege of eleven days took it by storm, without the loss of a single man. Outradurg was also taken on the 24th of December, by assault, without any loss on the English side. The troops of the Sultaun were so panic-struck, that as soon as the Europeans mounted the wall, they all fled. Ramgurry and several other small forts were also reduced, with little trouble; and all the whole of the strong country between Bangalore and the Kavery, acknowledged the sovereignty of the conqueror.

While the British forces were thus actively employed, the army of the Nizam was occupied in the siege of Gurrumcondah (this fort was made over to the Marattas by the Nabob of Kuddapah, in the year 1758, but was taken from them by Hyder Ali), from August to November. Their efforts were only crowned by the capture of the lower fort, or Pettah, when the season being arrived for again forming a junction with Lord Cornwallis, a considerable detachment was left, under the command of an officer, named Hafizjie, for the protection of their new conquest; and the remainder of the army proceeded about the middle of December, under the orders of the Nawab Sekunder Jah, towards Kolar.

On the 21st of December, the detachment of the Nizam's troops, left to guard the town or lower fort of Gurrumcondah, was surprised by Prince Hyder Sahib, the eldest son of the Sultaun, who having with 12,000 horse advanced with great rapidity, stormed the Pettah, and took the whole of the Moguls prisoners. After reinforcing the garrison, and withdrawing the families of several chiefs from the fort, he returned unmolested to Seringapatam.

It was before stated, that on the separation of the allied army in the month of June, the Marattas, under the command of Purseram Bao, had proceeded towards Chitteldurg, one of the strongest forts in the Mysore dominions. On their arrival in its neighbourhood, the Bao, finding there was no probability of taking it by force, endeavoured to bribe the Governor to surrender his trust; but failing in this expedient, he encamped for some time in its neighbourhood, and laid waste the country; after which he proceeded to the westward, and by the assistance of the English detachment under Captain Little, succeeded in capturing Huly Honore, and some other small forts.

The provinces of Canara and Bednore being the only part of the Sultaun's dominions which had not been overrun by, or in possession of the allies, he continued to draw his supplies from them, but apprehensive that the Marattas would cross the Tumbudra, and invade these districts, he sent a considerable force under the command of his cousin, the Nawab Aly Riza Sahib, to defend them. This officer took post near the western bank of the Tum, with the fortress of Simoga in his rear.

On the 25th of December, 1791, the Marattas crossed the river Budra, and on the following day, the Tum, both of which were fordable. On the 28th the English detachment, supported by their allies, attacked the Mysorean army, and after a very severe contest, obtained a complete victory. The Nawab escaped with 1,500 infantry and 400 cavalry to the fort of Culydurg, situated thirteen miles from Bednore, to which place he had previously sent off his elephants and treasure.

On the 31st of December, batteries were erected against Simoga, and, after a siege of four days, the garrison capitulated.

The Marattas remained in the neighbourhood of Simoga until the middle of January, 1792, when the Bao proceeded towards Bednore. On the 28th, he came within sight of that fortress, and ordered an attack to be made on some of the outworks; but, on the following day receiving intelligence that Cummeraddin, one of the Sultaun's most esteemed generals, was advancing with a large army to the defence of Bednore, he resolved to retire, and, according to his agreement, join Lord Cornwallis in the siege of the Sultaun's capital. He accordingly commenced his march, but did not arrive at Seringapatam until after the treaty of peace had been settled.

When the Sultaun received intelligence of the defeat of his cousin, Ali Riza, he immediately ordered Cummeraddin Khan to proceed to the defence of Bednore, and instructed him not to pursue the Marattas, but, having driven them away, to employ his army in collecting supplies, which he was to forward, whenever an opportunity offered, to Seringapatam.

About the same time, the Sultaun detached a party of predatory horse to lay waste the Carnatic, hoping thereby to withdraw some of the British troops employed against him, in defence of their own territory. His parties advanced within three miles of Madras, killed several people, and burnt some of the villages. The Sultaun, however, finding that little success was likely to attend such operations, now renewed his applications to Lord Cornwallis, and requested permission to send ambassadors for the adjustment of all differences; but his lordship, irritated at the Sultaun's late breach of faith, immediately sent back his messengers with a verbal answer that no amicable communication could be held with him, until he had released the prisoners taken at Coimbatore, whom he had detained contrary to the terms of capitulation.

Lord Cornwallis having collected immense supplies of every kind of provision, and having prepared his battering train of artillery with every other requisite for the siege, finding it in vain to wait longer for the Marattas under Purseram Bao, advanced, on the 1st of February, 1792, from Outradurg, accompanied by the armies of the Nizam and Harrypunt. During this and the following day's march, about one thousand of the Sultaun's cavalry attempted to cut off some of the baggage; but failing in this, they set fire to the villages, and drove away the cattle and inhabitants. On the 5th, the allies encamped within sight of Seringapatam, about five miles to the north of the river Kavery. The Sultaun had drawn up his army in a very strong position, nearly on the ground occupied by his father in the year 1767; but the whole space, excepting the rear, was now surrounded by a thick-bound hedge, and strengthened with formidable redoubts, amply supplied with artillery, and covered by the heavy guns of the fort. His force consisted of forty-five thousand infantry, five thousand cavalry, and one hundred pieces of cannon.

Lord Cornwallis, having reconnoitred this truly formidable position, resolved to attack it, and without informing the allies of his intention, marched at nine o'clock of the night of the 6th of February, with eight thousand seven hundred of the British infantry (without cannon) divided into three columns, and, after a severe contest, he not only obliged the Sultaun to abandon his position, leaving all his artillery behind him, but also succeeded in securing the ford of the river, and occupying the eastern part of the island.

During the 7th the Sultaun made several attempts to regain possession of the redoubts on the north side of the river, and to drive the English out of the island; but all his efforts proved ineffectual, and the spirit of his troops being quite broken, they deserted in great numbers; and even the French in his service, either wearied with his capricious humour, or supposing everything lost, gave themselves up to Lord Cornwallis.

On the eastern point of the Island of Seringapatam is situated a very delightful garden, named Lal Bag, ornamented with several palaces, and rendered sacred by the mausoleum of Hyder Ali: this garden was taken possession of on the night of the 6th, when the British troops crossed the river; and it being found impossible to procure any other materials for making fascines or gabions, Lord Cornwallis was under the necessity of permitting the cypress and other beautiful trees to be cut down for that purpose. The palaces and cloisters were, at the same time, converted into hospitals for the sick and wounded.

The Sultaun's proud mind was much irritated at seeing this charming spot, to ornament which he had bestowed so much pains, thus laid waste, and the tomb of his father contaminated by those whom he considered as infidels. He vented his rage in a continual discharge of cannon from the fort, directed at the garden, and every other post within sight, occupied by his enemies. Some of his shot even ranged into the English camp on the other side of the river; but the distance was so considerable, that this ineffectual cannonade only served to shew the state of the Sultaun's mind, without benefitting his cause, or destroying a man of his enemies.

When this ebullition of passion had evaporated, the Sultaun began seriously to reflect on his perilous situation; and seeing no hopes but in the forbearance and clemency of the victors, he resolved again to address Lord Cornwallis on the subject of peace. To this end he directed Lieutenants Chalmers and Nash, who had been taken prisoners at Coimbatore (and whom, although he had detained them contrary to the orders of capitulation, he had treated with more indulgence than any European that had ever fallen into his power), to be brought to him. On the evening of the 8th of February, these officers were introduced: they found the Sultaun seated under the fly of a tent, pitched on the south glacis of the fort, apparently much dejected, very plainly dressed, and with very few attendants. He informed them it was his intention immediately to release them; and that, as he had been long desirous of peace, he wished to make them the bearers of letters to Lord Cornwallis on that subject; to which he requested Lieutenant Chalmers would return with an answer. Then having given the letters in charge to that gentleman, he presented him with two shawls and 500 rupees; after which he promised that his baggage and servants should be shortly sent, and ordered horses and attendants to convey him and his companions to the English camp, where they safely arrived early in the next day.

On the morning of the 10th, a party of the Sultan's horse being mistaken for a troop of the allies, were permitted to enter the British camp. They inquired for the tent of the commander-in-chief, but the person whom they addressed, supposing they meant the commandant of artillery, pointed out to them the tent of Colonel Duff, towards which they immediately galloped, cutting down every person they met on the road; but the alarm being given, they were fired on by some of the Park guards, and obliged to make a speedy retreat.

On the 16th of February, Lord Cornwallis was joined by the Bombay army, under the command of General Abercromby, consisting of 2,000 Europeans and 4,000 Sepoys.

On the night of the 18th, a formidable battery was erected on the north side of the fort, at the distance of only 800 yards; and on the 19th, the army under General Abercromby crossed the Kavery, and took post on the south-west side. This manœuvre was opposed by the Sultaun in person, with a very considerable force of both cavalry and infantry; but after a sharp contest, the Sultaun was obliged to return to Seringapatam, leaving his adversaries in possession of the ground they had chosen.

On the 22nd, General Abercromby's advanced posts were vigorously attacked; but after a contest which lasted the greater part of the day, the Mysoreans were again compelled to retire, without effecting their purpose. During these operations, negociations for peace were also carrying on. On the 14th, the agents of the Sultaun were met, at a tent pitched for the purpose, by those of the allies, and their discussions continued on the 16th, 19th, and 21st; but nothing decisive was adopted until the 23rd; when, everything being prepared for erecting a breaching battery within 500 yards of the fort, and the numerous Maratta army, under Purseram Bao, daily expected to assist in the operations of the siege, the Sultaun at length agreed to cede to the allies one-half of his dominions, the annual revenues of which were worth 90 lacs of rupees (£900,000); to pay them, in the course of twelve months, the sum of three krore, and 30 lacs of rupees (£3,030,000); to restore all prisoners taken by himself or his father; and to deliver up two of his sons as hostages for the due performance of the treaty.

On the morning of the 24th of February, hostilities ceased; and on the 26th, the Princes arrived in camp with considerable pomp. They were mounted on an elephant richly caparisoned, accompanied by several other elephants preceded by a number of persons mounted on camels bearing flags, and 100 running footmen armed with polished javelins, a guard of 200 Sepoys, well dressed and disciplined, with a party of cavalry, brought up the rear. Lord Cornwallis, attended by the principal officers of his army, met the Princes at the door of his state tent, and after embracing them, seated them one on each side. The eldest, named Prince Abdul Khalic, was about ten; the younger, Prince Moaz Addeen, nearly eight years of age. As soon as the ceremonies were adjusted, Ghulam Ali, the Sultaun's principal agent, addressed his Lordship: "This morning, these children were the sons of the Sultaun, my master; their situation is now changed, and they must, for some time to come, look up to your Lordship as their father."

Lord Cornwallis assured the agent and the Princes (through

the medium of an interpreter), that every attention possible would be shewn to them; and that nothing in his power should be wanting to render their situation pleasant. He then presented each of the Princes with a gold watch, mounted with diamonds, as a testimony of his friendship; after which, the beetel-nut and perfumes being distributed, his Lordship accompanied the princes to their elephant, where, having again embraced them, they were conducted to a handsome suite of tents (sent for their use by the Sultaun), with the same ceremony they had entered the camp.

The following day, Lord Cornwallis returned the Princes' visit; on which occasion he was received with much state and ceremony, and on his departure was presented with two Persian scimetars.

The politeness and attention shown to the Princes by his Lordship was a source of much satisfaction to the Sultaun, and to the ladies of his family, whose affection and fears had led them to suppose that the hostages would be kept under a rigid and irksome confinement.

Notwithstanding the delivery of hostages, and the payment of one krore of rupees to the allies, it was evident that the Sultaun was still procrastinating, and seeking for some subterfuge by which he might evade the fulfilment of the treaty. After the first week, no more money was sent to the camp; and the Sultaun's agents pretended that the revenue accounts of many of the provinces were lost. They also attempted to give in statements overrating the districts adjoining the dominions of the allies, and underrating those they supposed not likely to be claimed. Their last effort to gain time was by overrating the specie, or coins of Mysore, much above their intrinsic value; all of which artifices caused some delay and much litigation.

During this period, it was observed that the Sultaun's people still continued to repair the ramparts, and even to erect new works inside the fort, contrary to the agreement of the armistice and the custom of war. On Lord Cornwallis remonstrating against this conduct, the Sultaun replied that his Lordship was misinformed; but if it would afford him any satisfaction, he would direct one of the bastions of the fort to be thrown down, in order that the English engineers might survey Seringapatam to advantage.

The Curg Raja having been found one of the most faithful and useful allies to the English during this war, Lord Cornwallis had early resolved to deliver him from the oppressions of the Sultaun. In compliance, therefore, with the first article of the treaty, the Sultaun was required to relinquish all authority over, and every claim to, the territories of that chief. The Curg province being contiguous to Seringapatam, and far removed from the territories of any of the allies, it had never entered the imagination of the Sultaun or his agents that it would be among the districts claimed. Such a demand was, therefore, quite unexpected by the Sultaun, who harbouring the utmost animosity against the Raja for his late conduct, had determined in his own mind to wreak his vengeance on that prince and his unfortunate subjects. On the perusal of this article, he was irritated to a state of frenzy: he vowed he would rather set fire to his capital, and perish with his whole family in the flames, than comply with this harsh requisition. He then ordered the agents to retire from his presence, and never again dare to mention the subject to him.

On the return of the agents to camp, and their report of the Sultaun's determination, Lord Cornwallis, resolving no longer to be trifled with, issued orders for the renewal of the siege. He at the same time directed the attendants of the Princes to be disarmed, and informed the hostages, that they must prepare to march next morning towards the Carnatic.

The Princes were much affected by this intelligence, and joined with the agents, in requesting that his Lordship would postpone his resolution for one day longer, during which time, they hoped the Sultaun would be induced to comply with his Lordship's wishes.

On the 16th of March, Purseram Bao, who, with his division, had joined the army a few days before, crossed the Kavery, and formed a junction with General Abercromby, to be in readiness to invest the south side of the fort; but the Marattas, either not considering themselves as included in the armistice, or the chiefs being unable to curb the predatory habits of the soldiery, commenced ravaging the country, and captured a number of camels and cattle, which they found in the neighbourhood of Mysore.

The Sultaun, whether forced by the desertion and disobedience of his troops, or persuaded by the entreaties of his friends, his mother, the Empress, and the Begums of his Seraglio, at length submitted, and affixed his seal and signature to the definitive treaty, which deprived him of half his dominions.

The Sultaun took this opportunity to remonstrate against the conduct of Purseram Bao and his Marattas, whom he requested Lord Cornwallis would either order to recross the river, or permit him to march out of the fort, and punish them with his own troops.

On the 19th of March the young Princes, attended and escorted as when they first arrived in camp, came to perform the ceremony of delivering the definitive treaty to Lord Cornwallis and the allies. They were received by his Lordship with the greatest kindness and attention; and after some general conversation, Prince Abdul Khalic arose, and delivered the definitive treaty in triplicate to his Lordship. The agents of the Nizam, and the Marattas, were not then present; but as soon as they arrived and were seated, Lord Cornwallis having returned two copies of the treaty to the young prince, desired him to deliver them to those persons: the prince complied, but apparently with much constraint and dissatisfaction. The Maratta, on receiving his copy, made use of some expression; to which the Prince replied, "At all events you may be silent, *your master* has no reason to complain."

The Princes having completed the ceremony, and delivered this testimony of their father's submission, took their leave, and returned to their tents. Thus ended the last scene of this important war.

It is stated, that for a considerable time after the allies had departed from the neighbourhood of Seringapatam, the Sultaun shut himself up in the most retired part of his palace, and was for many days inaccessible to any person; at length, wearied by brooding over his misfortunes, he yielded to the solicitations of the Begums of the Seraglio, and admitted his favourites, Mir Saduc and Purniah, in order to consult with them on the posture of his affairs, and on the means of replenishing his treasury. It was soon determined, in this council, that it was the duty of all loyal subjects to contribute a portion of their wealth, to make good to their monarch the sums forced from him by his enemies. The Sultaun, however, to evince his moderation and generosity, consented to relinquish thirty lacs of the sum he had been compelled to pay; and orders were issued for three krore of rupees (£3,000,000), in addition to the usual taxes, to be levied in regular proportions from the diminished number of his subjects. Had this contribution been impartially and scrupulously assessed, it would not have been attended with any great distress to the subject; but the collectors took advantage of the order, not only to make their own fortunes, but to bribe the Asophs, or lord-lieutenants of the provinces; and in lieu of three, ten krore were collected, the burden of which fell principally on the cultivators of the soil, whose complaints could never reach the ears of the Sultaun, who, after his late humiliation, had become inaccessible to his subjects.

The Sultaun had, soon after his accession to the throne, formed a new code of revenue regulations, in which he had increased not only the number, but also the power of the officers; and instead of imitating the wise conduct of his father, in protecting the cultivator from the oppressions of the collector, he appeared indifferent to the conduct of the latter, provided the revenue due to government was realized.

The Sultaun's next care was to recruit his army, and although it was represented to him that his diminished revenues were not adequate to the expense of so great an establishment, he declared he would not reduce a single battalion. He, however, gave orders for several forts, which had not made that resistance against the allies which he had expected, to be dismantled; and was so disgusted with Bangalore for having served as the grand depôt of the English army, that, although its fortifications had cost him and his father many millions, he directed them to be levelled with the ground.

The garden called Lal Bag, which had proved so useful to the allies during the siege, and which had been injudiciously used as a burying-place for the Europeans, was purified by digging up all the bodies, and throwing them into the river, the mausoleum of Hyder Ali was thoroughly repaired and new painted, and every possible measure taken to efface the vestiges of its late possessors. These (with the exception of replacing the trees) were soon obliterated. But the besiegers had left a trace on the mind of the Sultaun, which no time could annul. Previous to the late war, the Sultaun had opened a correspondence with Timur Shah, King of the Affghans, or Abdallies, whose dominions are situated between Persia and India. To the successor of that Prince he now addressed himself, imploring him to form a league with the Mohammedan chiefs in Hindustan, and to advance to the conquest of Dhely. Agents were also employed at the Courts of the Peshwa, Dowlet Rao Scindia, and the Nizam, to foment jealousies, to excite disturbances, and to break their connection with the English. Even the court of the old and supposed faithful ally of the British nation, Mahommed Ali of the Carnatic, was not free from the intrigues and machinations of the Sultaun. This plot commenced almost immediately after the arrival of his sons at Madras; and, long before these hostages were released, the British President at Puna gave information to the Governor-General, that a secret correspondence was carrying on between the Sultaun and the Peshwa. In short, from the conclusion of the war, to the year 1796, letters or embassies were, from time to time, sent to every chief, or person of consequence, from

Taheran in Persia, to the mountains of Nepal, who was supposed either to bear any enmity to, or likely to benefit by the downfall of the English; exciting them to unite with the Sultaun, the defender of the Mohammedan faith, in driving that ambitious nation from India. During this period, fortune seemed inclined again to favour the views of the Sultaun, in raising up new enemies against the English, and by exciting domestic dissensions, at the courts of the allies. In the year 1794, Fyzullah Khan, the Rohilla Chief of Rampore, died, and was succeeded by his eldest son. This prince, in the course of a few days, was assassinated by his younger brother, Ghulam Mohammed, who forcibly took possession of the government. The English, having espoused the cause of the son of the murdered prince, defeated and took Ghulam Mohammed prisoner. He was conveyed to Calcutta, where under a pretence of going on a pilgrimage to Mecca, he embarked on board a ship, probably landed at one of the ports in the Sultaun's dominions, and thence made his way to the court of Kabul, where he united with the agents of the Sultaun in clamours against the English, and in urging Zeman Shah to invade Hindostan, promising that, on his approach to Dhely, he should be joined by the whole tribe of Rohillas.

The extensive conquests of Dowlet Rao Scindia, and the great increase of his power, having awakened the jealousy of the court of Puna, that chief had been required to pay a proportion of his revenues into the public treasury, but instead of so doing, he made out very extensive demands against the government, and marched to the capital with a numerous army to enforce his claims, thereby setting at defiance the authority of the Peshwa, and laying the foundation of the civil wars, which have since shaken every part of the Maratta empire.

At the court of Hyderabad, the great age and indisposition of the Nizam rendering it probable that his life would not be of long duration, his sons began to intrigue for the succession. The Sultaun clandestinely espoused the cause of Feridun Jah, and detached a well appointed army, under the command of Syed Ghuffar, towards that quarter, under pretence of collecting his revenues from the tributary chiefs; but with secret orders to act as circumstances might require. Another army was at the same time assembled in the vicinity of Seringapatam under the immediate command of the Sultaun. All these circumstances served to awaken the jealousy, rouse the vigilance, and stimulate the exertions of the British government.

In the year 1796, the Mysore Raja Chiaum Ray died, leaving an only son, then an infant of three years old, to inherit the dignity of his ancestors, but the Sultaun would not now condescend to acknowledge even a nominal superior.

In the end of this year, or the commencement of 1797, an army of Affghans crossed the river Attock, and attempted to proceed towards Dhely. They were, however, so warmly opposed by the Seik chiefs, that, after losing a considerable number of men, they were obliged to retreat. This expedition was probably undertaken by Zeman Shah, in compliance with the proposals made by the Sultaun to that Prince, in his first plan, for attacking the English; and it so far alarmed the British government, that a large force was assembled at Mindy Ghat, on the western bank of the Ganges, avowedly for the purpose of opposing the invasion.

The intrigues and military movements of the Sultaun at this period (although his correspondence with the Shah was not then known) rendering it probable that he meant to take advantage of these circumstances to invade the Carnatic, the Madras army was also ordered to take the field; and an expedition which was fitting out against the Spanish islands in the China seas was, in consequence, relinquished.

The retreat of Zeman Shah's army from Hindustan, the premature discovery of the intrigues of Feridun Jah, and the menacing position of the English armies, combined to prevent the Sultaun from engaging in any open scene of hostility or any overt act of insult against the

British nation; although several months previous to this period, he had privately despatched ambassadors to the Mauritius, to renew his connexions with France, and to solicit the aid of 10,000 Europeans and 30,000 negro troops. The discovery of this transaction, and the ineffectual assistance sent to him by his friends, drew again on the Sultan the vengeance of the British arms before he was properly prepared to resist them.

In the month of June, 1798, the Governor-General of India (Marquis Wellesley, then Lord Mornington) received an authentic account of the arrival of the Sultaun's ambassadors at the Mauritius, and of all their subsequent proceedings. This glaring proof of the Sultaun's intentions leaving no room for doubt or hesitation, orders were immediately issued for assembling the armies, and the most active preparations for war were made throughout British India. The Governor-General did not, however, confine his precautions and preparations to his own territories; effectual measures were at the same time taken to annihilate the party of the Sultaun and the French at the court of Hyderabad, and to enable the Nizam to co-operate against the common enemy. An attempt was also made to unite the discordant parties at the court of Punah; but the mutual jealousies of the Maratta chiefs, some of whom were probably in the interest of the Sultaun, rendered it impossible for the Peshwa to fulfil his engagements, or to take any part in this war.

The Governor-General being thus prepared, but averse to rush unnecessarily into an expensive and uncertain war, deemed it proper first to admonish the Sultaun, and leave it in his power to terminate the differences between the two governments in an amicable manner by proper apologies. He in consequence addressed several letters to the Sultaun, in which he carefully avoided every hostile expression, merely apprising him that his intercourse with the French was perfectly known, and proposing that Major Doveton might be sent to him on the part of the allies, for the purpose of forming an amicable arrangement. The answers to these letters were replete with prevarication, and the proposal respecting Major Doveton entirely evaded.

During this period, intelligence reached the Governor-General of the operations of the French in Egypt, and of the embarkation of Monsieur Dubuc at Tranquebar, ambassador from the Sultaun to the French Government. A knowledge of these circumstances rendered any further delay inexpedient; and orders were in consequence issued on the 3rd of February, 1799, for the British armies, and those of the allies, immediately to invade the Sultaun's dominions. Ten days subsequent to these orders, a letter was received by the Governor-General from the Sultaun, in which the latter stated that, "being frequently disposed to make excursions, and hunt, he was "accordingly proceeding upon a hunting excursion, and that his "Lordship might despatch Major Doveton to him slightly attended."

On the 11th of February, the grand army, under the command of General Harris, marched from Vellore, and, on the 28th of the same month, was joined at Karimungalum by the Nizam's forces, with 6,000 subsidiary British troops in his Highness's pay.

On the 4th of March, the combined armies encamped near Ryacotta, on the frontier of Mysore; whence a letter from the Governor-General was despatched to the Sultaun, acknowledging the receipt of his last epistle, and referring him to General Harris for further explanation.

On the 5th of March, hostilities commenced by the capture of the forts of Neeldurgum and Anchitty; and on the 9th, the united army, consisting of nearly 37,000 fighting men, which had advanced in several columns, was assembled in the vicinity of Kelamungalum. Previous to this period, the Bombay army, consisting of nearly 70,000 men, had marched from the Malabar coast, and having entered the district of the Curg Raja, had taken post at the head of the Sedapore and Sedasir passes.

Whilst the enemies of the Sultaun thus advanced in formidable array, *his* army was essentially diminished in numbers, and much inferior in discipline to what it had been at the commencement of the last war. His finances were also deranged, and his councils perplexed by contrary opinions; in addition to which, his spirits were dejected and broken by the disappointment of his hopes of French assistance, by the retreat of Zeman Shah from Hindustan, and by the failure of his intrigues at the Court of Hyderabad. He, however, again despatched ambassadors to Kabul, and sent either agents or letters to Persia, to Puna, and to every chief from whom he could have the smallest hopes of assistance.

On the Sultaun's being convinced that his enemies were about to enter his territories, he marched with the greater part of his army from the neighbourhood of Seringapatam, and took post at Madur, on the high road leading to Bangalore; whence he detached several bodies of horse, to lay waste the country, and to burn all the forage on the route by which the allies should advance. The Sultaun continued in this situation until his spies brought him intelligence that the Bombay army had approached his western frontier, and were encamped in several divisions at Sedasir, Sedapore, and Ahmutinat. Judging from this disposition, that General Stuart had no expectation of being attacked, and hoping to find him unprepared, the Sultaun decamped suddenly from Madur on the 3rd of March, and on the morning of the 6th, having drawn up his army, amounting to 12,000 men, in three columns, advanced under cover of a thick wood to attack the British advanced post, consisting of three battalions of Sepoys, under the command of Lieut.-Colonel Montresor. These he completely surrounded; and, although they defended themselves with much perseverance and resolution, they must shortly have been annihilated, had they not been reinforced by a large detachment of Europeans, headed by General Stuart, who joined them about three o'clock. The Sultaun's troops then gave way and retreated, leaving a great number dead on the field, and several of their principal officers wounded.

After this discomfiture, the Sultaun returned to Periapatam, where he remained until the 11th of March. He then proceeded to Seringapatam, where, having rested his troops for four days, he again marched to meet the army under General Harris.

The allied army moved, on the 10th of March, from Kelamun gulum, and on the 14th encamped within sight of Bangalore. During these four days' march, the Sultaun's horse were actively employed in burning the forage, and destroying the villages on the route. The army halted at this encampment during the 15th, which circumstance induced the officer commanding the Mysore cavalry to suppose it was intended again to make Bangalore the grand depôt, as it had been during the former war. He therefore set fire to all the villages in that neighbourhood, and even spared not the Pettah or the suburbs of that city, the fortifications of which had been demolished during the peace.

On the morning of the 16th, General Harris marched to the south-west, having determined to proceed to Seringapatam by Cankanelly and Sultan Pettah. This movement was the cause of great surprise and disappointment to the Mysoreans, who, wishing to spare their own country as much as possible, had hitherto neglected to destroy the villages or burn the forage on *that* route.

On the 23rd of March, the Sultaun very imprudently quitted his strong position on the banks of the Madur river, the passage of which he might have disputed with great advantage, and encamped at Malavelly. On the following day, the allied army encamped on the ground so lately occupied by the Sultaun.

On the 27th, General Harris marched towards Malavelly, and, on his arrival at that place, found the Sultaun's army drawn up in readiness to receive him. As soon as the British line could be formed, it advanced in regular order, and commenced a heavy fire, both of cannon and musketry, which was returned with great spirit; but the Sultaun, finding he could not effect anything, thought it prudent to retreat; and as no advantage could be derived from a pursuit, General Harris ordered the troops to return and encamp at Malavelly. The Sultaun lost, on this occasion, three of his best officers, and had 1000 men killed or wounded.

On the 29th, the allied army marched towards Sosillay, and, immediately commenced crossing the Kavery. This manœuvre was also totally unexpected by the Sultaun, who concluded that General Harris would advance by Arakery, and take up the position occupied by Lord Cornwallis during the last war, on the northern bank of the river. The Sultaun was so strongly impressed with the idea of General Harris pursuing the same route, that he neglected to give orders for the destruction of the grain and forage on the southern side of the river; and fearing that a sudden attack would be made on his camp he obliged his troops to lie under arms during two nights.

As soon as the Sultaun perceived his mistake he ordered his infantry and artillery to proceed to Seringapatam, while he himself crossed the river with his cavalry, and on the 2nd of April, approached sufficiently near to reconnoitre the British camp. Having made his observations, he gave orders for his infantry to cross the river with twenty pieces of cannon, and to occupy some rising ground, by which the allies would be obliged to pass, on their way to Seringapatam. Reflecting, however, that it might be more prudent to preserve his troops for the defence of his capital, he countermanded these orders, and directed the infantry to encamp close under the east and south faces of the fort.

During the period which had intervened since the year 1792, the Sultaun had been constantly employed in strengthening the fortifications of Seringapatam; but with the exception of a large battery, consisting of ten guns, which he had erected on the north-west angle of the fort, his improvements had been confined to the south and east sides. Here he had also thrown up strong entrenchments, extending from the Dowlet Bag to the Periapatam Bridge, which, being within seven or eight hundred yards of the fort, were perfectly commanded by its guns, and afforded an excellent shelter for a number of his troops, for whom he had not room inside the fortress.

On the 5th of April, the army under General Harris took up its ground in a strong position, opposite the west face of Seringapatam, at the short distance of 3,500 yards. On the following day, the General succeeded, after a severe contest, in dislodging some parties of the Sultaun's troops, who had taken post in an aqueduct, and several ruined villages in front of the camp, and compelled them to retire.

When the Sultaun saw the position his enemies had chosen, against which his improvements and entrenchments on the south and east sides were of no avail, he gave orders for two new entrenchments to be thrown up along the western face of the fort, one on each side of the river. That on the western bank extended from the Periapatam Bridge to the south bank of the Kavery, inclosing the whole of the ground occupied by his cavalry during the last siege.

On the 9th the Sultaun, being seriously alarmed, endeavoured to open a correspondence with the British commander-in-chief, and addressed to him the following letter:—"The Governor-General, "Lord Mornington Behadur, sent me a letter, a copy of which is "enclosed; you will understand it. I have adhered firmly to treaties. "What then is the meaning of the advance of the English armies, "and the occurrence of hostilities? Inform me: what need I say "more?" To this General Harris briefly replied, by referring the Sultaun to the letters of the Governor-General, in which he would find every circumstance minutely explained.

On the 11th, the Sultaun's new entrenchments on the island being completed, part of his infantry were encamped within it, and on the following day he opened a heavy cannonade on the British camp, which only served to show the great distance his guns carried, one of the shot having nearly reached the tent of the commander-in-chief at the distance of two miles and-a-half.

On the evening of the 14th, the Bombay army joined General Harris, and took post in the rear of his encampment; but early on the morning of the 16th they crossed the Kavery, and occupied a strong position on the northern bank of that river.

On the evening of the 20th, General Harris attacked the entrenchment on the south west bank of the river, which, although occupied by 1,800 of the Sultaun's infantry, was carried without the loss of a man on the British side. In retaliation of this injury, the Sultaun ordered a select corps of 6,000 of his infantry, led on by all the French troops in his service, to cross the river as soon as it became dark on the night of the 21st, and proceed to attack the army of General Stuart. This service was intrusted to Mir Ghulam Hussein and Mohammed Halim, both of them esteemed generals, who executed their orders with great spirit, and at two o'clock in the morning of the 22nd, assaulted the whole line of the advanced posts of the Bombay army; but after maintaining the attack for several hours, having lost six or seven hundred men, and fearing the advance of General Stuart with all his force, they prudently retired.

On the 20th, the Sultaun again addressed a letter to General Harris, expressing a desire for peace; and, on the 22nd, a draft of the terms, on which it would be granted by the allies, was sent to him.

The proposed preliminary treaty consisted of eleven articles, the principal points of which were, that the Sultaun should immediately dismiss all Europeans from his service; that he should for ever renounce his connexion with the French nation; that he should cede one-half of his dominions to the allies, and pay them the sum of two krore of rupees (two millions sterling), one-half immediately, and the remainder in six months; that he should immediately release all prisoners, and that he should deliver four of his sons, and four principal officers, as hostages for the due performance of the treaty. Twenty-four hours only were allowed to the Sultaun to signify his assent to or rejection of these terms.

Although the operations of the siege had not commenced until the 9th of April, nevertheless by the evening of the 24th, all the guns on the west face of the fort were silenced, the west cavalier and north-west bastion were also dismantled, and the fire of the fort reduced to a few guns in the south face, and some distant cavaliers; but as the Sultaun's troops still retained possession of part of the entrenchment and a redoubt on the western bank of the river, which impeded the erection of breaching batteries, General Harris issued orders for their being attacked. Notwithstanding the entrenchment was within reach of the musketry of the fort, and was defended by Syed Ghofar, with 1,500 men, a successful assault was made on the evening of the 26th; and although the Sultaun's troops behaved with great bravery, they were not able to withstand the persevering attacks of the European columns, but were forced to retreat across the river, with the loss of 150 men.

On the morning of the 28th, the Sultaun addressed the following letter to General Harris:

"I have the pleasure of your friendly letter (of the 22nd), and "understand its contents. The points in question are weighty, and "without the intervention of ambassadors, cannot be brought to a "conclusion. I am therefore about to send two gentlemen to you, "and have no doubt but a conference will take place. They will "personally explain themselves to you. What more can I write?"

To this proposition the General replied, by referring the Sultaun to the terms which he had forwarded on the 22nd, as the only conditions on which the allies would treat. General Harris also declined to admit the ambassadors unless accompanied by the hostages and specie required, and insisted on an answer before three o'clock of the following day.

On the night of the 1st of May, all the batteries having been completed, next morning at sunrise the besiegers opened a dreadful fire on the fort. Their guns were principally directed against the western curtain, about sixty yards distant from the north-west bastion, and with such effect, that before night a breach was made in the fausse-braie wall, and the main rampart very much shattered.

On the evening of the 3rd, the breach being reported practicable, scaling-ladders, fascines, and other materials, were sent to the trenches, and before the day broke on the following morning, all the troops destined for the assault were placed under cover, ready to rush on as soon as the signal should be given.

During the last fortnight of the siege, the Sultaun inhabited an apartment in one of the gateways, called Cullaly Didy, on the northern rampart, in order to be near the place of attack; he having frequently said, " that he would defend the fort to the last extremity, " and that, *as a man could die only once, it was of little consequence,* " *when the period of his existence might terminate.*" He, however, was strongly impressed with an idea that Seringapatam could not be taken, which idea was supported by his courtiers, who, if sensible of the danger, were afraid to tell him the truth, and were daily saying to him, " *that the English would be obliged to raise the siege for want of* " *provisions, and that their shot had produced little effect on the walls.*"

Early on the morning of the 4th of May, the Sultaun repaired to the western rampart, and, having carefully inspected the breach, perceived that his situation had now become very critical. He, however, did not betray any symptoms of fear, but gave his orders to Mir Ghofar, who commanded the troops in the vicinity of the breach, with great coolness and precision.

On the Sultaun's return to his apartment, an incident occurred which tended much to depress his spirits, and to diminish the courage of his attendants. A procession of Brahmin astrologers now waited on him, and announced that some dreadful misfortune would befall him on *that day*, unless averted by the prayers of the righteous and pious offerings.

Whether the Sultaun's mind was now depressed by fear, or tainted by superstition, he repaired to his palace, and issued orders for *all the ceremonies* prescribed by the Brahmins to be duly performed, and having given them several presents, requested their prayers for the prosperity of his government. He also ordered to be sacrificed two elephants with all their golden trappings; in the four corners of each of the cloth covers were placed an immense quantity of pearls, sapphires, rubies, and emeralds, and a large sum of gold mohurs were distributed amongst the beggars.

About noon, the Sultaun again quitted the palace, without visiting his family. He was dressed in a light-coloured jacket, with trowsers of fine chintz, a sash of red silk, and a rich turban. He wore two embroidered belts with precious stones, in one of which was his sword and from the other was suspended a cartouch box. He had also tied on his right arm a talisman, composed of prayers and verses of the Koran, enclosed in a silver case. On his arrival at the Cullaly Didy, the Sultaun received intelligence, both from his spies and the officers on duty, that, from the preparations making in camp, and the number of men seen in the trenches, it was evident that the English would make an attack, either during the course of that day or at night. He replied, that it was improbable they would make an attack during the day, and that in the evening he should take such precautions as would baffle every attempt of his enemies. A short time after this conversation, information was brought to the Sultaun that Syed Ghofar, who commanded at the breach, had been killed by a cannon shot. He was a good deal agitated on this intelligence, and exclaimed, "Syed "Ghofar was a brave man, and feared not death: he has obtained the "crown of martyrdom. Let Mohammud Casim take charge of the "breach."

It being the hour of dinner, the Sultaun's repast was served up; but, before he had time to finish it, he was disturbed by the noise of the attack. He instantly washed his hands, buckled on his sword, and ordered his fusils to be loaded. He then hastened along the northern rampart towards the breach, followed by a number of servants carrying various arms, and attended by several chiefs, with a select guard. When the Sultaun had arrived within 200 yards of the breach, he was met by the fugitives, and perceived that the head of the English column had forced the breach and mounted the ramparts. He endeavoured to stop his flying troops, and having taken post behind one of the traverses, encouraged his men, both by his voice and example, to make a determined stand. He repeatedly fired on the assailants; and his servants declare that several of the Europeans fell by his hand. Notwithstanding these exertions, when the front of the English column approached the spot where he stood, most of his attendants having deserted him, the Sultaun was obliged to retreat. While any of his troops remained with him, he continued to dispute the ground; till having arrived at a bridge leading to the inner fort, he mounted his horse and endeavoured to enter the town; but on his arrival at the gate, the passage was so much crowded by the fugitives, that he could not make his way through them. Whilst in this situation, a party of his pursuers fired into the gateway, and wounded the Sultaun in the left breast. He, however, attempted to push on, but was stopped by the fire of a party of Europeans (the light infantry of the 12th Regiment, soon after mounting the breach, discovered a narrow passage over the ditch into the inner fort, which much facilitated the capture), from withinside the gate. From these he received a second wound in the right side: his horse at the same time sunk under him, being severely wounded, and his turban fell to the ground. The fallen Sultaun was immediately raised by some of his faithful adherents, and placed upon his palankin, under the arch, in one of the recesses of the gateway. It was at this time proposed to the Sultaun, by one of his servants, that he should make himself known to the English, from whose general character there could be no doubt he would meet with every attention compatible with his situation; but this he disdainfully refused. After a short interval, some European soldiers entered the gateway, and one of them attempting to take off the Sultaun's sword belt, the wounded Prince, who still held his sword in his right hand, made a cut at the soldier, and wounded him about the knee; when the latter instantaneously fired his musket and shot him through the temple, which caused immediate death. Thus fell the haughty and ambitious Sultaun, preserving, to the last moment of his existence, *that* animosity against the British nation to which, under the decree of Divine Providence, may be ascribed his ruin, and the subversion of his empire.

The English having got complete possession of the fort, and having obtained information respecting the fate of the Sultaun, the commanding officer (General Baird) came in the evening to the gateway, attended by the Keladar and several of the Sultaun's servants, to search for the body. After much labour it was found, and brought from among a heap of slain. His eyes were open, and the body was so warm, that for a few moments Colonel Wellesley and others were doubtful whether he was not alive: on feeling his pulse and heart, that doubt was removed. He had four wounds, three in the body, and one in the temple, the ball having entered a little above the right ear, and lodged in the cheek. The countenance was no way distorted, but had an expression of stern composure. The turban, sash, sword, and belt were gone, but the body was perfectly recognised by the attendants, and, being again placed on the palankin was conveyed to the court of the palace, where it remained under a guard during the night.

During the time which elapsed from the death of the Sultaun until the discovery of his body, the English had taken nine of the princes, his sons, prisoners, and had placed guards upon every part of the palace, to prevent the escape of any person from it; also to take care of the treasure, and other valuables therein. It next became requisite to secure the families of the chiefs, who, in consequence of the jealousy or mistaken policy of the Sultaun, were all compelled to reside at Seringapatam. Safeguards were immediately sent to every house, and thankfully received by the inhabitants. This measure much facilitated the conquest of Mysore; as these officers, finding their honour and property respected by the conquerors, threw themselves on the clemency of the English, and submitted themselves and their troops to the disposal of General Harris. Twelve of the Sultaun's sons were made prisoners. Such of them as had arrived at the age of manhood, were sent with their families to Vellore, at which place, in the year 1806, under the administration of Sir William Bentinck, evil-disposed persons fomented disaffection and mutiny amongst the East India Company's native troops in garrison, and they rose against their officers and tried to destroy the Europeans, the real cause of which was disagreements between their commanders and themselves. In the course of this disturbance, the dangers of which the princes and their families shared with all others residing within the fort, some of the mutineers made use of the name of one of the princes, and so raised a suspicion that was quite unfounded, of their having been instigators of the plot and conspiracy that produced that outbreak. It was in consequence determined, after the mutiny was suppressed, in order to prevent a similar use being again made of their name, to take the princes and their families away from Vellore, and to require all the members of their family to fix their residence at Calcutta, where they have resided submissively ever since, and it is generally known they are extremely grateful for the continued justice and kindness they have received from the British government.

There were found in the fort 929 pieces of ordnance, and 287 were mounted on the fortifications, 99,000 muskets and carbines,

83 powder magazines, and an immense number of shot, shells, etc. The value of the treasure and jewels was estimated at £11,143,216 sterling. The number of troops in the fort, and on the island, on the morning of the assault, was 21,839; of these several thousands shared the fate of their master, and many were killed in attempting to escape over the ramparts.

General Harris having given orders that every possible respect should be paid to the remains of the deceased Sultaun, the preparations for the funeral were superintended by the principal Cazy of Seringapatam. No expense was omitted on this occasion, and the ceremony was performed with as much pomp as time and circumstances would admit. The bottom of a *state palankin* served as a bier, on which the body was placed, wrapped up in muslins, and covered by a rich brocade.

On the afternoon of the 5th of May the funeral procession, escorted by four companies of Europeans, moved from the fort. The bier was carried by the servants of the deceased, and was attended by Prince Abdul Khalic (the second son) as chief mourner, the Keladar, the Cazies, and other Mussulmans of Seringapatam, and was met at the entrance of the Lal Bag by all the Mohammedan chiefs of the Nizam's army. The streets through which the procession passed were lined with inhabitants, many of whom prostrated themselves before the body, and expressed their grief in loud lamentations. When the procession reached the gate of Hyder Ali's Mausoleum, the troops formed a street, and, as the body passed, *presented arms*. The Cazy then read the funeral service; after which the Sultaun was laid close to the remains of his father, and a charitable donation of 12,000 rupees was distributed to the different fakirs and poor persons who attended the funeral.

From the time the procession commenced until the body was deposited in the ground minute guns were fired from the ramparts, and, to add to the solemnity of the scene, the evening closed with a most dreadful storm of thunder, lightning, and rain.

A plain tomb of marble has since been erected over the grave (which has been carefully preserved in good order, and all the ceremonies usual to the Mohammedan faith are strictly observed by Government, for which treatment of his memory his family are sincerely grateful), and the following epitaph, supposed to be written by one of the Nizam's officers, suspended near it. In Roman characters, it may be rendered—

"Typu Sultan, chu kurd, âzmi jihad, huk 'bdu munsebi shehadat, dad
Sali tarikhi o, shehir biguft, hamy din, shahi zemaneh, biruft

"Gooftu e syed Abd ul Cadir

"A. H. 1213." "Shehir Takhallus.

Thus translated by a celebrated Oriental philologer:

"As Tippoo Sultaun vowed to wage a holy war, the Almighty "conferred the rank of Martyrdom upon him, the date of which "Shuheer declares thus: 'The Defender of the Faith, and the "Sovereign of the World, hath departed.'

"Composed by Syed Abd al Cadir,

"A. H. 1213." "Called, poetically, Shehir.

N.B.—Each of the letters of the fourth line having a numerical power, when added together make 1213, being the date of the event.

Tippoo Sultaun, at the time of his death, had nearly completed his sixtieth year. He was not of a dark complexion, as it is generally said, but, for an Indian, was reckoned fair, inclined to corpulency, and

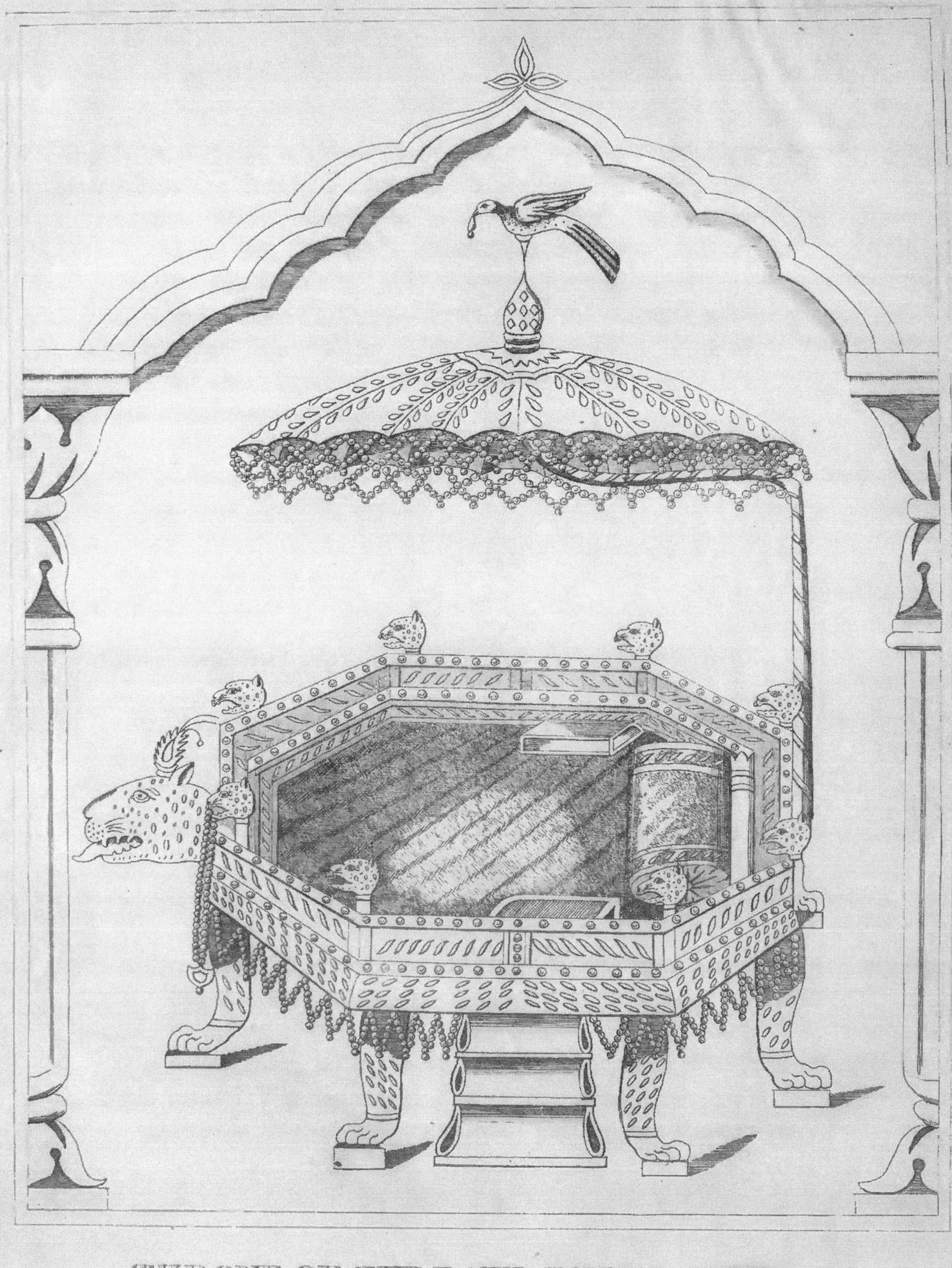

THRONE OF THE LATE TIPPOO SULTAUN

about five feet nine inches high. He had a round face, with large black eyes, and an aquiline nose, which gave much animation and expression to his countenance. He wore mustachios, but shaved his beard. He was naturally active, fond of riding—hunting especially the lion and tiger, which is performed on horseback—and what is very uncommon in princes of the East, frequently took long walks. He, however, passed a great portion of the day in his study. He, notwithstanding, contrived by his real or pretended zeal for the Mohammedan faith, and the support and encouragement which he gave to its followers, to attach to him all the high and lower classes, who to this hour consider him as a martyr to the faith, and as a prince who fell gloriously in the cause of his religion. (Many of the circumstances attending the death of Tippoo Sultaun and the fall of Seringapatam bear a strong resemblance to the fate of Palæologus, the last of the Greek emperors, and the capture of Constantinople by the Turks, A.D. 1453. Vide "Gibbon's Decline and Fall of the Roman Empire," chap. 68.)

Marquis Wellesley, the late Governor-General, sensible of the utility and importance of a library at the new Institution at Fort William, Calcutta, was pleased to order that the immense and valuable library of the late Sultaun should be transferred to that place, which was accordingly done—a part of the same, with other valuables, being sent to the East India House in England.

The valuable Bird of Paradise, formed with precious stones, and other parts of the Sultaun's throne, his armour, swords, muskets, and other curious articles, were placed in Windsor Castle, one of the residences of our beloved Sovereign.

General Baird, who had now taken an active part in defeating the Sultaun, had formerly suffered three years confinement in this prison. There was also a descendant of the Hindoo Rajah of Mysore, whom Hyder Ali dethroned.

COPY OF A LETTER

FROM

MM. DUBUC TO TIPPOO SULTAUN,

DATED 10TH DECEMBER, 1798.

GRAND PACHA,

Health and respect. The men have fortunately arrived, but we are in want of the most essential thing, the *letters* which they left on their way. I, however, hope they will arrive in a few days. They have been four months on their journey; and you may judge of their dispatch and of their punctuality in their services to you. The Hurkarras whom I despatched to you on the 11th of last month, returned yesterday with your Majesty's answer of the 29th of the same month, and I hasten to send them back, as they are very faithful persons, and I wish them to be liberally rewarded. The person who was to have furnished the money has not made his appearance, and I fear there will be considerable difficulty in getting them paid. I think it indispensably necessary for you to expedite an order for taking up immediately all the money which is at Mercieu's, and to annex it to a letter of credit, as I had requested of you, on the Republic. The importance of my mission is such, and the result of it must prove so advantageous to your Majesty, that I cannot too often repeat, money must be considered as nothing when affairs of such immense moment are carrying on. It will be necessary for me to depart, and without money I cannot. In all countries money is the sinew of war, and if your Majesty does not wish to be ruined by the English, and lose the assistance of your good friends the French, give me a sufficient demonstration of your confidence in giving me the proper means of proceeding. Socars with money will not be stopped, more particularly if it be in pagodas with stars. Use dispatch in sending it to me, and I shall instantly set off. The clothes are not yet come, and I have despatched people to forward them. I request your Majesty will authorise me to take a year's salary in advance, as you promised me, in order to provide for the subsistence of my family in my absence, since the six months for which I have been paid expire on the 8th of next month, and that I have been compelled to expend everything in my possession. The English having taken my ship and my property, you will consider my demand just in every point of view, when you reflect that my family are in a foreign country, deprived of every resource. I once more repeat my earnest desire that your Majesty will give me full powers in that respect, and order me immediately to be provided with the necessary funds. The Hurkarras have promised to return within thirty days, and I shall be able to depart in forty. It would be prudent to have some other Hurkarras here, that you may receive intelligence every eight days. I beg leave to recommend earnestly to you the Vakeel, who is not sufficiently paid, and has received nothing for eight months past; he also should have a palanquin, for the envoy of a great Prince, so truly noble and generous as you are, ought not to walk on foot like a Cooly. Are you content with my conduct? Speak candidly; you know how much I am attached to you, and you shall have certain proofs of my fidelity. I beseech your Majesty to countenance your bounty and protection to my good friend and colleague, General Chapins; see him often, and the more you shall see him, the more you shall know that he is worthy of your esteem as a man of honour and prudence.

I have learned that your Majesty has written to the Government of Madras and to Lord Mornington. What will be the issue of their answer? Be on your guard against them: be either ready to defend yourself or to make an attack. The preparations for war are going on with great rapidity. The army of the Nizam is already on its march: it must be stopped. The English were desirous of carrying away Vakeel Sacha Chidevaran, but I discovered the plot, and it has not succeeded. It is necessary that your Majesty should instantly write to the Government of Tranquebar, by a swift courier, to demand its immediate protection for your General-in-chief, Du Buc; his Major, Fillietag; the Interpreter, De Bay, and your Vakeel. Lord Mornington, Governor-General of Bengal, and General Clarke are coming to the coast about the end of this month for the purpose of entering into negociations with your Majesty, which, if they are not advantageous to them, they will cause you to declare war against them. The result of that measure will be the invasion of your country, and the dethroning of you, by substituting for you and your heirs a Nabob of their own making. Your Majesty must perceive that nothing less is in agitation than the destruction of your kingdom. You must exert yourself, and negociate everywhere for to maintain your power, until the moment when I shall be able to secure it for ever for yourself and your august children. It is very easy for the English, in consequence of their intrigues in every part of India, to cause troubles of a serious kind, and deprive you of all your allies. Should they succeed in the war against your Majesty, they would afterwards effect the destruction of the power of the Marattas, and deprive them of every possession which might be ceded to them by a new treaty of peace. It is, therefore, evidently their interest to treat jointly with you for the purpose of finding a certain and mutual guarantee, and that each member may defend the stipulations and cessions made by each at the peace which you signed in your capital with the contracting parties. The English threaten you, the Marattas are bound to support you and not suffer you to be overcome. The barrier which separates you from the former should exist without any encroachment. You may rely on your allies as long as you possess interests in common, and you would be abandoned by them were these common interests to cease.

The time is short and precious: you must give proofs of your good intentions and gain over the English, and, at the same time, throw obstacles in the way of their negociations at Poona. In such a conjuncture, the Marattas ought to give to the law of treaties all possible weight, and not to omit recalling to the minds of the English the assistance granted by them against your Majesty. Should their remonstrances be neglected, and the means of conciliation prove fruitless, let them instantly take up arms and threaten the nation guilty of a breach of the treaties. Such a proceeding would, perhaps, stop all military designs and operations against your Majesty. But if the event should prove different, the sword must be drawn and the sheath thrown so far as to render every search for it useless. We have no intelligence of any peculiar interest from Europe. The Republic is uniformly victorious, and continues to refuse peace to England. Scindia * has already taken Delhi, and I think that he must have also finished the conquest of Agra. It would be prudent in your Majesty to despatch couriers to him to acquaint him with the situation in which you are placed. I entreat your Majesty to read my letter attentively; it has been dictated by candour, truth, and a sense of your interest.

I pray God to grant success to the exertions of your Majesty, to whom I have the honour to be, with respect,

(Signed) DUBUC,

Commander-in-chief, Naval Captain of the French Republic, one and indivisible.

---

* A Maratta.

APPENDIX.

TRANSLATION.

Letter from Sultaun Selim to the Indian Sovereign, Tippoo Sultaun, dated Constantinople, 20th September, 1798, *delivered to Mr. Spencer Smith, his Britannic Majesty's Minister Plenipotentiary, etc.*

MOST NOBLE SOVEREIGN.

WE take this opportunity to acquaint your Majesty, when the French Republic was engaged in a war with most of the powers of Europe within this latter period, our Sublime Porte not only took no part against them, but, regardful of the ancient amity existing with that nation, adopted a system of the strictest neutrality, and showed them even such acts of countenance, as have given rise to complaints on the part of other Courts.

Thus friendly disposed towards them, and reposing a confidence in those sentiments of friendship which they appeared to profess for us, we gave no ear to many propositions and advantageous offers which had been made to us to side with the belligerent powers; but, pursuant to our maxims of moderation and justice, we abstained from breaking with them without a direct motive, and firmly observed the line of neutrality—all which is notorious to the world.

In this posture of things, when the French having witnessed the greatest marks of attention from our Sublime Porte, a perfect reciprocity was naturally expected on their side, when no cause existed to interrupt the continuance of the peace betwixt the two nations, they, all of a sudden, have exhibited the unprovoked and treacherous proceedings, of which the following is a sketch:—

They began to prepare a fleet in one of their harbours, called Toulon, with most extraordinary mystery; and when completely fitted out and ready for sea, embarked a large body of troops; and they put also on board several people versed in the Arabic language, and who had been in Egypt before. They gave the command of that armament to one of their generals, named Bonaparte, who first went to the Island of Malta, of which he took possession, and thence proceeded direct for Alexandria; where, being arrived on the 17th Muharem, all of a sudden landed his troops, and entered the town by open force, publishing soon after manifestoes in Arabic among the different tribes, stating in substance that the object of their enterprise was not to declare war against the Ottoman Porte, but to attack the Beys of Egypt, for insults and injuries they had committed against the French merchants in time past—that peace with the Ottoman Empire was permanent—that those of the Arabs who should join would meet the best treatment, but such as showed opposition would suffer death; with this further insinuation, made in different quarters, but more particularly to certain courts at amity with us, that the expedition against the Beys was with the privity and consent of the Sublime Porte, which is a horrible falsity. After this they also took possession of Rosetta, not hesitating to engage in a pitched battle with the Ottoman troops, who had been detached from Cairo to assist the invaded.

It is a standing law amongst all nations, not to encroach upon each other's territories, whilst they are supposed to be at peace. When any such events take place as lead to a rupture, the motives so tending are previously made known between the parties, nor are any open aggressions attempted against their respective dominions, until a formal declaration of war takes place.

Whilst, therefore, no interruption of the peace, nor the smallest symptom of misunderstanding appeared between our Sublime Porte and the French Republic, a conduct so audacious, so unprovoked, and so deceitfully sudden on their part, is an undeniable trait of the most extreme insult and treachery.

The province of Egypt is considered as a region of general veneration, from the immediate proximity of the noble city of Mecca, the Keblah of the Mussulmen (the point of the compass to which all Turks turn their face in performing their prayers), and the sacred town of Medina, where the tomb of our Blessed Prophet is fixed; the inhabitants of both these sacred cities deriving from thence their subsistence.

Independent of this, it has been actually discovered from several letters which have been intercepted, that the further project of the French is to divide Arabia into various republics; to attack the whole Mahomedan sect in its religion and country; and, by a gradual progression, to extirpate all Mussulmans from the face of the earth.

It is for these cogent motives and considerations, that we have determined to repel this enemy, and to adopt vigorous measures against these persecutors of the faith; we placing all confidence in the Omnipotent God, the source of all succour, and in the intercession of him, who is the Glory of Prophets.

Now it being certain, that, in addition to the general ties of religion, the bonds of amity and good understanding have ever been firm and permanent with your Majesty, so justly famed for your zeal and attachment to our faith; and that more than once such public acts of friendly attention have been practised between us, as to have cemented the connection subsisting between the two countries; we, therefore, sincerely hope, from your Majesty's dignified disposition, that you will not refuse entering into concert with us, and giving our Sublime Porte every possible assistance, by such an exertion of zeal as your firmness and natural attachment to such a cause cannot fail to excite.

We understand, that in consequence of certain secret intrigues, carried on by the French in India (after their accustomed system) in order to destroy the settlements, and to sow dissensions in the provinces of the English there, a strict connection is expected to take effect between them and your Majesty, for whose service they are to send over a corps of troops by the way of Egypt.

We are persuaded, that the tendency of the French plans cannot in the present days escape your Majesty's penetration and notice; and that no manner of regard will be given to their deceitful insinuations on your side: and whereas the Court of Great Britain is actually at war with them, and our Sublime Porte engaged on the other hand in repelling their aggressions, consequently the French are enemies to both; and such a reciprocity of interest must exist between those Courts, as ought to make both parties eager to afford every mutual succour which a common cause requires.

It is notorious, that the French, bent upon the overthrow of all sects and religions, have invented a new doctrine, under the name of liberty; they themselves professing no other belief, but that of Dehrees (Epicureans, or Pythagoreans) that they have not even spared the territories of the Pope of Rome; a country, since time immemorial, held in great reverence by all the European Nations, that they have wrested and shared with others the whole Venetian State, notwithstanding that fellow Republic had not only abstained from taking part against them, but had rendered them service during the course of the war; thus effacing the name of the Republic of Venice from the annals of history.

There is no doubt that their present attempt against the Ottomans, as well as their ulterior designs (dictated by their avaricious view towards Oriental riches) tend to make a general conquest of that country, (which may God never suffer to take effect) and to expel every Mussulman from it, under pretence of annoying the English. Their end is to be once admitted in India, and then to develope what really lies in their hearts, just as they have done in every place where they have been able to acquire a footing.

In a word, they are a nation whose deceitful intrigues and perfidious pursuits know no bounds; they are intent on nothing but on depriving people of their lives and properties, and on persecuting religion, wherever their arms can reach.

Upon all this, therefore, coming to your Majesty's knowledge, it is sincerely hoped that you will not refuse every needful exertion towards assisting your brethren Mussulmans, according to the obligations of religion, and towards defending Hindostan itself against the effect of French machinations, should it be true, as we hear, that an intimate connection has taken place between your court and that nation, we hope that by weighing present circumstances as well as every future inconvenience which would result from such a measure, your Majesty will beware against it; and in the event of your having harboured any idea of joining with them, or of moving against Great Britain, you will lay such resolutions aside. We make it our especial request, that your Majesty will please to refrain from entering into any measures against the English, or lending any compliant ear to the French. Should there exist any subject of complaint with the former, please to communicate it; certain as you may be of the employment of every good office on our side to compromise the same. We wish to see the connection above alluded to exchanged in favour of Great Britain.

We confidently expect, that upon consideration of all that is stated in this communication, and of the necessity of assisting your brethren

Mussulmans in this general cause of religion, as well as of co-operating towards the above precious Province being delivered from the hands of the Enemy, your Majesty will employ every means, which your natural zeal will point out, to assist the common cause, and to corroborate, by that means, the ancient good understanding, so happily existing between our Empires. Certified Translation and Copy.

(A True Copy.)

(Signed) SPENCER SMITH,

„ F. A. GRANT, *Sub-Secretary.*

(A True Copy.)

N. B. EDMONSTONE,

P. T. to the Government.

Copy of Tippoo Sultaun's reply to the Letter addressed to him by the Grand Seignior.

In the name of the most merciful God.

Praise to the Supreme King of Kings, who hath made just and high-minded princes the instruments of exalting the standard of the established religion of Mohumed, and committed the governance and prosperity of the people and dominions of Islaum to their able management and guidance! Be abundance of praise also the offering at the throne of that leader, by the aid of whose prophetic mission the benignant channels of the faith retain their course—and salutations unnumbered to that consecrated person whose Divine Mission is the pride of the followers of Islaum, and to his illustrious offspring and companions; every one of whom was the extirpator of Heretics, and of those who know not the way of the Lord!—After this, it is humbly represented to the exalted presence; the seat of justice, expanded as the heavens, resplendent as the sun; to the luminous star of the firmament ef dominion; the bright planet of the empyreum of glory and fortune; the bloom of the power of greatness; the refresher of the spring of supremacy; the ornament of the throne of pomp and splendor; the supporter of the seat of happiness and prosperity—with troops numerous as the stars; with angels his guards; whose throne is exalted as the skies; whose dignity is as Solomon's; ray of the benignity of God, the Sultaun of the sea and land; may the vessels of his state continue to traverse the seas of success and prosperity, unperishable! And may the effects of his justice continue to pervade every corner of the earth! The august and gracious letter written the 11th of Rubbeeh-oo-Sauny, 1213 Hidj (answering to 23rd September 1798) which was issued through the British Envoy conveyed upon me boundless honour and distinction; the foundations of concord and attachment acquired new strength from its contents, and the fabric of friendship obtained renovated firmness by the gracious expressions it contains.

The venerated pen did me the honour to write of the irruption of the French nation, those objects of the Divine anger, by the utmost treachery and deceit, into the venerated region of Egypt, notwithstanding the strict observance of long subsisting amity and friendship on the part of the Sublime Porte.—Of the views of that irreligious turbulent people—of their denial of God and his prophets—of the determination of the Sublime Porte to adopt the most vigorous measures of the overthrow of that nation of Rebels—and desiring me, for the sake of the whole body of the faith and religious brotherhood, to afford assistance to our brethren Mussulmans; support our Holy Theology, and not withhold my power and endeavours in defending the region of Hindostan from the machinations and evils of these enemies—that I will explain to the Sublime Porte whatever ground of uneasiness and complaint the English may have given me, when by the Divine aid and the intervention of your good office, all difference will be compromised, and opposition and estrangement be converted into cordiality and union—this gracious communication I have understood.

Through the Divine favour and prophetic grace, all the votaries of Islaum united in brotherhood by the ties of religion—especially the Sublime Porte and this state, the good gift of God; for the foundations of friendship and attachment are firmly cemented between them and repeated tokens of mutual regard have been manifested—both in word and deed are they aiding and assisting to each other. This labourer in the way of the Lord (I) am obedient to your highness's world-subjecting will—There is absolutely no difference between us—Let me be informed of and employed to promote that which your exalted mind proposed for the prosperity and due ordinance of the faith and its followers, and the aid of God will alone ensure success. As the French nation are stranged from, and are become the opponents of the Sublime Porte, they may be said to have rendered themselves the enemy of all the followers of the faith, all Mussulmans shonld renounce friendship with them, (quotation from the Koraun) "Consider not Heretics as friends, consider none such but Mussulmans."—I confidently hope that the gates of friendly correspondence between the two states may be always open, and the sentiments of our friendly minds be disclosed to each other.—May the sun of Dominion and Prosperity be resplendent in the East of Greatness!

Dated the 10th of Ramzaun the blessed, 1213 Hedgiree (answering to 16th Feb. 1799).

(True Translations.)

N. B. EDMONSTONE,

P. T. to the Government.

THE MUSSULMAUN'S LAMENT

OVER

THE BODY OF TIPPOO SULTAUN,

WRITTEN (ON THE SPOT WHERE HE FELL) IN AUGUST, 1823.

I.

Light of my faith! thy flame is quenched
In this deep night of blood:
The sceptre from thy race is wrenched,
And of the brave who stood
Around thy Musnud, strong and true,
When this day's sunbeams on the brow
Of yonder mountains glanced, how few
Are left to weep thee now!

Chorus—Allah! 'tis better thus to die,
With war-clouds hanging redly o'er us,
Than to live a life of infamy,
With years of grief and shame before us.

II.

Star of the battle! thou art set;
But thou didst not go down,

As others who could fame forget
Before the tempest's frown,—
As others who could stoop to crave
Pardon and peace from their haughty foes;
Better to perish with the brave
Than to live and reign with those.

CHORUS—Allah! 'tis better thus to die,
With war-clouds hanging redly o'er us,
Than to live a life of infamy.
With years of grief and shame before us.

III.

No! thou hast to thy warrior bed
Sunk like that burning sun,
Whose brightest, fiercest rays are shed
When his race is nearest done,
Where death-fires flash'd and sabres rang,
And quickest sped the parting breath,
Thou, from a life of empire sprang
To meet a soldier's death.

CHORUS—Allah! 'tis better thus to die,
With war-clouds hanging redly o'er us,
Than to live a life of infamy,
With years of grief and shame before us.

IV.

Thy mighty father joyfully
Look'd from his throne on high;
He mark'd his spirit live in thee;
He smiled to see thee die,—

To see thy sabre's last faint sweep
Tinged with a foeman's gore,
To see thee go to the hero's sleep
With thy red wounds all before.

CHORUS—Allah! 'tis better thus to die,
With war-clouds hanging redly o'er us,
Than to live a life of infamy,
With years of grief and shame before us

V.

The faithful in their emerald bowers
The Tooba tree beneath,
Have 'twin'd thee, of unfading flowers,
The martyr's glorious wreath:
The dark-eyed girls of paradise
Their jewell'd kerchiefs wave,
And welcome to their crystal skies
The sultaun of the brave.

CHORUS—Allah; 'tis better thus to die,
The martyr's death, with bliss before us,
Than to draw the breath of infamy,
With the victor's banner waving o'er us.

BERNARD WYCLIFFE.

THE DIRGE OF TIPPOO SULTAUN, FROM THE CANARA.

I.

How quickly fled our Sultaun's state!
  How soon his pomp has pass'd away!
How swiftly sped Seringa's fate,
  From wealth and power to dire decay:
How proud his conquering banners flew,
  How proudly marched his dread array.
Soon as the King of Earth withdrew
  His favouring smile, they pass'd away.

II.

His peopled kingdoms stretching wide,
  A hundred subject leagues could fill,
While dreadful frown'd in martial pride,
  A hundred Droogs from hill to hill:
His hosts of war a countless throng,
  His Franks, impatient for the fray;
His horse, that proudly pranc'd along,—
  All in a moment pass'd away,—

III.

His mountain-forts of living stone
  Were hewn from every massy rock,
Whence bright the sparkling rockets shone,
  And loud the vollied thunder spoke:
His silver lances gleam'd on high,
  His spangled standards flutter'd gay.
Lo! in the twinkling of an eye,
  Their martial pride has pass'd away.

COMMISSION FOR MYSORE:

DATED 4TH JUNE, 1799.

RICHARD, EARL OF MORNINGTON, &c., &c., &c., GOVERNOR-GENERAL FOR ALL THE FORCES AND AFFAIRS OF THE BRITISH NATION IN INDIA, TO ALL TO WHOM THESE PRESENTS SHALL COME, GREETING:

WHEREAS, the glorious success of the British and Allied Arms in Mysore, under the favour of Providence, has reduced the territories of the late Tippoo Sultaun to the joint power and authority of the Honourable the English East India Company, and of his Highness the Soubah of the Deccan, their friend and ally; and whereas his said Highness has given full power and authority to the Right Honourable Richard, Earl of Mornington, Governor-General for all the Forces and Affairs of the British nation in India, to conduct and order the interests of his Highness in the said possessions, and to conclude such an arrangement thereof as shall appear to his Lordship to be most expedient for the security and welfare of the country, and for the common benefit of the Allies; now know ye, that for the more speedy conclusion of such a salutary arrangement, and for the restoration of order and tranquillity, by the settlement of the said conquered territories, I, the said Richard, Earl of Mornington, Governor-General, as aforesaid, do hereby constitute, nominate, and appoint, Lieutenant-General George Harris, the Honourable Colonel Arthur Wellesley, the Honourable Henry Wellesley, Lieutenant-Colonel William Kirkpatrick, Lieutenant-Colonel Barry Close, or any three or more of them, to be Commissioners for the settlement of the territories so recently conquered from the said Tippoo Sultaun, and to be, and be styled, Commissioners for the Affairs of Mysore, with full powers to negotiate and conclude, in my name, all such treaties, and to make and issue all such temporary and provisional regulations, for the ordering and management of the civil and military government, and of the revenues of the said territories, as may be necessary for the immediate administration and settlement thereof: the said Commissioners to be, nevertheless, subject to such orders and instructions as they shall, from time to time, receive from me, and regularly to report their proceedings to me, keeping an exact diary, or daily record thereof, under the signature of one of their Secretaries. And I do hereby empower the said Commissioners to hold their meetings at such places, either within the territories of the late Tippoo Sultaun, or elsewhere, as they shall judge most convenient, and to adjourn, from time to time, and to change the place of their meeting according to the exigency of the public service. And I authorize and direct the said Commissioners to communicate, from time to time, with Meer Allum Bahauder, touching the objects of this Commission. And I nominate and appoint Captain Malcolm and Captain Munro to be Secretaries, and Mr. Edward Golding to be Assistant Secretary to the said Commission, during my pleasure. And before the said Commissioners, or any of them, shall proceed to act in the execution of any of the powers or trusts vested in them by this Commission, save only the power of administering the oath hereinafter mentioned, he or they shall severally take and subscribe the following oath; that is to say:

I, *A. B.*, do faithfully promise and swear, that as a Commissioner for the affairs of Mysore, I will execute the several powers and trusts reposed in me, according to the best of my skill and judgment, without favour or affection, prejudice or malice, to any person whatever. I will not disclose or make known any of the orders or instructions which shall be transmitted to me, or to the said Commissioners, by the Governor-General, or by his order, or any of the proceedings of the said Commissioners, save only to the other members of this Commission, or to the person or persons who shall be duly nominated and employed in transcribing or preparing the same, respectively, or in recording the proceedings of the said Commissioners, or unless I shall be authorised by the Governor-General to disclose or make known the same. I do further promise and swear, that I will not demand, take, or accept, directly or indirectly, by myself, or by any other person, for my use, or on my behalf, or on the behalf, or for the use of any other person, any sum of money, or other valuable thing, by way of gift, present, or otherwise; and that to the Governor-General in Council I will justly and truly account for, answer, and pay, all the rents, duties, and other revenues, and sums of money, which shall come to my hands, or to the hands of any person or persons in trust for, or employed by me, in execution of the powers and authorities vested in the said Commissioners by the said Governor-General.

So help me God.

Which oath, any two of the said Commissioners shall, and are hereby empowered to administer to the others of them. And the said oath shall be entered by one of the Secretaries to the Commission amongst the acts of the Board, and be duly subscribed and attested by the said Commissioners, at the time of their taking and administering the same to each other, respectively; and the several Secretaries and other officers of the said Board of Commissioners shall also take and subscribe before the said Board such oath of secresy, and for the execution of the duties of their respective stations, and the integrity of their conduct therein, as the said Board shall direct. And when any three of the said Commissioners shall have taken the oath, they shall immediately constitute a Board, and proceed to act under the Commission. And I do hereby empower and direct the said Commissioners to take charge, and render an exact account to me, of all such public property as has been, or shall be, found within the territories of the late Tippoo Sultaun, and also to collect, and bring to account, all such arrears of revenue, and all such sums of money as were due to the Sircar on the 4th of May, 1799, or have, or shall become due to the Government of the Allies, from and after that day. Provided always, that this order shall not be construed to prevent or impede the distribution, among the Allied army, of the prize taken in the fort of Seringapatam, on the 4th of May, according to the General Order issued by the Governor-General in Council, under date the 4th June, 1799: and provided also, that nothing contained in this Commission shall be deemed to preclude the right of the captors of any fort or place, taken on or before the said 4th day of May, 1799, to obtain from the Commissioners an attested account of the public property contained therein, in order that the claims of all such captors may be heard and determined by the Governor-General in Council, or by the Honourable the Court of Directors, or by his Majesty in Council, according to the nature of the case. And I do hereby authorise and direct the said Commissioners, immediately upon entering on their duties under this Commission, to issue a proclamation, notifying the restoration of tranquillity, and promising to all the inhabitants of the territories of the late Tippoo Sultaun, security of person and of private property, encouraging them to resume their ordinary occupations, under the protection of the Allies. And I further direct, that the said proclamation shall contain the strictest injunctions, under the most severe penalties, to all persons within the said territories, to abstain from acts of violence, outrage, and plunder.

INSTRUCTIONS TO THE COMMISSIONERS OF MYSORE.

DATED 4TH OF JUNE, 1799.

(Secret.)

To the Commissioners for the Affairs of Mysore.

GENTLEMEN,

1. The Commission which accompanies this letter will apprise you of the nature and extent of the powers which I have deemed it advisable to entrust to you. These powers necessarily supersede those which I had delegated during the campaign to the Commission appointed to assist Lieut.-General Harris in all matters relating to political negotiation. The favourable situation of affairs in Mysore appearing to render my presence at Seringapatam quite unnecessary, I have again taken the resolution of remaining at Madras; and I therefore propose to confide to you such a portion of my authority as may enable you, under my orders, to effect a settlement of the country without my presence. Whatever three members of the Commission shall be present at Seringapatam, on the arrival of this despatch, will proceed immediately to act under the Commission, and to execute the instructions contained in this letter.

2. The restoration of the representative of the ancient family of the Rajahs of Mysore, accompanied by a partition of territory between

the Allies, in which the interests of the Marattas should be conciliated, appearing to me under all circumstances of the case to be the most advisable basis on which any new settlement of the country can be rested, I have resolved to frame, without delay, a plan founded on these principles, and I hope, in the course of to-morrow, to be able to forward to you the articles of a treaty, with proper instructions annexed, for the purpose of carrying the above-mentioned plan into effect.

3. In the meanwhile it is absolutely necessary that certain measures of precaution should be immediately adopted in order to facilitate the intended arrangement. These measures relate, first, to the satisfaction of the principal Musselmen sirdars, and of the killedars of the several forts; secondly, to the mode of removing the family of Tippoo Sultaun from Mysore with the least practicable injury to their feelings. With regard to the first object, I have already forwarded to the Honourable Mr. Henry Wellesley a letter to Meer Allum, and a copy of a letter from the Nizam to me, which I trust will enable you to give complete satisfaction to Kummeer-ud-Deen; and unless you expect any considerable advantage from his influence at Seringapatam, in conciliating others of his religion, I desire that you will take the earliest measures to induce him to repair to Gurrumcondah. With the other leading Musselmen you should immediately enter into such specific engagements as shall preclude the possibility of any alarm in their minds, with respect to their situation and prospects, under any new arrangement of the country.

4. I rely on your discretion to conclude such an arrangement with as little burthen to the finances of the Company as circumstances will admit. The whole body of Tippoo's sirdars ought not to become an exclusive charge upon the Company. They must be employed and provided for by the Allies, and by the Rajah of Mysore, collectively; the families of the sirdars slain during the campaign must also be provided for in the same manner.

5. The killedars who have surrendered, and those who still hold forts in their possession, should be paid their arrears for the month of April at least, with their pay for the month of May, and for as long a time as we may leave them in charge of their forts. On dismissing any of them, liberal gratuities should be given them for the purpose of conciliation. All these charges may hereafter be adjusted between the Allies.

6. As soon as you shall judge that your arrangements with the remnant of the Musselmen interest are in sufficient forwardness, you will proceed to take the necessary measures for removing the family of the Sultaun. The details of this painful, but indispensable measure, cannot be entrusted to any person more likely to combine every office of humanity with the prudential precautions required by the occasion, than Colonel Wellesley; and I therefore commit to his discretion, activity, and humanity, the whole arrangement, subject always to such suggestions as may be offered by the other members of the Commission. I have appointed Lieut.-Colonel Doveton to take the command of the fortress of Vellore, which is destined for the future residence of the Sultaun's family. Colonel Doveton is also appointed paymaster of stipends to the family; and he has been directed to make every possible preparation for their accommodation at Vellore. After their arrival, no reasonable expense will be spared to render their habitation suitable to their former rank and expectations; and it is my intention to give them a liberal pecuniary allowance. Colonel Wellesley will judge whether it may be necessary to give either to the whole, or to any branch of the family, any specific assurance of the exact amount of the sums to be allotted to them respectively. If any such particular explanation should appear necessary for their satisfaction, I authorise you to make the allotment of stipend to each of them, as well for the establishment of the Zenana, provided that the total sum for the maintenance of the whole family be not stated at more than three, or, at the utmost, four lacs of pagodas. The sons of the late Sultaun may

be accompanied by such attendants as they may select, provided the number be not so great as to endanger the public tranquillity, or to form a point of union for the adherents of the late Sultaun. It might be desirable that Ali Reza should accompany the princes, as he appears to be attached to the interests of the Company, and at the same time to entertain considerable affection for the princes. The females and children of the several families must follow the princes as speedily as possible. Colonel Wellesley, in my name, will give the most unequivocal assurances of protection and indulgence to every branch of the family; and at a proper time he will deliver the letters for the four eldest sons of Tippoo Sultaun, forwarded by the Persian translator to Mr. Henry Wellesley. If General Harris should be at Seringapatam, or within reach of it, I am persuaded that his humanity will induce him to exert every effort to mitigate all the rigorous parts of this revolution in Mysore, which I feel myself bound, by every principle of duty towards the British interests in India, to accomplish without delay.

7. I have learned, with the utmost degree of surprise and concern, that the Zenana in the palace of the Sultaun was searched for treasure* some time after the capture of the place: I could have wished, for the honour of the British name, that the apartments of the women had not been disturbed. In the heat and confusion of an assault, such excesses are frequently unavoidable; but I shall for ever lament, that this

---

* "We feel great satisfaction in being able to assure your Lordship, that before the Zenana was searched for treasure, separate apartments were prepared for the ladies, and no precaution omitted to secure them from the possibility of being exposed to any inconvenience. No treasure was found in the Zenana, nor was any article whatever conveyed from thence."—*Extract: Letter from the Commissioners to the Governor-General, dated 8th June,* 1799.

scene should have been acted long after the contest had subsided, and when the whole place had submitted to the superiority of our victorious arms. If any personal ornaments, or other articles of value, were taken from the women in that unfortunate moment, I trust that the Commander-in-chief will make it his business to vindicate the humanity of the British character, by using the most zealous exertions to obtain a full restitution of the property in question.

8. After this observation, it is superfluous to add my most anxious expectation, that the utmost degree of care will be taken to secure the personal property of the princes and of the women, when the period of their removal shall arrive.

9. You will of course apply to the Commander-in-chief for such an escort as may be necessary to convey the family of Tippoo Sultaun to the place of their destination; and you will arrange the time and mode of their departure, so as to preclude the possibility of any commotion or escape. It is desirable that some officer, conversant in the language, manners, and customs of the natives, and of approved humanity, should accompany the princes until Lieut.-Colonel Doveton can meet them. His qualifications for the trust which I have reposed in him are too well known to require any illustration.

10. In exercising the general powers vested in you by the accompanying Commission, I desire that you will not interfere in the management of the province of Canara, until you shall receive further instructions from me. I have directed General Stuart to make a temporary arrangement for the government of that province; and until I shall have received his report, I cannot decide the system of measures most eligible to be adopted in that quarter. You will apprise the Commissioners, whose power is superseded by this new Commission, of my entire approbation of their services; and you will return them my thanks accordingly.

11. The present regulation is founded on an opinion that the Commander-in-chief may not always be at liberty to act in a political

capacity, and that he may not be able to spare more than one of his confidential staff from about his person. My selection of Lieut.-Colonel Close has been directed, not only by my knowledge of his extraordinary talents, proficiency in the native languages, and experience in the native manners and customs, but my determination to establish him in the important office of Resident with the Rajah of Mysore, as soon as that prince shall be placed on the Musnud. You will observe, that the Commission enjoins all the Commissioners, and persons employed under them, to take an oath of secresy previously to their entering upon their functions ; you will therefore communicate a copy of the Commission to any member who may happen to be absent from Seringapatam when the despatch shall arrive; but the contents of this despatch must not be communicated by the person to whom it is addressed to any person who shall not have taken the oath of secresy prescribed in the Commission, excepting Meer Allum.

12. It has occurred to me, that the removal of your meetings to Bangalore might have an useful effect in drawing the multitude of Mussulmen from Seringapatam. This would enable the commandant of the fort to commence the repair or improvement of the fortification, and to proceed in clearing the place, and making it strictly a military station. I recommend the earliest possible attention to this measure, as being of essential importance to our security in Mysore.

I have the honour to be, &c. &c. &c.

(Signed) MORNINGTON.

Fort St. George, 4th June, 1799.

PARTITION TREATY OF MYSORE.

Treaty for strengthening the Alliance and Friendship subsisting between the English East India Company Behauder, His Highness the Nabob Nizam-ud-Dowlah Asoph Jah Behauder, and the Paishwah Row Pundit Purdhan Behauder, and for effecting a Settlement of the Dominions of the late Tippoo Sultaun.

WHEREAS the deceased Tippoo Sultaun, unprovoked by any act of aggression on the part of the Allies, entered into an offensive and defensive alliance with the French, and admitted a French force into his army, for the purpose of commencing war against the Honourable English Company Behauder, and its Allies, Nizam-ud-Dowlah Asoph Jah Behauder, and the Paishwah Row Pundit Purdhan Behauder; and the said Tippoo Sultaun having attempted to evade the just demands of satisfaction and security made by the Honourable English Company Behauder and its Allies, for their defence and protection against the joint designs of the said Sultaun and of the French, the allied armies of the Honourable English Company Behauder, and of his Highness Nizam-ud-Dowlah Asoph Jah Behauder, proceeded to hostilities, in vindication of their rights, and for the preservation of their respective dominions from the perils of foreign invasion, and from the ravages of a cruel and relentless enemy.

And whereas it has pleased Almighty God to prosper the just cause of the said Allies, the Honourable English Company Behauder and his Highness Nizam-ud-Dowlah Asoph Jah Behauder, with a continued course of victory and success, and finally to crown their arms, by the reduction of the capital of Mysore, the fall of Tippoo Sultaun, the utter extinction of his power, and the unconditional submission of his people; and whereas the said Allies, being disposed to exercise the right of conquest with the same moderation and forbearance which they have observed from the commencement to the conclusion of the late successful war, have resolved to use the power which it hath pleased Almighty God to place in their hands, for the purpose of obtaining reasonable compensation for the expenses of the war, and of establishing permanent security and genuine tranquillity for themselves and their subjects, as well as for all the powers contiguous to their respective dominions: wherefore a treaty, for the adjustment of the territories of the late Tippoo Sultaun, between the English East India Company Behauder and his Highness the Nabob Nizam-ud-Dowlah Asoph Jah Behauder, is now concluded by Lieutenant-General George Harris, Commander-in-chief of the forces of his Britannic Majesty and of the English East India Company Behauder in the Carnatic and on the coast of Malabar, the Honourable Colonel Arthur Wellesley, the Honourable Henry Wellesley, Lieutenant-Colonel William Kirkpatrick, and Lieutenant-Colonel Barry Close, on the part and in the name of the Right Honourable Richard, Earl of Mornington, K.P., Governor-General for all affairs, civil or military, of the British nation in India; and by the Nabob Meer Allum Behauder, on the part and in the name of his Highness the Nabob Nizam-ud-Dowlah Asoph Jah Behauder, according to the under-mentioned articles, which, by the blessing of God, shall be binding on the heirs and successors of the contracting parties, as long as the sun and moon shall endure, and of which the conditions shall be reciprocally observed by the said contracting parties.

Article 1.

It being reasonable and just that the Allies, by this treaty, should accomplish the original objects of the war (viz., a due indemnification for the expenses incurred in their own defence, and effectual security for their respective possessions against the future designs of their enemies,) it is stipulated and agreed, that the districts specified in Schedule A, hereunto annexed, together with the heads of all the passes leading from the territory of the late Tippoo Sultaun to any part of the possessions of the English East India Company Behauder, of its allies or tributaries, situated below the Ghauts on either coast, and all forts situated near to and commanding the said passes, shall be subjected to the authority, and be for ever incorporated with, the dominions of the English East India Company Behauder, the said Company Behauder engaging to provide effectually, out of the revenues of the said districts, for the suitable maintenance of the whole of the families of the late Hyder Ali Khan, and of the late Tippoo Sultaun, and to apply to this purpose, with the reservation hereinafter stated, an annual sum of not less than two lacs of star pagodas, making the Company's share as follows:—

Estimated value of district enumerated in the Schedule A, according to the statement of Tippoo Sultaun in 1792.

Canteria pagodas	7,77,170
Deduct provision for the families of Hyder Ali Khan and Tippoo Sultaun two lacs of star pagodas, in Canteria pagodas	2,40,000
Remains to the East India Company ..	5,37,170

Article 2.

For the same reason stated in the preceding article, the districts specified in the Schedule B, annexed hereunto, shall be subject to the authority, and for ever united with the dominions of the Nabob Nizam-ud-Dowlah Asoph Jah Behauder, the said Nabob having engaged to provide liberally, from the revenues of the said districts, for the support of Meer Kummer-ud-Deen Behauder, and of his family and relations, and to grant him for this purpose a personal jaghire in the district of Gurrumcondah, equal to the annual sum of rupees 2,10,000, or of Canteria pagodas 70,000, over and above, and exclusive of a jaghire, which the said Nabob has also agreed to assign to the said Meer Kummer-ud-Deen Khan, for the pay and maintenance of a proportionate number of troops, to be employed in the service of his said Highness, making the share of his Highness as follows:—

Estimated value of the territory specified in Schedule B, according to the statement of Tippoo Sultaun in 1792	6,07,332
Deduct personal jaghire to Meer Kummer-ud-Deen Khan, Rupees 2,10,000, or Canteria pagodas	70,000
Remains to the Nabob Nizam-ud-Dowlah Asoph Jah Behauder	5,37,332

Article 3.

It being further expedient, for the preservation of peace and tranquillity, and for the general security on the foundations now established by the contracting parties, that the fortress of Seringapatam should be subjected to the said Company Behauder, it is stipulated and agreed that the said fortress, and the island on which it is situated (including the small tract of land, or island, lying to the westward of the main island, and bounded on the west by a nullah called the Mysore Nullah, which falls into the Cavery near Chungal Ghaut) shall become part of the dominions of the said Company, in full right and sovereignty for ever.

Article 4.

A separate government shall be established in Mysore; and for this purpose it is stipulated and agreed, that Maha Rajah Mysore Kistna Rajah Oodiaver Behauder, a descendant of the ancient Rajahs of Mysore, shall possess the territory hereinafter described, upon the conditions hereinafter mentioned.

Article 5.

The contracting powers mutually and severally agree, that the districts specified in Schedule C, hereunto annexed, shall be ceded to the said Maha Rajah Mysore, upon the conditions hereinafter mentioned.

Article 6.

The English East India Company Behauder shall be at liberty to make such deduction, from time to time, from the sums allotted by the First Article of the present treaty, for the maintenance of the family of Hyder Ali Khan and Tippoo Sultaun, as may be proper, in consequence of the decease of any member of the said families, and in the event of any hostile attempt, on the part of the said family from any member of it, against the authority of the contracting parties, or against the peace of their respective dominions, or the territory of the Rajah of Mysore, then the said English East India Company Behauder shall be at liberty to limit, or suspend entirely, the payment of the whole, or any part of the stipend hereinbefore stipulated to be applied to the maintenance and support of the said families.

Article 7.

His Highness the Paishwah Row Pundit Purdhan Behauder shall be invited to accede to the present treaty; and although the said Paishwah Row Pundit Purdhan Behauder has neither participated in the expense or danger of the late war, and therefore is not entitled to share any part of the acquisitions made by the contracting parties (namely, the English East India Company Behauder, and his Highness the Nabob Nizam-ud-Dowlah Asoph Jah Behauder), yet for the maintenance of the relations of friendship and alliance between the said Paishwah Row Pundit Purdhan Behauder, the English East India Company Behauder, his Highness the Nabob Nizam-ud-Dowlah Asoph Jah Behauder, and Maha Rajah Mysore Kishna Rajah Behauder, it is stipulated and agreed, that certain districts, specified in Schedule D, hereunto annexed, shall be reserved for the purpose of being eventually ceded to the said Paishwah Row Pundit Purdhan Behauder in full right and sovereignty, in the same manner as if he had been a contracting party to this treaty; provided, however, that the said Paishwah Row Pundit Purdhan Behauder shall accede to the present treaty, in its full extent, within one month from the day on which it shall be formally communicated to him by the contracting parties; and provided also, that he shall give satisfaction to the English East India Company Behauder and to his Highness the Nabob Nizam-ud-Dowlah Asoph Jah Behauder, with regard to certain points now depending between him, the said Paishwah Row

Pundit Purdhan Behauder, and the said Nabob Nizam-ud-Dowlah Asoph Jah Behauder; and also with regard to such points as shall be represented to the said Paishwah, on the part of the English East India Company Behauder, by the Governor-General, or the English Resident at the Court of Poonah.

Article 8.

If, contrary to the amicable expectation of the contracting parties, the said Paishwah Row Pundit Purdhan Behauder shall refuse to accede to this treaty, or to give satisfaction upon the points to which the Seventh Article refers, then the right to, and sovereignty of, the several districts hereinbefore reserved for eventual cession to the Paishwah Row Pundit Purdhan Behauder shall rest jointly in the said English East India Company Behauder, and the said Nabob Nizam-ud-Dowlah Asoph Jah Behauder, who will either exchange them with the Rajah of Mysore for other districts of equal value more contiguous to their respective territories, or otherwise arrange and settle respecting them, as they shall judge proper.

Article 9.

It being expedient, for the effectual establishment of Maha Rajah Mysore Kishna, Rajah in the Government of Mysore, that his Highness should be assisted with a suitable subsidiary force, it is stipulated and agreed, that the whole of the said force shall be furnished by the English East India Company Behauder, according to the terms of a separate treaty to be immediately concluded between the said English East India Company Behauder and his Highness the Maha Rajah Mysore Kishna Rajah Oodiaver Behauder.

Article 10.

This treaty, consisting of ten Articles, being settled and concluded this day, the 22nd of June, 1799 (corresponding with the 17th of Mohurrum, 1214, Anno Higeree) by Lieutenant-General Harris, the Honourable Colonel Arthur Wellesley, the Honourable Henry Wellesley, Lieutenant-Colonel William Kirkpatrick, and Lieutenant-Colonel Barry Close, on the part, and in the name, of the Right Honourable Richard, Earl of Mornington, Governor-General aforesaid, and by Meer Allum Behauder, on the part, and in the name, of his Highness the Nabob Nizam-ud-Dowlah Asoph Jah Behauder, the said Lieutenant-General Harris, the Honourable Colonel Arthur Wellesley, the Honourable Henry Wellesley, Lieutenant-Colonel William Kirkpatrick, and Lieutenant-Colonel Barry Close, have delivered to Meer Allum Behauder one copy of the same, signed and sealed by themselves; and Meer Allum Behauder has delivered to Lieutenant-General George Harris, the Honourable Colonel Arthur Wellesley, The Honourable Henry Wellesley, Lieutenant-Colonel William Kirkpatrick, and Lieutenant-Colonel Barry Close, another copy of the same, signed and sealed by himself; and Lieutenant-General George Harris, the Honourable Colonel Arthur Wellesley, the Honourable Henry Wellesley, Lieutenant-Colonel William Kirkpatrick, and Lieutenant-Colonel Barry Close, and Meer Allum Behauder, severally and mutually engage, that the said treaty shall be respectively ratified by the Right Honourable the Governor-General, under his seal and signature, within eight days from the date hereof, and by his Highness the Nabob Nizam-ud-Dowlah Asoph Jah Behauder, within twenty-five days from the date hereof

(L.S.) MEER ALLUM.

Witnessed, by order of the Commissioners,

(Signed) J. MALCOLM, *Secretary.*

Separate Articles of the Treaty between the Company and the Nizam.

1. With a view to the prevention of future altercations, it is agreed between his Highness the Nabob Nizam-ud-Dowlah Asoph Jah Behauder, and the Honourable English East India Company Behauder, that to whatever amount the stipends appropriated to the maintenance of the sons, relatives, and dependents of the late Hyder Ali Khan and Tippoo Sultaun, or the personal jaghire of Meer Kummer-ud-Deen Khan, shall hereafter be diminished, in consequence of any of the stipulations of the treaty of Mysore, the contracting parties shall not be accountable to each other on this head.

2. And it is further agreed between the contracting parties, that in the event provided for in the Eighth Article of the treaty of Mysore, two-thirds of the share reserved for Row Pundit Purdhan Behauder shall fall to his Highness the Nabob Nizam-ud-Dowlah Asoph Jah Behauder, and the remaining third to the Honourable English East India Company Behauder.

Schedule A.

1. The Company's Share.

The following districts from Nuggur or Bednore:

	Cant. Pagodas.	Fanams.		
Korial (Mangalore), Bekul and Neleseram	1,33,662	7¼		
Karcul	11,393	2¼		
Barkoo	48,389	8½		
Carried forward			1,93,444	18

	Cant. Pagodas.	Fanams.		
Brought forward	1,93,444	18		
Khoosaulpore	26,361	7½		
Bulkull	9,177	0¼		
Garsopa	9,192	0½		
Hunawur (Onore)	17,842	9½		
Mirjaun	8,953	4¾		
Ancola, Punchmahl and Shedasheoghur (or Soonda Payen Ghaut)	28,332	2		
Bilghuy	18,929	4¼		
			3,11,874	6¾

Coimbatore, viz.:

	Cant. Pagodas.	Fanams.		
Coimbatore	80,000	0		
Danaigincottah	35,000	0		
Cheoor	27,000	0		
Chinjerry	27,000	0		
Darapoor Chuckergary	64,000	0		
Settimungalum	30,000	0		
Undoor	8000	0		
Peroondora	14,000	0		
Vizimungul or Aravacoorchy ..	20,000	0		
Erroade	20,000	0		
Caroor	41,000	0		
Coodgully	15,000	0		
Caveryporam	4,000	0		
			3,85,000	0
Carried forward			6,96,874	6¾

Wynaad (from Amudnugur Chickloor) from Talooks, belonging to Seringapatam.

	Cant. Pagodas.	Fanams.		
Brought forward			6,96,874	6¾
Punganoor	15,000	0		
Sutticul, Alumbaddy, Koodahully	15,200	0		
Oussore	18,096	0		
Decani-Cottah, and Ruttungherry ..	14,000	0		
Vencatigeri-Cottah	6,000	0		
Ankusgeery and Sooligeery	4,000	0		
Bangalore	3,000	0		
Talamulla and Talwaddy, half Talooks of Hurdaluelly	5,000	0		
			80,296	0
Total			7,77,170	6¾
Deduct provision for the maintenance of the families of Hyder Ali Khan and of Tippoo Sultaun, Star pagodas 2,00,000, or Canteria pagodas ..			2,40,000	0
Remains to the Company, Canteria pagodas ..			5,37,170	6¾

Schedule B.

2. The Nizam's Share.

Gooty.

Fuze Huzzoor Kubal	15,568	0		
Kona Koomlah	7,500	0		
Carried forward . ..			23,068	0

	Cant. Pagodas.	Fanams.		
Brought forward	23,068	0		
Pamri	11,000	0		
Wunjur Kurroor	8,998	1		
Yursutty Muracherroo	5,902	0		
Beem Rapah	4,800	0		
Muttoor	2,700	0		
Pravalli Mumnimong	9,426	3		
Chunumpilly	8,951	8		
Mulkairva Kotoo	22,251	8¾		
Kurtooni	8,800	0		
Yarky	22,673	1		
Pennacoonda..	60,000	0		
Munug Seera..	8,000	0		
Hundytenaatpoor	16,000	0		
Koorgoor, remainder of	11,629	0		
Kunchindgoondy, ditto of	10,000	0		
Of Gurrumcondah.				
All the districts not added in 1792 ..	1,85,810	0		
Puttungeery, from Seringapatam ..	10,000	0		
Rydroop (6 talooks)	1,02,856	0		
Kunnoul Peshcush	66,666	0		
From Chittledroog.				
Jerymullah (1 talook)	7,800	0		
			6,07,332	1¾
Deduct for a personal jaghire to Cumeer-ud-Deen Khan and relations			70,000	0
Remains to the Nizam, ...	Canteria pagodas		5,37,332	1¾

Schedule C.

District ceded to Maha Rajah Mysore Kistna Rajah Oodiaver Behauder.

Talooks belonging to Seringapatam.

	Cant. Pagodas.	Fanams.	
Puttun Attacran	11,000	0	0
Mysore Attacran or Rechmut Nuzzur	11,500	0	0
Nuzzur Bar	14,000	0	0
Hardunhelly	15,000	0	0
Periapatam	6,200	0	0
Muddoor	13,200	0	0
Hetghur Deivan-Cottah	8,000	0	0
Betudapoor	7,000	0	0
Tyour	8,000	0	0
Yelandoor	10,000	0	0
Mallivelly Gullinabad	9,000	0	0
Tulkar Sosilah	8,100	0	0
Nurzipore	10,200	0	0
Yestonah	7,200	0	0
Bailoor	15,700	0	0
Astrulgoor	4,300	0	0
Chenapatam	12,100	0	0
Bullum Mungirabad	10,000	0	0
Hussin	7,900	0	0
Honavelly	9,400	0	0
Nagmungul	4,700	0	0
Bellore	3,100	0	0
Mahorage Droog	10,000	0	0
Gram	3,500	0	0
Ramgherry	7,400	0	0

	Cant. Pagodas.	Fanams.	
Turkanemb	7,400	0	0
Ahmud Nuggur Chickloor ..	10,000	0	0
Kurp	12,000	0	0
Toory Khaira	9,000	0	0
Coonydghul	5,008	9	0
Hoolioordroog	4,000	0	0
Kirkairy	4,065	0	0
Chennyputtun	9,138	0	0
Noorgairly	3,000	0	0
Mairlabah or Kishmaghessoor ..	6,100	0	0
Sucknyputtun	6,200	0	0
Banorawar Gurradungilly .. .. .. Harrunhilly	10,000	0	0
Boodihall	7,000	0	0
Nidgul	6,000	0	0
Posgur	10,000	0	0
Hagulwary	12,000	0	0
Goomairpollam	10,000	0	0
Bangalore	55,000	0	0
Maugry	8,400	0	0
Mudgherry	36,000	0	0
Coorghurry	4,000	0	0
Cankanelly	8,900	0	0
Nalwungle and Doorbilla ..	16,000	0	0
Anikul	10,300	0	0
Byroodroog	4,000	0	0
Hyboor	7,000	0	0
Dewanhully	20,045	0	0
Ootradroog	5,000	0	0
Chinroydroog	8,000	0	0

	Cant. Pagodas.	Fanams.				
Toomkoor and Deoroy	18,000	0	0			
Nidgegul and Maclydroog ..	16,000	0	0			
Kundakeera and Chellnaighelly..	16,000	0	0			
Chota Balapoor	80,000	0	0			
Colar	80,000	0	0			
Jungum-Cottah	13,000	0	0			
Chuckmogalam	8,134	4	0			
Kudoor	7,129	7	4			
				7,78,322	0	4

Sera, remainder of.

Sera and Amerapoor	55,000	0	0			
Ooscotah	50,754	0	0			
Burra Balapoor	44,000	0	0			
				1,49,754	0	0

Nuggur, above Ghaut.

Kusbah	29,145	$4\frac{3}{4}$	2
Coolydroog	28,818	$0\frac{3}{4}$	2
Koompsee	8,094	$2\frac{1}{2}$	0
Kope	22,864	$5\frac{1}{4}$	2
Wastara	6,818	9	0
Eekairy and Sagur	39,411	$0\frac{1}{2}$	2
Gooty (Hoobly)	11,006	8	$\frac{3}{4}$
Surbtonanundy	10,458	$0\frac{1}{4}$	2
Terryanwitty	17,424	0	0
Shikarpor	11,774	$0\frac{3}{4}$	0
Annuntapoor	10,191	$0\frac{1}{2}$	9

	Cant. Pagodas.	Fanams.			
Lakooley Dannass	11,629 6¾	1			
Oodgunny	13,614 1¾	0			
Simoga	16,883 5	0			
Hooly Honore	6,583 5¾	1			
Biddary	10,835 5	2			
Chingeery, Beswapattam ..	22,091 1¾	3			
Turrykeera	14,076 4¼	2			
Azeimpoor	10,696 2¾	3			
.. .. ..			3,02,417	6	6

Chittledroog, remainder of 12 *talooks.*

Kusbah	20,874 7¾	1			
Beemsumunder	12,148 4	2			
Dideary	12,984 9½	0			
Husdroog	11,936 2¾	3			
Multoor	10,392 3½	2			
Murkal Moroo	12,662 9¼	3			
Tullick	11,854 0¾	0			
Burnm Sagur	10,163 6¼	0			
Kunkopa	12,542 0½	2			
Bilchoor	10,683 1	2			
Hinoor	10,010 0	5			
Goody-Cottah	11,330 5	3			
			1,48,583	1	7
			13,79,076	8	1
Deduct two Purgunnahs of Hurdenhally, viz.: Talmale and Talwaddy, included in the Company's share			5,000	0	0
			13,74,076	8	1

Schedule D.

THE PEISHWAH'S SHARE.

		Cant. Pagodas.		Fanams.
Harpoonelly (6 talooks)		1,10,030	8¾	0
Soonda (above the Ghauts)		59,377	0	0
Annagoondy		60,101	0	0
From Chittledroog, 2 talooks, viz.:				
Holul Kaira	11,425 6 0			
Mycomdo	12,226 9 0			
		23,652	5	0
From Bednore, 1 talook, viz.:				
Hurryhur..		10,796	0	0
Total Canteria pagodas		2,63,957	3¾	0

Ratified at Hyderabad by his Highness the Nizam, on the 13th day of July, Anno Domini 1799.

(Signed) J. A. KIRKPATRICK,
Resident.

MEMORIAL, EXPLANATORY OF THE PARTITION TREATY OF MYSORE.

1. The principle of partition between the Nizam and the Company, assumed in the first and second articles, is, that each party should retain, in direct sovereignty, an equal share of unencumbered territorial revenue, deduction being made from both sides of the amount of the pensions for jaghires, of which each party has agreed to bear the charge.

2. The allowances made by Tippoo Sultaun to his family, and that of Hyder, including the whole expenses of the maintenance of every branch of the families, did not exceed 1,12,116 Canteria pagodas.

3. It was, however, thought advisable to allot a larger sum for this purpose, as well with a view to meet the first expenses of settling the families in the Carnatic, as the increased charge of maintaining the younger sons of the late Sultaun (nine in number) as they shall advance in years. The youngest of the four princes, now at Vellore, is about fifteen years of age. It is not intended to make the nine younger sons now at Seringapatam, the eldest of whom is about eleven years of age, so large an allowance as that enjoyed by each of the four elder now at Vellore. The four elder sons have been accustomed to a degree of state, of which it would be indelicate to deprive them: the same reasons do not apply to the younger sons,

who have scarcely ever been suffered to pass beyond the limits of the Zenana.

4. The estimate of the revenues of Tippoo Sultaun, on which the partition has been founded, is the same as that admitted by the allies at Seringapatam in 1792, deducting the sum of nine lacs of pagodas, which had been added by the Allies to the estimate given in by the vakeels of Tippoo Sultaun on that occasion. There is every reason to suppose, that this estimate is much below the real produce of the revenues of the country, especially in its valuation of the Company's share. Tippoo Sultaun had made a fictitious increase of his revenues, by an arbitrary addition to the nominal value of his coin, and by other capricious and extravagant operations, the nature of which is explained in the papers annexed to this despatch: by this contrivance he had raised the apparent amount of his revenues to the sum of Canteria pagodas 83,67,549: this sum, certainly, much exceeded their real amount. In No. 3,* a comparison is instituted between the extravagant statements lately found at Seringapatam, and the depreciation of Tippoo Sultaun's remaining revenue imposed upon the Allies in 1792. By this comparison it appears that, at the lowest valuation, the Company's share of the present partition may be expected, within a short period of time, to produce not less than 14,78,698 Star pagodas,† provided the revenues be ably and honestly administered.

5. A map, constructed by Captain Marriott, will be found in No. ——. It is recommended to the attention of your Honourable Court, as exhibiting a curious and interesting view of the new and capricious division of territory introduced by Tippoo Sultaun, by which he had changed many of the names, and all the divisions of every part of his kingdom, loading his establishments with innu-

---

* Appendix. Captain Macleod's Statement of Revenue, etc.

† N.B. This is the gross amount; about twelve lacs net revenue.

merable Mahomedan officers of revenue, and entirely subverting the wise and economical system established by Hyder Ali. In No. 4* will also be found a note, relating to the produce and commercial powers of Mysore. Having already stated, in paragraphs 13, 14 and 15 of this despatch, the principles which have regulated the selection of the particular districts allotted to each of the contracting parties, it is unnecessary to add anything on that subject to this memorial.

6. The third article does not appear to require any explanation. The small tract of land retained in addition to the island of Seringapatam is necessary to the effectual strength of the place, and to its constant supply with water. By the next despatch, it is hoped, that an accurate report of the value of the acquisitions made under this article may be forwarded to your Honourable Court.

7. Articles 4 and 5. These articles are so expressed as to exclude any claim of right to the throne on the part of the Rajah, and also to prevent many of the Polygars, descended from the ancient possessors of various parts of the territories of Tippoo Sultaun, from preferring obsolete pretensions, founded on alleged rights of inheritance.

8. Article 6 requires no explanation. The first separate article refers to this, and will hereafter be explained.

9. Article 7 refers to an intended treaty with the Maratta empire, the negotiation of which is now depending at Poonah, with every prospect of a favourable issue.

10. The eighth article requires no particular comment; it is connected with the second separate article, which will be hereafter explained.

11. The ninth article is founded upon the equitable right of the Company, arising from a superior share in the expenses and dangers

---

* Appendix. Captain Macleod's Statement of Revenue, etc.

of the war, to the principal benefit of any collateral arrangements to be made with the new government at Mysore. It is evident that his Highness the Nizam, the existence of whose throne has confessedly been saved, and is now protected by the British power, will derive a considerable additional security from the establishment of the British influence in Mysore. On the other hand, the pensions to be made to the Marattas will be employed to purchase certain immunities of the most valuable kind for his Highness; or if the Maratta power should decline such an accommodation, the second separate article (as hereafter explained) will place his Highness's interests, under the operation of this treaty, on a level with those of the Company.

Separate Articles.

Article 1.

This article was inserted with a view to exclude the Nizam from any interference in the affairs of the families of Hyder Ali and Tippoo Sultaun: its operation is reciprocal, as it renounces the Company's right of interference between Nizam Ali and Kummer-ud-Deen.

Article 2.

If the Paishwah should accede to the terms to be proposed to him under the seventh article of the treaty, it has already been remarked, that the Nizam will derive considerable benefit from that arrangement. The precise nature of the benefit, which his Highness may expect, is now a matter of negotiation at Poonah. If Nizam Ali should be disappointed in his expectation at Poonah, he will be amply imdemnified by receiving two-thirds of the territory now reserved for eventual cession to the Paishwah, while the Company shall receive only one-third.

SUBSIDIARY TREATY OF SERINGAPATAM.

A Treaty of perpetual friendship and alliance, concluded, on the one part, by his Excellency Lieutenant-General George Harris, Commander-in-Chief of the forces of his Britannic Majesty and of the English East India Company Behauder, in the Carnatic and on the Coast of Malabar, the Honourable Colonel Arthur Wellesley, the Honourable Henry Wellesley, Lieutenant-Colonel William Kirkpatrick, and Lieutenant-Colonel Barry Close, on behalf, and in the name, of the Right Honourable Richard, Earl of Mornington, K.P., Governor-General for all affairs, civil and military, of the British nation in India, by virtue of full powers vested in them for this purpose, by the said Richard, Earl of Mornington, Governor-General; and, on the other part, by Maha Rajah Mysore Kistna Rajah Oodiaver Behauder, Rajah of Mysore.

Whereas it is stipulated in the treaty concluded on the 22nd of June, 1799, between the Honourable English East India Company Behauder, and the Nabob Nizam-ud-Dowlah Asoph Jah Behauder, for strengthening the alliance and friendship subsisting between the said English East India Company Behauder, his Highness Nizam-ud-Dowlah Asoph Jah Behauder, and the Paishwah Row Pundit Purdhan Behauder, and for effecting a settlement of the territories of the late Tippoo Sultaun, that a separate government shall be established in Mysore, and that his Highness Maha Rajah Mysore Kistna Rajah

Oodiaver Behauder shall possess certain territories, specified in Schedule C, annexed to the said treaty, and that for the effectual establishment of the government of Mysore, his Highness shall be assisted with a suitable subsidiary force, to be furnished by the English East India Company Behauder:

Wherefore, in order to carry the said stipulations into effect, and to increase and strengthen the friendship subsisting between the said English East India Company and the said Maha Rajah Mysore Kistna Rajah Oodiaver Behauder, this treaty is concluded by Lieutenant-General George Harris, Commander-in-chief of the forces of his Britannic Majesty, and of the said English East India Company Behauder, in the Carnatic and on the coast of Malabar, the Honourable Colonel Arthur Wellesley, the Honourable Henry Wellesley, Lieutenant-Colonel William Kirkpatrick, and Lieutenant-Colonel Barry Close, on the part, and in the name, of the Right Honourable Richard, Earl of Mornington, Governor-General aforesaid, and by his Highness Maha Rajah Mysore Kistna Rajah Oodiaver Behauder, which shall be binding upon the contracting parties, as long as the sun and moon shall endure.

Article 1.

The friends and enemies of either of the contracting parties shall be considered as the friends and enemies of both.

Article 2.

The Honourable the East India Company Behauder agrees to maintain, and his Highness Maha Rajah Mysore Kistna Rajah Oodiaver Behauder agrees to receive a military force for the defence and security of his Highness's dominions; in consideration of which protection, his Highness engages to pay the annual sum of seven lacs of star pagodas to the said East India Company; the said sum to be paid in equal monthly instalments, commencing from the 1st of July, Anno Domini 1799. And his Highness further agrees that the disposal of the said sum, together with the arrangement and employment of the troops to be maintained by it, shall be left entirely to the Company.

Article 3.

If it shall be necessary for the protection and defence of the territories of the contracting parties, or either of them, that hostilities shall be undertaken, or preparations made for commencing hostilities against any state or power, his said Highness Maha Rajah Mysore Kistna Rajah Oodiaver Behauder agrees to contribute towards the discharge of the increased expense, incurred by the augmentation of the military force, and the unavoidable charges of war, such a sum as shall appear to the Governor-General in Council of Fort William, on an attentive consideration of the means of his said Highness, to bear a just and reasonable proportion to the actual net revenues of his said Highness.

Article 4.

And whereas it is indispensably necessary, that effectual and lasting security should be provided against any failure in the funds destined to defray, either the expenses of the permanent military force in time of peace, or the extraordinary expenses described in the third article of the present treaty, it is hereby stipulated and agreed, between the contracting parties, that whenever the Governor-General in Council of Fort William, in Bengal, shall have reason to apprehend such failure in the funds so destined, the said Governor-General in Council shall be at liberty, and shall have full power and right, either to introduce such regulations and ordinances, as he shall deem expedient for the internal management and collection of the revenues, or for the better ordering of any other branch and department of the government of Mysore, or to assume and bring under the direct management of the servants of the said Company Behauder, such part or parts of the territorial possessions of his Highness Maha Rajah Mysore Kistna Rajah Oodiaver Behauder, as shall appear to him, the said Governor-General in Council, necessary to render the funds efficient and available, either in time of peace or war.

Article 5.

And it is hereby further agreed, that whenever the said Governor-General in Council shall signify to the said Maha Rajah Mysore Kistna Rajah Oodiaver Behauder, that it is become necessary to carry into effect the provision of the fourth article, his said Highness Maha Rajah Mysore Kistna Rajah Oodiaver shall immediately issue orders to his aumils, or other officers, either for carrying into effect the said regulations and ordinances, according to the tenor of the fourth article, or for placing the territories required under the exclusive authority and control of the English Company Behauder. And in case his Highness shall not issue such orders within ten days from the time when the application shall have been formally made to him, then the said Governor-General in Council shall be at liberty to issue orders, by his own authority, either for carrying into effect the said regulations or ordinances, or for assuming the management and collection of the revenues of the said territories, as he shall judge most expedient, for the purpose of securing the efficiency of the said military funds, and of providing for the effectual protection of the country, and the welfare of the people. Provided always, that whenever, and so long as any part or parts of his said Highness' territories shall be placed, and shall remain under the exclusive authority and control of the said East India Company, the Governor-General in Council shall render to his Highness a true and faithful account of the revenues and produce of the territories so assumed. Provided also, that in no case whatever shall his Highness's actual receipt of annual income, arising out of his territorial revenue, be less than the sum of one lac of star pagodas, together with one-fifth part of the net revenues of the whole of the territories ceded to him by the fifth article of the treaty of Mysore; which sum of one lac of star pagodas, together with the amount of one-fifth of the said net revenues, the East India Company engages, at all times, and in every possible case, to secure and cause to be paid for his Highness' use.

Article 6.

His Highness Maha Rajah Mysore Kistna Rajah Oodiaver Behauder engages, that he will be guided by a sincere and cordial attention to the relations of peace and amity now established between the English Company Behauder and their allies; and that he will carefully abstain from any interference in the affairs of any State in alliance with the said English Company Behauder, or of any State whatever. And for securing the object of this stipulation, it is further stipulated and agreed, that no communication or correspondence with any foreign State whatever, shall be holden by his said Highness, without the previous knowledge and sanction of the said English Company Behauder.

Article 7.

His Highness stipulates and agrees, that he will not admit any European foreigners into his service, without the concurrence of the English Company Behauder; and that he will apprehend and deliver to the Company's Government all Europeans, of whatever description, who shall be found within the territories of his said Highness, without regular passports from the English government, it being his Highness's determined resolution not to suffer, even for a day, any European foreigners to remain within the territories now subjected to his authority, unless by consent of the said Company.

Article 8.

Whereas the complete protection of his Highness' said territories requires that various fortresses and strong places, situated within the territories of his Highness, should be garrisoned and commanded, as well in time of peace as of war, by British troops and officers, his Highness Maha Rajah Mysore Kistna Rajah Oodiaver Behauder engages, that the said English Company Behauder shall, at all times, be at liberty to garrison, in whatever manner they may judge proper, such fortresses and strong places within the said Highness' territories, as it shall appear to them advisable to take charge of.

Article 9.

And whereas, in consequence of the system of defence which it may be expedient to adopt for the security of the territorial possessions of his Highness Maha Raja Mysore Kistna Rajah Oodiaver Behauder, it may be necessary that certain forts and strong places within his Highness's territories should be dismantled or destroyed, and that other forts and strong places should be strengthened and repaired, it is stipulated and agreed, that the English East India Company shall be the sole judges of the necessity of any such alterations in the fortresses. And it is further agreed, that such expenses as may be incurred on this account, shall be borne and defrayed, in equal proportion, by the contracting parties.

Article 10.

In case it shall become necessary for enforcing and maintaining the authority and government of his Highness in the territories now subjected to his power, that the regular troops of the English East India Company Behauder should be employed, it is stipulated and agreed, that upon formal application being made for the service of the said troops, they shall be employed in such manner as to the said

Company shall seem fit; but it is expressly understood by the contracting parties, that this stipulation shall not subject the troops of the English East India Company Behauder to be employed in the ordinary transactions of revenue.

Article 11.

It being expedient, for the restoration and permanent establishment of tranquillity in the territories now subjected to the authority of his Highness Maha Rajah Mysore Kistna Rajah Oodiaver Behauder, that suitable provision should be made for certain officers of rank in the service of the late Tippoo Sultaun, his said Highness agrees to enter into the immediate discussion of this point, and fix the amount of the funds (as soon as the necessary information can be obtained) to be granted for this purpose, in a separate article, to be hereafter added to this treaty.

Article 12.

Lest the garrison of Seringapatam should, at any time, be subject to inconvenience from the high price of provisions and other necessaries, his Highness Maha Rajah Mysore Kistna Rajah Oodiaver Behauder agrees, that such quantities of provisions, and other necessaries, as may be required for the use and consumption of the troops composing the said garrison, shall be allowed to enter the place, from all and every part of his dominions, free of any duty, tax, or impediment whatever.

Article 13.

The contracting parties hereby agree to take into their early consideration the best means of establishing such a commercial intercourse between their respective dominions, as shall be mutually beneficial to the subjects of both governments, and to conclude a commercial treaty, for this purpose, with as little delay as possible.

Article 14.

His Highness Maha Rajah Mysore Kistna Rajah Oodiaver Behauder hereby promises to pay, at all times, the utmost attention to such advice as the English government shall occasionally judge it necessary to offer to him, with a view to the economy of his finances, the better collection of his revenues, the administration of justice, the extension of commerce, the encouragement of trade, agriculture, and industry, or any other objects connected with the advancement of his Highness' interests, the happiness of his people, and the mutual welfare of both States.

Article 15.

Whereas it may hereafter appear, that some of the districts declared by the treaty of Mysore to belong, respectively, to the English Company Behauder and to his Highness, are inconveniently situated, with a view to the proper connection of their respective lines of frontier, it is hereby stipulated between the contracting parties, that in all such cases they will proceed to such an adjustment, by means of an exchange, or otherwise, as shall be best suited to the occasion.

Article 16.

This treaty, consisting of sixteen articles, being this day, the 8th of July, Anno Domini 1799, corresponding the 3rd of Suffer, Anno Higeree 1214, and to the 7th of the month Hassar, of the 1721 year of the Salwant æra, settled and concluded at the fort of Nuzzerbah, near Seringapatam, by his Excellency Lieutenant-General George Harris, Commander-in-chief of the forces of his Britannic Majesty, and of the Honourable English East India Company in the Carnatic and on the coast of Malabar, the Honourable Colonel Arthur Wellesley, the Honourable Henry Wellesley, Lieutenant-Colonel

William Kirkpatrick, and Lieutenant-Colonel Barry Close, with the Maha Rajah Mysore Kistna Rajah Oodiaver Behauder, the aforesaid gentlemen have delivered to the said Maha Rajah one copy of the same in English and Persian, sealed and signed by them, and his Highness the Maha Rajah has delivered to the gentlemen aforesaid another copy, also in Persian and English, bearing his seal, and signed by Luchuma, widow of the late Kistna Rajah, and sealed and signed by Purnea, dewan to the Maha Rajah Kistna Rajah Oodiaver.

And the aforesaid gentlemen have engaged to procure and deliver to the said Maha Rajah, without delay, a copy of the same, under the seal and signature of the Right Honourable the Governor-General, on the receipt of which by the said Maha Rajah, the present treaty shall be deemed complete and binding on the Honourable the English East India Company, and on the Maha Raja Mysore Kistna Rajah Oodiaver Behauder, and the copy of it now delivered to the said Maha Rajah shall be returned.

MEMORIAL EXPLANATORY OF THE SUBSIDIARY TREATY OF SERINGAPATAM.

Article 1 requires no explanation.

Article 2. The amount of subsidy was fixed after full communication with Purnea. It may, perhaps, be necessary to indulge the Rajah with the payment of a less sum, for the first year of the new Government; but no doubt exists, that after that period, the full subsidy may be realized without any inconvenience to the Rajah's affairs, or any pressure upon the country. It was thought more advisable to undertake the defence of the country, without any specification of the force to be employed, than to bind the Company to maintain a specified number of troops in Mysore.

Article 3. The principle established in this article, connected with the fourth and fifth articles, will enable the Company to command the whole resources of Mysore, in the event of actual or approaching war.

Articles 4 and 5. These articles secure to the Company the power, not only of assuming the management of the Rajah's revenues, either in time of peace or war, whenever such a measure may appear necessary, but also of introducing any improvement into any or each of the Rajah's administration, which the Governor-General in Council may deem advisable; it may therefore be hoped, that it will not be necessary to resort to the extreme measure of assuming the Rajah's country. The powers, both of regulation and assumption, are secured in the most unqualified manner, for the purpose of avoiding the embarrassments which have occasioned so much inconvenience in Oude, Tanjor, and the Carnatic. The sum of one lack of star pagodas, in addition to one-fifth of the net revenue, is reserved for the Rajah, lest in time of war, such a defalcation of revenue should take place, as should reduce his income below the amount of his necessary expenses. It is not intended that the Rajah, in time of peace, should ever be required to pay to the Company a larger sum than the amount of the subsidy; namely, seven lacks of star pagodas, excepting only in the case of preparation for hostilities.

Articles 6 to 10 require no explanation.

Article 11. It is intended by this article to reserve the right of charging the Rajah with the provision to be made for the principal sirdars and killedars in the service of the late Tippoo Sultaun. The measures which have already been taken, with a view to the execution of this article, will appear in a letter from the Commissioners in the Mysore, under the date 12th June. The total amount of the annual charge already incurred on this head is 23,000 star pagodas. Some addition must certainly be made to this sum; but it is not probable that they will increase the annual charge beyond the amount of 40,000 pagodas.† This sum cannot be deemed a considerable sacrifice to the important object of conciliating the good will of the principal surviving officers of the late Sultaun. It must, however, be observed, that the whole of this sum is not to be stated as a permanent charge, several pensions having been granted conditionally, during the good behaviour

† Tippoo's allowances to his officers, civil and military, were framed on the most parsimonious scale, although the number of his subordinate officers of revenue was extravagant.

of the pensioner, or until he shall be employed by the Company or its Allies. The provisions which have been made for the families of those who have fallen during the campaign are included in this calculation, and amount to a sum which bears no proportion to the credit which has resulted to the character of the Company from this transaction.

Article 12 requires no explanation.

Article 13. The subject of this article has already occupied the attention of the Commissioners; some time, however, will necessarily be required, before a plan can be thoroughly digested for this important subject.

Articles 14 and 15 require no explanation.

CAPTAIN MACLEOD TO THE MYSORE COMMISSIONERS,

Dated 8th July, 1799.

To the Commissioners for the Affairs of Mysore.

Gentlemen,

In compliance with the desire of the Right Honourable the Governor-General, conveyed in his letter to you, dated the 21st June, extract of which was forwarded to me by your directions, I have the honour to transmit to you a statement of the revenues of the territories lately acquired for the Honourable Company, in which you will please to observe the grounds on which I am led to believe that those acquisitions are capable to yield a gross revenue, equal to the sums in column 4.

The late Tippoo Sultaun raised his jummabundy, in the year 1796, by augmenting his land-rent three Canteria fanams on each pagoda (ten fanams), supposing the country to be capable of bearing this augmentation. He also charged his jummabundy with half a fanam, as a tax on shroffs, and a quarter of a fanam as a duty on tobacco. The two last articles were absurdly added to the land-rent, as well as the first, the whole amounting to $3\frac{3}{4}$ fanams on every ten fanams;

so that by this increase every ten by the preceding jummabundy became $13\frac{3}{4}$ for the new jummabundy, or 40 was raised to 55.

There were, however, some inconsiderable articles of the revenue excluded from contributing towards this augmentation; such as the rent of lands farmed for portions of the produce, and also the road duties; but as I could not procure an exact account of the amount of items left out in forming the increase, I have supposed, for the convenience of calculation, that the increase of 1796 extended to the whole gross revenue, and by following this mode, I have estimated the increase in column 2 of the statement greater than it really was; consequently, column 3 or 4 is estimated lower than it otherwise should be, if the detail of the whole increase had been accurately ascertained.

The sums in Canteria pagodas in the third column, or in star pagodas in the fourth, may, in my opinion, be considered as nearly the fair jummabundy which may hereafter be expected; though I cannot take upon myself to assert, that the several districts ought to yield revenue equal to this valuation of them.

If some of the districts should be over-rated in this estimate, it is probable that others are under-valued. I think it is not unreasonable to expect, that in the aggregate the whole may, in the course of three or four years, produce a revenue equal to the amount of column 4; and if from this sum one-fifth be deducted, for the several heads of enaums to pagodas, &c., and for defraying all charges of collection, there would remain to the Company a clear revenue of near twelve lacks of star pagodas annually.

Should this estimate of the new acquisitions be hereafter found, through better information, to be materially erroneous, I hope it will be remembered that I followed the truest scale which can at present be procured. Much will always depend on the skill and talents of persons employed in the management of revenue.

I have an account of the amount of the rent of each aumildarrie composing the jumma in the first column: and I have materials and information sufficient to prove, that the schedule of the Mysore revenue, given to the Confederates in 1792, was a false statement of the jummabundy.

I have the honour to be, &c., &c., &c.,

(Signed) William Macleod.

Seringapatam, 8th July, 1799.

FROM CAPTAIN MACLEOD TO GENERAL HARRIS,

Dated Seringapatam, 22nd May, 1799,

Inclosing Abstracts of Tippoo Sultaun's Jummabundy.

Sir,

I have the pleasure to lay before you an abstract of the jummabundy, and a list of the several forts of the late Tippoo Sultaun. As he had given new names to all forts and the residence of his asophs, the proper, or former name, is affixed to each division and fort, for the convenience of geographical information.

The Sultaun's mistaken system of revenue collection operated in a great degree towards reducing his receipts, by his having increased the number of aumildarries to ten times as many as had usually been the proportion under all former Governments of the Mysore dominions.

The Sultaun raised his jummabundy in the year 1795, by adding about nineteen lacks of Canteria pagodas to his former jumma: but this increase was only ideal; as I am informed by men, of whose veracity I have a high opinion, that since the year 1792, his receipts were annually from twenty-five to thirty-five lacks of Canteria pagodas. His actual annual disbursements are estimated at forty lacks of Canteria pagodas, since the treaty of 1792; so that it appears a considerable portion of his expenses must have been taken from the treasure collected by his father.

All the asophs and aumildars under his Government were Moormen, who were seldom chosen for any other reason than their being Mahomedans; and although the whole of them had an oath of fidelity administered to them, the embezzlement of public revenue by the several classes of servants is supposed to have amounted annually to fifteen or twenty lacks of Canteria pagodas. The jagheers for the support of troops, which amount to about five lacks of Canteria pagodas, do not appear in the statement; the valuation of them is included in the revenue.

I have the honour to be, &c., &c., &c.,

(Signed) WILLIAM MACLEOD,

Acting Superintendent of Revenue.

CAPTAIN MACLEOD'S MEMORANDA OF THE COMMERCE OF THE MYSORE COUNTRY.

EXPORTS.

Beetle, Areka (or Sissauris)	Those articles generally allude to the Exports from Ballaghaut to the Coast of Coromandel. The first four articles are the most considerable.
Black Pepper	
Cardamums	
Sandal Wood	
Wax	
Ivory	
Rubies	
Thick Diamonds	
Cotton Thread	
Coarse painted Cloths of Pombrie, etc.	
Raw Cotton	

IMPORTS, *chiefly from the Eastward.*

Salt	The principal articles are Salt, Cloth, Raw Silk and Tobacco.
Coarse and fine Cloths of different sorts	
Silk of different sorts	
Velvets	
Damasks	
Copper	
Lead	
Tutenaigue	
Masulipatam Chintz	
Burhunpoor ditto	
Flat Diamonds	
Pearls	
Broad Cloths	
Dried Fruits	
Coral	
Raw Silk	
Spices	
Drugs	
Tobacco	

It would greatly encourage trade, if the road duties on all articles were abolished throughout the Mysore territories; but as this measure would occasion an immediate diminution of revenue, amounting perhaps to two lacs of pagodas, it cannot be carried into execution, at least until the land-rent may rise, in consequence of a few years' peace and good management.

It would, however, be of importance to the Company's possessions and manufactures, if all duties on raw cotton and thread were discontinued throughout the Rajah's country, as it is in the Company's territories.

(Signed) WILLIAM MACLEOD.

Seringapatam, 12*th July*, 1799.

After the mutiny at Vellore, Lord Minto, on the 19th October, 1807, after considerable and mature deliberation, made a minute and resolution for the Mysore princes, the same being but a full and just carrying out of the spirit of the treaty of Mysore, for to use his words, "We have to inquire, therefore, what change in these principles, "the events of Vellore and the transplantation of this family to "Bengal should induce. I confess that, to me, the principle "appears to remain the same, and that a change only in some "particulars of the arrangements is rendered advisable by the "new occurrences just adverted to. It still becomes us to show "as much generosity towards these families as is consistent with "public security under present circumstances, and these, I think, will "be found on consideration rather to admit of relaxation than to "require any augmentation of restraint. We could not at any time "propose to purchase the friendly mind of this family by any liberality "we showed them. It was contrary to nature that they should "conceive affection or attachment towards the immediate authors of "such calamities as had fallen upon their house, or that they should "in their hearts renounce the pretensions to their father's Crown, "which they had been taught and accustomed from their infancy to "consider as their inheritance. It was with this knowledge that we "determined to treat them in their misfortunes with liberality and "kindness. The conquered family of Hyder Ali and Tippoo Sultaun "by falling under the absolute power came for that very reason under "the protection of the conqueror, and found themselves by the "civilised spirit of European warfare, and by the peculiar character of "the European enemy who had subdued them, entitled to the tender "and liberal treatment which they have in reality experienced. But "they were felt, by the generous character of our country, to be persons "entitled to all the considerations which belongs to illustrious birth, "and to the tenderness which is due to misfortune, especially in a "vanquished enemy."

There remains, now, but one surviving son of the late Tippoo Sultaun, His Highness Prince Gholam Mohumed, who with his and his deceased brother's sons, the junior princes, and daughters, live at Calcutta, submissively, quietly, and thankfully, under the protection of the British Government.

A GENEALOGICAL MEMORIAL*

OF THE ANCESTORS OF

HYDER SHAH,

ALIAS

HYDER ALI KHAN BAHADUR.

THE illustrious Husun, son of Yahya, who was one of the heads of the noble family of Korish, combined in his person bodily grace with mental accomplishments, obtained a commission from the Sublime Porte, a shureef of Mecca and Medina, in his 35th year. He had two sons, Mohummud and Ulee, the latter of whom died while only ten years of age; the former, however, ruled to maturity and left a son named Uhmud, at the time of his death, which occurred in 874 A.H. The old Husun did not long survive his beloved son, but soon followed him to the grave, the next year on the 15th Rumzaun 875, A.H. The Grand Seignior received the melancholy intelligence of his demise with regret, and authorised Davood Pasha to appoint some one to the important post of shureef. The Pasha, considering

* This Genealogical Memorial was translated from the Persian book entitled "Carnamah Hydery."

Uhmud son of Mohummud too young, though he was fifteen, elected Syud Ubdool Mulik, a clever and respectable gentleman, as shureef of Mecca. This so grieved Uhmud that he took his departure for Yumun (Arabia Felix), and after a short stay at Aden, which lay in his way, arrived at Sunaa, where he had an interview with the governor of the place, and placed his services at his disposal. The chief was no sooner informed of his great respectability and superior talents, than he gave him his daughter in marriage and put the reins of government in his hands, which he held with uninterrupted peace for twenty years; when his father-in-law fell dangerously sick, he called a council of the nobility, and in their presence intrusted the education of his child, then five years of age, to his care, and conjured him to treat the boy as his own, and govern the country with justice. The old man having expired, thirteen years more elapsed in tranquillity, when a hypocrite, by name Solim, reviled him in the presence of his younger brother-in-law, excited hatred between the two parties, and conspired against his life, binding himself by strong oaths to assassinate him, and put the youth on the Musnud, provided he would secure the post of commander-in-chief for him. From that day forward Solim began secretly to ingratiate himself with the soldiery, and at the same time professed the greatest attachment to Uhmud, but waited impatiently to carry on his fatal wicked design into execution as soon as a fit opportunity would offer. After one year's uneasiness, however, a day was fixed for the inhuman deed, when the assassin armed himself with a poisoned dagger, and went to Uhmud with the pretence of paying his respects to him; immediately on his arrival there, he gave him a mortal wound, returned with joy to the young chief and advised him to have the deceased's son also murdered, so as not to leave any impediment in his way. One of the faithful slaves of Uhmud, named Qumbur, was apprised of this approaching calamity, and directed another slave to flee with the boy to Bagdad, as he himself was resolved to revenge the death of his master though he should lose his own life in the attempt. Having said this, he went in pursuit of Solim, saw him just coming out of the house, cut off his head at one blow, and tried to escape; but the attendants of Solim surrounded him and cut him to pieces. The other slave having related the circumstance of his father's death to Mohummud, his son, now in his thirteenth year, conveyed him in safety to Bagdad, where they took their lodging in Tohir Uffindu's house. His pleasing manners and whole conduct attracted the admiration of the host, who gave him the hand of his daughter, by whom he left three sons at the time of his death. The two elder died without issue, but the younger Ubdool Ghunee, who had married a merchant's daughter, died in 1030 A.H. leaving a son named Ibraheem and a daughter. Ibraheem followed the occupation of his father as merchant, and died in 1057 A.H. having left three daughters and a son, Hussun. This infant being only one year old when his father departed this life, those persons who had dealings with him dishonestly withheld from him the money which they owed him, so that till he attained his majority, there was nothing left but two or three thousand dinars, which circumstance, combined with others of a similar nature, compelled him to leave that country, and accordingly he embarked with his family and arrived at Ajmere. There he settled in the house of one of the votaries of Khajah Moeenoodeen Chishtee, and soon after married his daughter. She had only advanced six months in pregnancy when her husband died, and three months after a son was born, who was named Vulee Mohumed. This youth was afterwards married to his cousin and had a son by her. A dispute having arisen between him and his uncle, he was quite disgusted, and journeyed over with his son to Dehlee, and after a short stay there, travelled to Duckan and arrived at Goolburga, which he chose for his abode. When his son Mohumed Ulee was grown up and had attained a complete knowledge of all the arts and sciences, he married him to the daughter of one of the votaries of the celebrated Saint Bundah

Newaz Gasooduraze, the long haired. After the death of his father Mohumed Ulee took his wife with him to Beejapore and thence to the town of Colar in the Carnatic upper ghauts. He died in 1109 A.H. and left four sons, named Shaik Mohumed, Mohumed Ilyas, Mohumed Imaum, and Futtah Allee, alias Futtah Mohumed, the eldest of whom took care of the whole family. In the meantime Futtah Mohumed, without asking the permission of his eldest brother, went over to the Carnatic lower ghauts, and Mohumed Ilyas proceeded himself shortly after to Tanjavur, and there died 1115 A.H. leaving a son named Hyder Shaib. Futtah Mohumed, who was living at Arcot, invited Boorhanooddeen, a very respectable person descended from a priest, from Tanjavur, and married his daughter, while his brother Imaum married his sister-in-law. A short time after he took his departure for Mysore, and there had two sons named Shahbaz and Vulee Mohumed, the latter of whom died an infant of two years; the death of his son grieved him much, and he took his family with him to the great Bolapore. In the year 1129 A.H. a glorious son was born named Hyder Shah, afterwards known as Hyder Ulee Khan Bahadur.

AUTHORITIES QUOTED IN THE PRECEDING MEMOIRS.

A Persian Manuscript, written by a native of Hyderabad, communinicated by Colonel Kirkpatrick.

Translations of Two Memoirs of Hyder Ali Khan, written by Syed Mohammed and Mohammed Imaum, formerly in the service of the Sultaun. Communicated by Colonel Kirkpatrick.

Orme's History of the Military Transactions of the British Nation in Indostan.

Dow's History of Hindostan.

Narrative of the Operations of Captain Little's Detachment, 1790-91.

Dirom's Narrative of Lord Cornwallis's Campaign of 1792.

Beatson's War in Mysore, 1799.

Dr. Buchanan's Journey through Mysore, 1801.

English Annual Registers; Asiatic Annual Registers. Compiled from Official Documents.

Historical and Political View of the Decan.

Memoirs of the Map of Hindostan.

Histoire de Mysore, par M. Michaud.

British Military Biography, from Alfred to Wellington.

The History of Hyder Ali Khan Bahadur, or New Memoirs concerning the East Indies, with historical notes, by M. M. D. L. T., General of 10,000 men in the Army of the Mogul Empire, written in London, 1784.

Authentic Memoirs of Tippoo Sultaun, by an Officer in the East India Service.

The History of Nadur Shah, by James Fraser.

The Dispatches, Minutes, and Correspondence of the Marquis Wellesley, K.G.

The East India Gazetteer, by Walter Hamilton.

The United Service Journal and Naval and Military Magazine for 1841, Part II.

Historical Sketches of the South of India, in an attempt to trace the History of Mysore, by Lieutenant-Colonel Mark Wilks.

Nishan Hydery, by Meer Hussein Ally Kirmaney, in the service of Nizam of Hyderabad.

Humeed Khaney, by Humeed Khan, Moonshee to Lord Cornwallis in 1792.

George Namah, by Moollah Feeroze, in Bombay.

Futoohat Hydery, by Lallah Kheym Narain.

Humlaut Hydery. Persian, by Mowlavee Abdool Ruheem.

A Persian Book, written by Moonshee Abdool Huck, in the service of Captain Conway, during the Siege of Seringapatam.

Captain Colin Mackenzie's work regarding the Dominions of the late Tippoo Sultaun.

The History of Hydur Naik, otherwise styled Nawaub Hydur Ali Khan, etc., etc., translated from an original Persian MS. by Colonel W. Miles, and other documents relating to the affairs of the Mysore Princes.